WORKERS OF ALL COUNTRIES, UNITE!

SELECTED WORKS
OF
MAO TSE-TUNG

Volume III

FOREIGN LANGUAGES PRESS
PEKING 1967

First Edition 1965
Second Printing 1967

The present volume is an English translation of the
second Chinese edition of the third volume of the
Selected Works of Mao Tse-tung, published by the
People's Publishing House, Peking, in April 1960.

Printed in the People's Republic of China

CONTENTS

*THE PERIOD OF THE WAR OF RESISTANCE
AGAINST JAPAN (II)*

Contents

THE PERIOD OF
THE WAR OF RESISTANCE
AGAINST JAPAN (II)

PREFACE AND POSTSCRIPT
TO *RURAL SURVEYS*

March and April 1941

PREFACE
March 17, 1941

The present rural policy of the Party is not one of Agrarian Revolution as during the ten years' civil war, but is a rural policy for the National United Front Against Japan. The whole Party should carry out the Central Committee's directives of July 7 and December 25, 1940,[1] and the directives of the forthcoming Seventh National Congress. The following material is being published to help comrades find a method for studying problems. Many of our comrades still have a crude and careless style of work, do not seek to understand things thoroughly and may even be completely ignorant of conditions at the lower levels, and yet they are responsible for directing work. This is an extremely dangerous state of affairs. Without a really concrete knowledge of the actual conditions of the classes in Chinese society there can be no really good leadership.

The only way to know conditions is to make social investigations, to investigate the conditions of each social class in real life. For those charged with directing work, the basic method for knowing conditions is to concentrate on a few cities and villages according to a plan, use the fundamental viewpoint of Marxism, *i.e.*, the method of class analysis, and make a number of thorough investigations. Only thus can we acquire even the most rudimentary knowledge of China's social problems.

To do this, first, direct your eyes downward, do not hold your head high and gaze at the sky. Unless a person is interested in turning his eyes downward and is determined to do so, he will never in his whole life really understand things in China.

11

Second, hold fact-finding meetings. Certainly, no all-round knowledge can be acquired merely by glancing this way and that and listening to hearsay. Of the data I obtained through fact-finding meetings, those on Hunan Province and on Chingkangshan have been lost. The materials published here consist mainly of the "Survey of Hsingkuo", the "Survey of Changkang Township" and the "Survey of Tsaihsi Township". Holding fact-finding meetings is the simplest, most practicable and most reliable method, from which I have derived much benefit; it is a better school than any university. Those attending such meetings should be really experienced cadres of middle and lower ranks, or ordinary people. In my investigations of five counties in Hunan Province and two counties in Chingkangshan, I approached responsible cadres of middle rank; in the Hsunwu investigation I approached cadres of the middle and lower ranks, a poor *hsiutsai*,[2] a bankrupt ex-president of the chamber of commerce and a petty official in charge of county revenue who had lost his job. All of these people gave me a great deal of information I had never even heard of. The man who for the first time gave me a complete picture of the rottenness of Chinese jails was a petty jailer I met during my investigation in Hengshan County, Hunan. In my investigations of Hsingkuo County and Changkang and Tsaihsi townships, I approached comrades working at the township level and ordinary peasants. These cadres, the peasants, the *hsiutsai*, the jailer, the merchant and the revenue clerk were all my esteemed teachers, and as their pupil I had to be respectful and diligent and comradely in my attitude; otherwise they would have paid no attention to me, and, though they knew, would not have spoken or, if they spoke, would not have told all they knew. A fact-finding meeting need not be large; from three to five or seven or eight people are enough. Ample time must be allowed and an outline for the investigation must be prepared; furthermore, one must personally ask questions, take notes and have discussions with those at the meeting. Therefore one certainly cannot make an investigation, or do it well, without zeal, a determination to direct one's eyes downward and a thirst for knowledge, and without shedding the ugly mantle of pretentiousness and becoming a willing pupil. It has to be understood that the masses are the real heroes, while we ourselves are often childish and ignorant, and without this understanding it is impossible to acquire even the most rudimentary knowledge.

I should like to repeat that the main purpose of publishing this reference material is to indicate a method for finding out the conditions prevailing at the lower levels; it is not to have comrades memorize the specific material and the conclusions drawn from it. Speaking generally, the infant bourgeoisie of China has not been able, and never will be able, to provide relatively comprehensive or even rudimentary material on social conditions, as the bourgeoisie in Europe, America and Japan has done; we have therefore no alternative but to collect it ourselves. Speaking specifically, people engaged in practical work must at all times keep abreast of changing conditions, and this is something for which no Communist Party in any country can depend on others. Therefore, everyone engaged in practical work must investigate conditions at the lower levels. Such investigation is especially necessary for those who know theory but do not know the actual conditions, for otherwise they will not be able to link theory with practice. Although my assertion, "No investigation, no right to speak", has been ridiculed as "narrow empiricism", to this day I do not regret having made it; what is more, I still insist that without investigation there cannot possibly be any right to speak. There are many people who "the moment they alight from the official carriage" make a hullabaloo, spout opinions, criticize this and condemn that; but, in fact, ten out of ten of them will meet with failure. For such views or criticisms, which are not based on thorough investigation, are nothing but ignorant twaddle. Countless times our Party suffered at the hands of these "imperial envoys", who rushed here, there and everywhere. Stalin rightly says that "theory becomes purposeless if it is not connected with revolutionary practice". And he rightly adds that "practice gropes in the dark if its path is not illumined by revolutionary theory".[3] Nobody should be labelled a "narrow empiricist" except the "practical man" who gropes in the dark and lacks perspective and foresight.

Today I still feel keenly the necessity for thorough research into Chinese and world affairs; this is related to the scantiness of my own knowledge of Chinese and world affairs and does not imply that I know everything and that others are ignorant. It is my wish to go on being a pupil, learning from the masses, together with all other Party comrades.

POSTSCRIPT

April 19, 1941

The experience of the period of the ten years' civil war is the best and most pertinent for the present period, the War of Resistance Against Japan. This refers to the aspect of how to link ourselves with the masses and mobilize them against the enemy, but not to the aspect of the tactical line. The Party's present tactical line is different in principle from that of the past. Formerly, the Party's tactical line was to oppose the landlords and the counter-revolutionary bourgeoisie; now, it is to unite with all those landlords and members of the bourgeoisie who are not against resisting Japan. Even in the latter stage of the ten years' civil war, it was incorrect not to have adopted differing policies towards the reactionary government and political party which were launching armed attacks on us on the one hand, and towards all the social strata of a capitalist character under our own rule on the other; it was also incorrect not to have adopted differing policies towards the different groups within the reactionary government and political party. At that time, a policy of "all struggle" was pursued towards every section of society other than the peasantry and the lower strata of the urban petty bourgeoisie, and this policy was undoubtedly wrong. In agrarian policy, it was also wrong to repudiate the correct policy adopted in the early and middle periods of the ten years' civil war,[4] whereby the landlords were given the same allotment of land as the peasants so that they could engage in farming and would not become displaced or go up into the mountains as bandits and disrupt public order. The Party's policy is now of necessity a different one; it is not "all struggle and no alliance", neither is it "all alliance and no struggle" (like the Chen Tu-hsiuism of 1927). Instead, it is a policy of uniting with all social strata opposed to Japanese imperialism, of forming a united front with and yet of waging struggles against them, struggles that differ in form according to the different degrees in which their vacillating or reactionary side manifests itself in capitulation to the enemy and opposition to the Communist Party and the people. The present policy is a dual policy which synthesizes "alliance" and "struggle". In labour policy, it is the dual policy of suitably improving the workers' livelihood and of not hampering the proper development of the capitalist economy. In agrarian policy, it is the dual policy of requiring the landlords to reduce rent and interest and of stipulating that the peasants should pay this reduced rent and interest. In the sphere of political rights, it is the dual policy of allowing all the anti-Japanese landlords and capitalists the same rights of person and the same political and property rights as the workers and peasants and yet of guarding against possible counter-revolutionary activity on their part. State-owned and co-operative economy should be developed, but the main economic sector in the rural base areas today consists not of state but of private enterprises, and the sector of non-monopoly capitalism in our economy should be given the opportunity to develop and be used against Japanese imperialism and the semi-feudal system. This is the most revolutionary policy for China today, and to oppose or impede its execution is undoubtedly a mistake. To preserve the communist purity of Party members scrupulously and resolutely, and to protect the useful part of the capitalist sector of the social economy and enable it to develop appropriately, are both indispensable tasks for us in the period of resisting Japan and building a democratic republic. In this period it is possible that some Communists may be corrupted by the bourgeoisie and that capitalist ideas may emerge among members of the Party, and we must fight against these decadent ideas; however, we should not mistakenly carry over the struggle against capitalist ideas within the Party to the field of social economy and oppose the capitalist sector of the economy. We must draw a clear line of demarcation between the two. The Communist Party of China is working in a complicated environment, and every Party member, and especially every cadre, must temper himself to become a fighter who understands Marxist tactics. A one-sided and over-simplified approach to problems can never lead the revolution to victory.

NOTES

[1] The Central Committee's directive of July 7, 1940 is the "Decision of the Central Committee of the Communist Party of China on the Present Situation and the Party's Policy". The Central Committee's directive of December 25, 1940 is included in the *Selected Works of Mao Tse-tung*, Vol. II, as the article "On Policy".

[2] A *hsiutsai* was a holder of the lowest degree in the imperial examinations.

[3] J. V. Stalin, "The Foundations of Leninism", *Problems of Leninism*, Eng. ed., FLPH, Moscow, 1954, p. 31.

⁴ The first period of the ten years' civil war lasted from late 1927 to late 1928 and is generally known as the Chingkangshan period; the middle period ran from early 1929 to the autumn of 1931, that is, from the establishment of the Central Red Base Area to the victorious conclusion of the campaign against the third "encirclement and suppression"; and the third period from late 1931 to late 1934, that is, from the victorious conclusion of that campaign to the enlarged meeting of the Political Bureau at Tsunyi in Kweichow Province called by the Central Committee of the Party. The Tsunyi Meeting of January 1935 put an end to the domination of the "Left" opportunist line in the Party, which had lasted from 1931 to 1934, and steered the Party back to the correct line.

REFORM OUR STUDY

May 1941

I propose that we should reform the method and the system of study throughout the Party. The reasons are as follows:

I

The twenty years of the Communist Party of China have been twenty years in which the universal truth of Marxism-Leninism has become more and more integrated with the concrete practice of the Chinese revolution. If we recall how superficial and meagre our understanding of Marxism-Leninism and of the Chinese revolution was during our Party's infancy, we can see how much deeper and richer it is now. For a hundred years, the finest sons and daughters of the disaster-ridden Chinese nation fought and sacrificed their lives, one stepping into the breach as another fell, in quest of the truth that would save the country and the people. This moves us to song and tears. But it was only after World War I and the October Revolution in Russia that we found Marxism-Leninism, the best of truths, the best of weapons for liberating our nation. And the Communist Party of China has been the initiator, propagandist and organizer in the wielding of this weapon. As soon as it was linked with the concrete practice of the Chinese revolution, the universal truth of Marxism-

Comrade Mao Tse-tung made this report to a cadres' meeting in Yenan. The report and the two articles, "Rectify the Party's Style of Work" and "Oppose Stereotyped Party Writing", are Comrade Mao Tse-tung's basic works on the rectification movement. In these he summed up, on the ideological plane, past differences in the Party over the Party line and analysed the petty-bourgeois ideology and style which, masquerading as Marxism-Leninism, were prevalent in the Party, and which chiefly manifested themselves in subjectivist and sectarian tendencies, their form

17

Leninism gave an entirely new complexion to the Chinese revolution. Since the outbreak of the War of Resistance Against Japan, our Party, basing itself on the universal truth of Marxism-Leninism, has taken a further step in its study of the concrete practice of this war and in its study of China and the world today, and has also made a beginning in the study of Chinese history. These are all very good signs.

II

However, we still have shortcomings, and very big ones too. Unless we correct these shortcomings, we shall not, in my opinion, be able to take another step forward in our work and in our great cause of integrating the universal truth of Marxism-Leninism with the concrete practice of the Chinese revolution.

First, take the study of current conditions. We have achieved some success in our study of present domestic and international conditions, but for such a large political party as ours, the material we have collected is fragmentary and our research work unsystematic on each and every aspect of these subjects, whether it be the political, military, economic or cultural aspect. Generally speaking, in the last twenty years we have not done systematic and thorough work in collecting and studying material on these aspects, and we are lacking in a climate of investigation and study of objective reality. To behave like "a blindfolded man catching sparrows", or "a blind man groping for fish", to be crude and careless, to indulge in verbiage, to rest content with a smattering of knowledge — such is the extremely bad style of work that still exists among many comrades in our Party, a style utterly opposed to the fundamental spirit of Marxism-Leninism. Marx, Engels, Lenin and Stalin have taught us that it is necessary to study conditions conscientiously and to proceed from objective reality and not from subjective wishes; but many of our comrades act in direct violation of this truth.

---

of expression being stereotyped Party writing. Comrade Mao Tse-tung called for a Party-wide movement of Marxist-Leninist education to rectify style of work in accordance with the ideological principles of Marxism-Leninism. His call very quickly led to a great debate between proletarian and petty-bourgeois ideology inside and outside the Party. This consolidated the position of proletarian ideology inside and outside the Party, enabled the broad ranks of cadres to take a great step forward ideologically and the Party to achieve unprecedented unity.

Second, take the study of history. Although a few Party members and sympathizers have undertaken this work, it has not been done in an organized way. Many Party members are still in a fog about Chinese history, whether of the last hundred years or of ancient times. There are many Marxist-Leninist scholars who cannot open their mouths without citing ancient Greece; but as for their own ancestors — sorry, they have been forgotten. There is no climate of serious study either of current conditions or of past history.

Third, take the study of international revolutionary experience, the study of the universal truth of Marxism-Leninism. Many comrades seem to study Marxism-Leninism not to meet the needs of revolutionary practice, but purely for the sake of study. Consequently, though they read, they cannot digest. They can only cite odd quotations from Marx, Engels, Lenin and Stalin in a one-sided manner, but are unable to apply the stand, viewpoint and method of Marx, Engels, Lenin and Stalin to the concrete study of China's present conditions and her history or to the concrete analysis and solution of the problems of the Chinese revolution. Such an attitude towards Marxism-Leninism does a great deal of harm, particularly among cadres of the middle and higher ranks.

The three aspects I have just mentioned, neglect of the study of current conditions, neglect of the study of history and neglect of the application of Marxism-Leninism, all constitute an extremely bad style of work. Its spread has harmed many of our comrades.

There are indeed many comrades in our ranks who have been led astray by this style of work. Unwilling to carry on systematic and thorough investigation and study of the specific conditions inside and outside the country, the province, county or district, they issue orders on no other basis than their scanty knowledge and "It must be so because it seems so to me". Does not this subjectivist style still exist among a great many comrades?

There are some who are proud, instead of ashamed, of knowing nothing or very little of our own history. What is particularly significant is that very few really know the history of the Communist Party of China and the history of China in the hundred years since the Opium War. Hardly anyone has seriously taken up the study of the economic, political, military and cultural history of the last hundred years. Ignorant of their own country, some people can only relate tales of ancient Greece and other foreign lands, and even this knowledge is quite pathetic, consisting of odds and ends from old foreign books.

For several decades, many of the returned students from abroad have suffered from this malady. Coming home from Europe, America or Japan, they can only parrot things foreign. They become gramophones and forget their duty to understand and create new things. This malady has also infected the Communist Party.

Although we are studying Marxism, the way many of our people study it runs directly counter to Marxism. That is to say, they violate the fundamental principle earnestly enjoined on us by Marx, Engels, Lenin and Stalin, the unity of theory and practice. Having violated this principle, they invent an opposite principle of their own, the separation of theory from practice. In the schools and in the education of cadres at work, teachers of philosophy do not guide students to study the logic of the Chinese revolution; teachers of economics do not guide them to study the characteristics of the Chinese economy; teachers of political science do not guide them to study the tactics of the Chinese revolution; teachers of military science do not guide them to study the strategy and tactics adapted to China's special features; and so on and so forth. Consequently, error is disseminated, doing people great harm. A person does not know how to apply in Fuhsien[1] what he has learned in Yenan. Professors of economics cannot explain the relationship between the Border Region currency and the Kuomintang currency,[2] so naturally the students cannot explain it either. Thus a perverse mentality has been created among many students; instead of showing an interest in China's problems and taking the Party's directives seriously, they give all their hearts to the supposedly eternal and immutable dogmas learned from their teachers.

Of course, what I have just said refers to the worst type in our Party, and I am not saying that it is the general case. However, people of this type do exist; what is more, there are quite a few of them and they cause a great deal of harm. This matter should not be treated lightly.

III

In order to explain this idea further, I should like to contrast two opposite attitudes.

First, there is the subjectivist attitude.

With this attitude, a person does not make a systematic and thorough study of the environment, but works by sheer subjective enthusiasm and has a blurred picture of the face of China today. With this attitude, he chops up history, knows only ancient Greece but not China and is in a fog about the China of yesterday and the day before yesterday. With this attitude, a person studies Marxist-Leninist theory in the abstract and without any aim. He goes to Marx, Engels, Lenin and Stalin not to seek the stand, viewpoint and method with which to solve the theoretical and tactical problems of the Chinese revolution but to study theory purely for theory's sake. He does not shoot the arrow at the target but shoots at random. Marx, Engels, Lenin and Stalin have taught us that we should proceed from objective realities and that we should derive laws from them to serve as our guide to action. For this purpose, we should, as Marx has said, appropriate the material in detail and subject it to scientific analysis and synthesis.[3] Many of our people do not act in this way but do the opposite. A good number of them are doing research work but have no interest in studying either the China of today or the China of yesterday and confine their interest to the study of empty "theories" divorced from reality. Many others are doing practical work, but they too pay no attention to the study of objective conditions, often rely on sheer enthusiasm and substitute their personal feelings for policy. Both kinds of people, relying on the subjective, ignore the existence of objective realities. When making speeches, they indulge in a long string of headings, A, B, C, D, 1, 2, 3, 4, and when writing articles, they turn out a lot of verbiage. They have no intention of seeking truth from facts, but only a desire to curry favour by claptrap. They are flashy without substance, brittle without solidity. They are always right, they are the Number One authority under Heaven, "imperial envoys" who rush everywhere. Such is the style of work of some comrades in our ranks. To govern one's own conduct by this style is to harm oneself, to teach it to others is to harm others, and to use it to direct the revolution is to harm the revolution. To sum up, this subjectivist method which is contrary to science and Marxism-Leninism is a formidable enemy of the Communist Party, the working class, the people and the nation; it is a manifestation of impurity in Party spirit. A formidable enemy stands before us, and we must overthrow him. Only when subjectivism is overthrown can the truth of Marxism-Leninism prevail, can Party spirit be strengthened, can the revolution be victorious. We must

assert that the absence of a scientific attitude, that is, the absence
of the Marxist-Leninist approach of uniting theory and practice,
means that Party spirit is either absent or deficient.

There is a couplet which portrays this type of person. It runs:

> *The reed growing on the wall — top-heavy, thin-stemmed and*
> *shallow of root;*
> *The bamboo shoot in the hills — sharp-tongued, thick-skinned*
> *and hollow inside.*

Is this not an apt description of those who do not have a scientific
attitude, who can only recite words and phrases from the works of
Marx, Engels, Lenin and Stalin and who enjoy a reputation un-
warranted by any real learning? If anyone really wishes to cure himself of his malady, I advise him to commit this couplet to memory
or to show still more courage and paste it on the wall of his room.
Marxism-Leninism is a science, and science means honest, solid
knowledge; there is no room for playing tricks. Let us, then, be honest.

Secondly, there is the Marxist-Leninist attitude.

With this attitude, a person applies the theory and method of
Marxism-Leninism to the systematic and thorough investigation and
study of the environment. He does not work by enthusiasm alone
but, as Stalin says, combines revolutionary sweep with practicalness.[4]
With this attitude he will not chop up history. It is not enough for
him to know ancient Greece, he must know China; he must know
the revolutionary history not only of foreign countries but also of
China, not only the China of today but also the China of yesterday
and of the day before yesterday. With this attitude, one studies the
theory of Marxism-Leninism with a purpose, that is, to integrate
Marxist-Leninist theory with the actual movement of the Chinese
revolution and to seek from this theory the stand, viewpoint and
method with which to solve the theoretical and tactical problems of
the Chinese revolution. Such an attitude is one of shooting the arrow
at the target. The "target" is the Chinese revolution, the "arrow" is
Marxism-Leninism. We Chinese Communists have been seeking this
arrow because we want to hit the target of the Chinese revolution
and of the revolution of the East. To take such an attitude is to seek
truth from facts. "Facts" are all the things that exist objectively,
"truth" means their internal relations, that is, the laws governing
them, and "to seek" means to study. We should proceed from the
actual conditions inside and outside the country, the province, county

or district, and derive from them, as our guide to action, laws which are inherent in them and not imaginary, that is, we should find the internal relations of the events occurring around us. And in order to do that we must rely not on subjective imagination, not on momentary enthusiasm, not on lifeless books, but on facts that exist objectively; we must appropriate the material in detail and, guided by the general principles of Marxism-Leninism, draw correct conclusions from it. Such conclusions are not mere lists of phenomena in A, B, C, D order or writings full of platitudes, but are scientific conclusions. Such an attitude is one of seeking truth from facts and not of currying favour by claptrap. It is the manifestation of Party spirit, the Marxist-Leninist style of uniting theory and practice. It is the attitude every Communist Party member should have at the very least. He who adopts this attitude will be neither "top-heavy, thin-stemmed and shallow of root" nor "sharp-tongued, thick-skinned and hollow inside".

IV

In accordance with the above views, I would like to make the following proposals:

1. We should place before the whole Party the task of making a systematic and thorough study of the situation around us. On the basis of the theory and method of Marxism-Leninism, we should make a detailed investigation and study of developments in the economic, financial, political, military, cultural and party activities of our enemies, our friends and ourselves, and then draw the proper and necessary conclusions. To this end, we should direct our comrades' attention to the investigation and study of these practical matters. We should get our comrades to understand that the twofold basic task of the leading bodies of the Communist Party is to know conditions and to master policy; the former means knowing the world and the latter changing the world. We should get our comrades to understand that without investigation there is no right to speak, and that bombastic twaddle and a mere list of phenomena in 1, 2, 3, 4 order are of no use. Take propaganda work, for instance; if we do not know the situation with regard to the propaganda of our enemies, our friends and ourselves, we shall be unable to decide on a correct

propaganda policy. In the work of any department, it is necessary to know the situation first and only then can the work be well handled. The fundamental link in changing the Party's style of work is to carry out plans for investigation and study throughout the Party.

2.   As for China's history in the last hundred years, we should assemble qualified persons to study it, in co-operation and with a proper division of labour, and so overcome the present disorganized state of affairs. First it is necessary to make analytical studies in the several fields of economic history, political history, military history and cultural history, and only then will it be possible to make synthetical studies.

3.   As for education for cadres whether at work or in schools for cadres, a policy should be established of focusing such education on the study of the practical problems of the Chinese revolution and using the basic principles of Marxism-Leninism as the guide, and the method of studying Marxism-Leninism statically and in isolation should be discarded. Moreover, in studying Marxism-Leninism, we should use the *History of the Communist Party of the Soviet Union (Bolsheviks), Short Course* as the principal material. It is the best synthesis and summing-up of the world communist movement of the past hundred years, a model of the integration of theory and practice, and so far the only comprehensive model in the whole world. When we see how Lenin and Stalin integrated the universal truth of Marxism with the concrete practice of the Soviet revolution and thereby developed Marxism, we shall know how we should work in China.

We have made many detours. But error is often the precursor of what is correct. I am confident that in the context of the Chinese revolution and the world revolution, which is so intensely alive and so richly varied, this reform of our study will certainly yield good results.

NOTES

[1] Fuhsien County is about seventy kilometres south of Yenan.

[2] The Border Region currency consisted of the currency notes issued by the Bank of the Shensi-Kansu-Ningsia Border Region Government. The Kuomintang currency was the paper currency issued by the four big Kuomintang bureaucrat-capitalist banks from 1935 onwards with British and U.S. imperialist support. Comrade Mao

Tse-tung was referring to the fluctuations in the rates of exchange between these two currencies.

[3] See Karl Marx, "Afterword to the Second German Edition" of *Capital* in which he wrote: "The latter [the method of inquiry] has to appropriate the material in detail, to analyse its different forms of development, to trace out their inner connexion. Only after this work is done, can the actual movement be adequately described." (*Capital*, Eng. ed., FLPH, Moscow, Vol. I, p. 19.)

[4] See J. V. Stalin, "The Foundations of Leninism", *Problems of Leninism*, Russ. ed., Moscow, 1952, p. 80.

EXPOSE THE PLOT
FOR A FAR EASTERN MUNICH

May 25, 1941

1. A compromise between Japan and the United States at the expense of China and the creation of an Eastern Munich against communism and against the Soviet Union — such is the new plot which is now being hatched by Japan, the United States and Chiang Kai-shek. We must expose this plot and fight it.

2. Now that the Japanese imperialists have ended their latest round of military attacks, which was designed to force Chiang Kai-shek to capitulate, there are bound to be moves to induce him to capitulate. This is a repeat performance of the enemy's old policy of using the stick and the carrot, either alternately or simultaneously. We must expose this policy and fight it.

3. Simultaneously with her military attacks, Japan has launched a rumour-mongering campaign alleging that "the Eighth Route Army does not want to fight in co-ordination with the Kuomintang Central Army", that "the Eighth Route Army is seizing every opportunity to expand its territory", that "it is opening up an international route", that "it is setting up another Central Government", etc. This is a cunning Japanese scheme to foment discord between the Kuomintang and the Communist Party and thus to make it easier for them to induce the Kuomintang to capitulate. The Kuomintang Central News Agency and the Kuomintang press are copying and spreading these rumours, showing no qualms about echoing Japan's anti-Communist propaganda, and their intentions are most dubious. This, too, we must expose and fight.

4. Although the New Fourth Army has been declared to be "in rebellion" and the Eighth Route Army has not received a single

---

This inner-Party directive was written by Comrade Mao Tse-tung for the Central Committee of the Communist Party of China.

bullet or a single copper from the Kuomintang, they have never for a moment ceased fighting the enemy. The Eighth Route Army, moreover, has taken the initiative in co-ordinating its operations with those of the Kuomintang troops in the fighting in the present campaign in southern Shansi,[1] and for the last two weeks it has been launching attacks on all fronts in northern China, where fierce battles are raging at this very moment. The armed forces and the people led by the Communist Party have already become the mainstay in the War of Resistance Against Japan. All the calumnies against the Communist Party are aimed at sabotaging the War of Resistance and paving the way for capitulation. We should extend the military successes of the Eighth Route and New Fourth Armies and oppose all the defeatists and capitulationists.

NOTES

[1] The Southern Shansi campaign refers to the campaign of the Chungtiao Mountains. In May 1941, a Japanese invading force 50,000 strong attacked the Chungtiao Mountains area to the north of the Yellow River in southern Shansi. Altogether seven Kuomintang corps were massed in that area, and another four in the Kaoping area to the northeast, making a total of 250,000 men. Since the fight against the Communists was the main job of the Kuomintang troops north of the Yellow River, they had never prepared themselves to fight the Japanese, and most of them tried to avoid combat when the Japanese aggressors attacked. Therefore, in spite of vigorous efforts by the Eighth Route Army to support the Kuomintang troops against the enemy in this campaign, the Kuomintang troops were completely routed, losing more than 50,000 men in three weeks, while the remainder fled to the south of the Yellow River.

ON THE INTERNATIONAL UNITED FRONT AGAINST FASCISM

June 23, 1941

On June 22 the fascist rulers of Germany attacked the Soviet Union. This is a perfidious crime of aggression not only against the Soviet Union but against the freedom and independence of all nations. The Soviet Union's sacred war of resistance against fascist aggression is being waged not only in its own defence but in defence of all the nations struggling to liberate themselves from fascist enslavement.

For Communists throughout the world the task now is to mobilize the people of all countries and organize an international united front to fight fascism and defend the Soviet Union, defend China, and defend the freedom and independence of all nations. In the present period, every effort must be concentrated on combating fascist enslavement.

For the Chinese Communist Party the tasks throughout the country are as follows:

1. Persevere in the National United Front Against Japan, persevere in Kuomintang-Communist co-operation, drive the Japanese imperialists out of China, and by these means assist the Soviet Union.

2. Resolutely combat all the anti-Soviet and anti-Communist activities of the reactionaries among the big bourgeoisie.

3. In foreign relations, unite against the common foe with everybody in Britain, the United States and other countries who is opposed to the fascist rulers of Germany, Italy and Japan.

This inner-Party directive was written by Comrade Mao Tse-tung for the Central Committee of the Communist Party of China.

SPEECH AT
THE ASSEMBLY OF REPRESENTATIVES
OF THE SHENSI-KANSU-NINGSIA
BORDER REGION

November 21, 1941

Members of the Assembly! Comrades! Today's inauguration of the Border Region Assembly of Representatives is of great significance. The Assembly has but one objective, the overthrow of Japanese imperialism and the building of a China of New Democracy or, in other words, a China of the revolutionary Three People's Principles. In the China of today there can be no other objective. For our chief enemies now are not domestic, but are the Japanese fascists and the German and Italian fascists. At this moment the Soviet Red Army is fighting for the destiny of the Soviet Union and of the whole of mankind, and we, for our part, are combating Japanese imperialism. Japanese imperialism is continuing its aggression with the purpose of subjugating China. The Communist Party of China stands for uniting all the anti-Japanese forces throughout the country to overthrow Japanese imperialism, and for co-operating with all anti-Japanese parties, classes and nationalities; everyone, excepting traitors, must unite in the common struggle. This has been the consistent stand of the Communist Party. For more than four years the Chinese people have been heroically waging the War of Resistance, a war that has been maintained through the co-operation of the Kuomintang and the Communist Party and of all classes, parties and nationalities. But it is not yet won, and to win it we have to fight on and ensure that the revolutionary Three People's Principles are put into effect.

Why must we put the revolutionary Three People's Principles into effect? Because up to the present time Dr. Sun Yat-sen's revolutionary Three People's Principles have not been translated into reality

in all parts of China. Why don't we demand that socialism be put
into effect now? Of course socialism is a superior system and has
long been in operation in the Soviet Union, but in China today the
conditions for it are still lacking. It is the revolutionary Three People's
Principles that have been put into effect in our Shensi-Kansu-Ningsia
Border Region. We have not gone beyond them in solving any of our
practical problems. As far as these principles are concerned, today
the Principle of Nationalism means overthrowing Japanese imperialism, and the Principles of Democracy and People's Livelihood mean
working in the interests not of just one section but of all the people
who are against Japan. Throughout the country the people should
enjoy freedom of the person, the right to take part in political activity
and the right to protection of property. Throughout the country the
people should have the opportunity of voicing their opinions, and
they should have clothes to wear, food to eat, work to do and schools
to attend; in short, some provision should be made for everyone.
Chinese society is small at both ends and big in the middle, that is,
the proletariat at one end and the landlord class and big bourgeoisie
at the other each constitute only a small minority, while the great
majority of the people consists of the peasants, the urban petty bourgeoisie and the other intermediate classes. No political party that
wants to run China's affairs properly can do so unless its policy gives
consideration to the interests of these classes, unless some provision
is made for the members of these classes, and unless they have the
right to voice their opinions. The policies put forward by the Chinese
Communist Party seek to unite all the people who oppose Japan
and take into account the interests of every class that does so, and
especially the interests of the peasants, the urban petty bourgeoisie
and the other intermediate classes. The policies of the Communist
Party, which give all sections of the people the opportunity to voice
their opinions and make sure they have work to do and food to eat,
are policies embodying the genuinely revolutionary Three People's
Principles. In agrarian relations, on the one hand we carry out reduction of rent and interest so that the peasants will have food, and on
the other we provide for the payment of the reduced rent and interest
so that the landlords, too, can live. In the relations between labour
and capital, on the one hand we help the workers so that they have
both work and food, and on the other we pursue a policy of developing industry so that the capitalists may obtain some profit. In all this
our purpose is to unite the people of the whole country in the common

endeavour of resistance to Japan. This is what we call the policy of
New Democracy. It is the kind of policy that really suits the conditions in present-day China, and we hope that its application will not
be limited to the Shensi-Kansu-Ningsia Border Region, or to the
anti-Japanese base areas in the rear of the enemy, but will spread
throughout the country.

We have pursued this policy with success and have won the
approval of the people all over China. But there have also been
shortcomings. Some Communists still do not know how to co-operate
with non-Party people in a democratic way and have an exclusive,
"closed-door" or sectarian style of work; they still do not understand
the basic principle that Communists are in duty bound to co-operate
with people outside the Party who are against Japan, and have no
right to shut them out. This principle means that we should listen
attentively to the views of the masses, keep in close touch with them
and not become alienated from them. There is an article in the
Administrative Programme of the Shensi-Kansu-Ningsia Border Region which stipulates that Communists should co-operate democratically with non-Party people and must not act arbitrarily or keep
everything in their own hands. It is directed precisely at the comrades
who still fail to understand the Party's policy. Communists must
listen attentively to the views of people outside the Party and let
them have their say. If what they say is right, we ought to welcome
it, and we should learn from their strong points; if it is wrong, we
should let them finish what they are saying and then patiently explain
things to them. A Communist must never be opinionated or dom-
ineering, or think that he is good in everything while others are
good in nothing; he must never shut himself up in his little room,
or brag and boast and lord it over others. Apart from the die-hard
reactionaries who are in league with the Japanese aggressors and with
the traitors and are sabotaging resistance and unity, and who of
course have no right to speak, everyone is entitled to freedom of
speech, and it does not matter even if what he says is wrong. Affairs
of state are the public affairs of the whole nation and not the private
affairs of a single party or group. Hence Communists have the duty
to co-operate democratically with non-Party people and have no
right to exclude them and monopolize everything. The Communist
Party is a political party which works in the interests of the nation
and people and which has absolutely no private ends to pursue. It
should be supervised by the people and must never go against their

will. Its members should be among the people and with them and must not set themselves above them. Members of the Assembly and Comrades, this Communist Party principle of democratic co-operation with non-Party people is fixed and unalterable. So long as parties exist, people who join them will always be a minority while those outside them will always be the majority; hence our Party members must always co-operate with non-Party people, and they should make a good start right here in the Assembly. With this policy of ours, I believe that Communist members of the Assembly will get very good training here and overcome their "closed-doorism" and sectarianism. We are not a small opinionated sect and we must learn how to open our doors and co-operate democratically with non-Party people, and how to consult with others. Perhaps even now there are Communists who may say, "If it is necessary to co-operate with others, then leave me out." But I am sure there are very few. I can assure you that the overwhelming majority of our members will certainly be able to carry out the line of the Central Committee of our Party. At the same time I wish to ask all non-Party comrades to realize what we stand for, to understand that the Communist Party is not a small sect or clique pursuing private ends. No! The Communist Party sincerely and honestly wishes to set the affairs of state to rights. But we still have many failings. We are not afraid to admit them and are determined to get rid of them. We shall do so by strengthening education within the Party and by co-operating democratically with non-Party people. It is only by subjecting our failings to such a cross-fire, both from within and from without, that we can remedy them and really set the affairs of state to rights.

Members of the Assembly! You have taken the trouble to come here for this meeting, and I am happy to greet this distinguished gathering and wish it success.

RECTIFY THE PARTY'S STYLE OF WORK

February 1, 1942

The Party School opens today and I wish it every success.

I would like to say something about the problem of our Party's style of work.

Why must there be a revolutionary party? There must be a revolutionary party because the world contains enemies who oppress the people and the people want to throw off enemy oppression. In the era of capitalism and imperialism, just such a revolutionary party as the Communist Party is needed. Without such a party it is simply impossible for the people to throw off enemy oppression. We are Communists, we want to lead the people in overthrowing the enemy, and so we must keep our ranks in good order, we must march in step, our troops must be picked troops and our weapons good weapons. Without these conditions the enemy cannot be overthrown.

What is the problem now facing our Party? The general line of the Party is correct and presents no problem, and the Party's work has been fruitful. The Party has several hundred thousand members who are leading the people in extremely hard and bitter struggles against the enemy. This is plain to everybody and beyond all doubt.

Then is there or is there not any problem still facing our Party? I say there is and, in a certain sense, the problem is quite serious.

What is the problem? It is the fact that there is something in the minds of a number of our comrades which strikes one as not quite right, not quite proper.

In other words, there is still something wrong with our style of study, with our style in the Party's internal and external relations and with our style of writing. By something wrong with the style of study we mean the malady of subjectivism. By something wrong with

---

This speech was delivered by Comrade Mao Tse-tung at the opening of the Party School of the Central Committee of the Communist Party of China.

our style in Party relations we mean the malady of sectarianism. By something wrong with the style of writing we mean the malady of stereotyped Party writing.[1] All these are wrong, they are ill winds, but they are not like the wintry north winds that sweep across the whole sky. Subjectivism, sectarianism and stereotyped Party writing are no longer the dominant styles, but merely gusts of contrary wind, ill winds from the air-raid tunnels. (*Laughter.*) It is bad, however, that such winds should still be blowing in the Party. We must seal off the passages which produce them. Our whole Party should undertake the job of sealing off these passages, and so should the Party School. These three ill winds, subjectivism, sectarianism and stereotyped Party writing, have their historical origins. Although no longer dominant in the whole Party, they still constantly create trouble and assail us. Therefore, it is necessary to resist them and to study, analyse and elucidate them.

Fight subjectivism in order to rectify the style of study, fight sectarianism in order to rectify the style in Party relations, and fight Party stereotypes in order to rectify the style of writing — such is the task before us.

To accomplish the task of overthrowing the enemy, we must accomplish the task of rectifying these styles within the Party. The style of study and the style of writing are also the Party's style of work. Once our Party's style of work is put completely right, the people all over the country will learn from our example. Those outside the Party who have the same kind of bad style will, if they are good and honest people, learn from our example and correct their mistakes, and thus the whole nation will be influenced. So long as our Communist ranks are in good order and march in step, so long as our troops are picked troops and our weapons are good weapons, any enemy, however powerful, can be overthrown.

Let me speak now about subjectivism.

Subjectivism is an improper style of study; it is opposed to Marxism-Leninism and is incompatible with the Communist Party. What we want is the Marxist-Leninist style of study. What we call style of study means not just style of study in the schools but in the whole Party. It is a question of the method of thinking of comrades in our leading bodies, of all cadres and Party members, a question of our attitude towards Marxism-Leninism, of the attitude of all Party comrades in their work. As such, it is a question of extraordinary, indeed of primary, importance.

Certain muddled ideas find currency among many people. There are, for instance, muddled ideas about what is a theorist, what is an intellectual and what is meant by linking theory and practice.

Let us first ask, is the theoretical level of our Party high or low? Recently more Marxist-Leninist works have been translated and more people have been reading them. That is a very good thing. But can we therefore say that the theoretical level of our Party has been greatly raised? True, the level is now somewhat higher than before. But our theoretical front is very much out of harmony with the rich content of the Chinese revolutionary movement, and a comparison of the two shows that the theoretical side is lagging far behind. Generally speaking, our theory cannot as yet keep pace with our revolutionary practice, let alone lead the way as it should. We have not yet raised our rich and varied practice to the proper theoretical plane. We have not yet examined all the problems of revolutionary practice — or even the important ones — and raised them to a theoretical plane. Just think, how many of us have created theories worthy of the name on China's economics, politics, military affairs or culture, theories which can be regarded as scientific and comprehensive, and not crude and sketchy? Especially in the field of economic theory: Chinese capitalism has had a century of development since the Opium War, and yet not a single theoretical work has been produced which accords with the realities of China's economic development and is genuinely scientific. Can we say that in the study of China's economic problems, for instance, the theoretical level is already high? Can we say that our Party already has economic theorists worthy of the name? Certainly not. We have read a great many Marxist-Leninist books, but can we claim, then, that we have theorists? We cannot. For Marxism-Leninism is the theory created by Marx, Engels, Lenin and Stalin on the basis of practice, their general conclusion drawn from historical and revolutionary reality. If we merely read their works but do not proceed to study the realities of China's history and revolution in the light of their theory or do not make any effort to think through China's revolutionary practice carefully in terms of theory, we should not be so presumptuous as to call ourselves Marxist theorists. Our achievements on the theoretical front will be very poor indeed if, as members of the Communist Party of China, we close our eyes to China's problems and can only memorize isolated conclusions or principles from Marxist writings. If all a person can do is to commit Marxist economics or philosophy to memory, reciting glibly from Chapter I to Chapter X, but is utterly unable to apply them, can he be considered a Marxist theorist? No! He cannot. What kind of theorists do we want? We want theorists who can, in accordance with the Marxist-Leninist stand, viewpoint and method, correctly interpret the practical problems arising in the course of history and revolution and give scientific explanations and theoretical elucidations of China's economic, political, military, cultural and other problems. Such are the theorists we want. To be a theorist of this kind, a person must have a true grasp of the essence of Marxism-Leninism, of the Marxist-Leninist stand, viewpoint and method and of the theories of Lenin and Stalin on the colonial revolution and the Chinese revolution, and he must be able to apply them in a penetrating and scientific analysis of China's practical problems and discover the laws of development of these problems. Such are the theorists we really need.

The Central Committee of our Party has now made a decision calling upon our comrades to learn how to apply the Marxist-Leninist stand, viewpoint and method in the serious study of China's history, and of China's economics, politics, military affairs and culture, and to analyse every problem concretely on the basis of detailed material and then draw theoretical conclusions. This is the responsibility we must shoulder.

Our comrades in the Party School should not regard Marxist theory as lifeless dogma. It is necessary to master Marxist theory and apply it, master it for the sole purpose of applying it. If you can apply the Marxist-Leninist viewpoint in elucidating one or two practical problems, you should be commended and credited with some achievement. The more problems you elucidate and the more comprehensively and profoundly you do so, the greater will be your achievement. Our Party School should also lay down the rule to grade students good or poor according to how they look at China's problems after they have studied Marxism-Leninism, according to whether or not they see the problems clearly and whether or not they see them at all.

Next let us talk about the question of the "intellectuals". Since China is a semi-colonial, semi-feudal country and her culture is not well developed, intellectuals are particularly treasured. On this question of the intellectuals, the Central Committee of the Party made the decision[2] over two years ago that we should win over the great numbers of intellectuals and, insofar as they are revolutionary and willing to take part in the resistance to Japan, welcome them one and all. It is entirely right for us to esteem intellectuals, for without revolutionary intellectuals the revolution cannot triumph. But we all know there are many intellectuals who fancy themselves very learned and assume airs of erudition without realizing that such airs are bad and harmful and hinder their own progress. They ought to be aware of the truth that actually many so-called intellectuals are, relatively speaking, most ignorant and the workers and peasants sometimes know more than they do. Here some will say, "Ha! You are turning things upside down and talking nonsense." (*Laughter.*) But, comrades, don't get excited; there is some sense in what I am saying.

What is knowledge? Ever since class society came into being the world has had only two kinds of knowledge, knowledge of the struggle for production and knowledge of the class struggle. Natural science and social science are the crystallizations of these two kinds of knowledge, and philosophy is the generalization and summation of the knowledge of nature and the knowledge of society. Is there any other kind of knowledge? No. Now let us take a look at certain students, those brought up in schools that are completely cut off from the practical activities of society. What about them? A person goes from a primary school of this kind all the way through to a university of the same kind, graduates and is reckoned to have a stock of learning. But all he has is book-learning; he has not yet taken part in any practical activities or applied what he has learned to any field of life. Can such a person be regarded as a completely developed intellectual? Hardly so, in my opinion, because his knowledge is still incomplete. What then is relatively complete knowledge? All relatively complete knowledge is formed in two stages: the first stage is perceptual knowledge, the second is rational knowledge, the latter being the development of the former to a higher stage. What sort of knowledge is the students' book-learning? Even supposing all their knowledge is truth, it is still not knowledge acquired through their own personal experience, but consists of theories set down by their predecessors in summarizing experience of the struggle for production and of the class struggle. It is entirely necessary that students should acquire this kind of knowledge, but it must be understood that as far as they are concerned such knowledge is in a sense still one-sided, something which has been verified by others but not yet by themselves. What is most important is to be good at applying this knowledge in life and in practice. Therefore, I advise those who have only book-learning but as yet no contact with reality, and also those with little practical experience, to realize their own short-comings and become a little more modest.

How can those who have only book-learning be turned into intellectuals in the true sense? The only way is to get them to take part in practical work and become practical workers, to get those engaged in theoretical work to study important practical problems. In this way our aim can be attained.

What I have said will probably make some people angry. They will say, "According to your explanation, even Marx would not be regarded as an intellectual." I say they are wrong. Marx took part in the practice of the revolutionary movement and also created revolutionary theory. Beginning with the commodity, the simplest element of capitalism, he made a thorough study of the economic structure of capitalist society. Millions of people saw and handled commodities every day but were so used to them that they took no notice. Marx alone studied commodities scientifically. He carried out a tremendous work of research into their actual development and derived a thoroughly scientific theory from what existed universally. He studied nature, history and proletarian revolution and created dialectical materialism, historical materialism and the theory of proletarian revolution. Thus Marx became a most completely developed intellectual, representing the acme of human wisdom; he was fundamentally different from those who have only book-learning. Marx undertook detailed investigations and studies in the course of practical struggles, formed generalizations and then verified his conclusions by testing them in practical struggles — this is what we call theoretical work. Our Party needs a large number of comrades who will learn how to do such work. In our Party there are many comrades who can learn to do this kind of theoretical research; most of them are intelligent and promising and we should value them. But they must follow correct principles and not repeat the mistake of the past. They must discard dogmatism and not confine themselves to ready-made phrases in books.

There is only one kind of true theory in this world, theory that is drawn from objective reality and then verified by objective reality; nothing else is worthy of the name of theory in our sense. Stalin said that theory becomes aimless when it is not connected with practice.[3] Aimless theory is useless and false and should be discarded. We should point the finger of scorn at those who are fond of aimless theorizing. Marxism-Leninism is the most correct, scientific and revolutionary truth, born out of and verified by objective reality, but many who study Marxism-Leninism take it as lifeless dogma, thus impeding the development of theory and harming themselves as well as other comrades.

On the other hand, our comrades who are engaged in practical work will also come to grief if they misuse their experience. True, these people are often rich in experience, which is very valuable, but it is very dangerous if they rest content with their own experience. They must realize that their knowledge is mostly perceptual and partial and that they lack rational and comprehensive knowledge; in other words, they lack theory and their knowledge, too, is relatively incomplete. Without comparatively complete knowledge it is impossible to do revolutionary work well.

Thus, there are two kinds of incomplete knowledge, one is ready-made knowledge found in books and the other is knowledge that is mostly perceptual and partial; both are one-sided. Only an integration of the two can yield knowledge that is sound and relatively complete.

In order to study theory, however, our cadres of working-class and peasant origin must first acquire an elementary education. Without it they cannot learn Marxist-Leninist theory. Having acquired it, they can study Marxism-Leninism at any time. In my childhood I never attended a Marxist-Leninist school and was taught only such things as, "The Master said: 'How pleasant it is to learn and constantly review what one has learned.' "[4] Though this teaching material was antiquated, it did me some good because from it I learned to read. Nowadays we no longer study the Confucian classics but such new subjects as modern Chinese, history, geography and elementary natural science, which, once learned, are useful everywhere. The Central Committee of our Party now emphatically requires that our cadres of working-class and peasant origin should obtain an elementary education because they can then take up any branch of study — politics, military science or economics. Otherwise, for all their rich experience they will never be able to study theory.

It follows that to combat subjectivism we must enable people of each of these two types to develop in whichever direction they are deficient and to merge with the other type. Those with book-learning must develop in the direction of practice; it is only in this way that they will stop being content with books and avoid committing dogmatist errors. Those experienced in work must take up the study of theory and must read seriously; only then will they be able to systematize and synthesize their experience and raise it to the level of theory, only then will they not mistake their partial experience for universal truth and not commit empiricist errors. Dogmatism and empiricism alike are subjectivism, each originating from an opposite pole.

Hence there are two kinds of subjectivism in our Party, dogmatism and empiricism. Each sees only a part and not the whole. If people are not on guard, do not realize that such one-sidedness is a short-coming and do not strive to overcome it, they are liable to go astray.

However, of the two kinds of subjectivism, dogmatism is still the greater danger in our Party. For dogmatists can easily assume a Marxist guise to bluff, capture and make servitors of cadres of working-class and peasant origin who cannot easily see through them; they can also bluff and ensnare the naive youth. If we overcome dogmatism, cadres with book-learning will readily join with those who have experience and will take to the study of practical things, and then many good cadres who integrate theory with experience, as well as some real theorists, will emerge. If we overcome dogmatism, the comrades with practical experience will have good teachers to help them raise their experience to the level of theory and so avoid empiricist errors.

Besides muddled ideas about the "theorist" and the "intellectual", there is a muddled idea among many comrades about "linking theory and practice", a phrase they have on their lips every day. They talk constantly about "linking", but actually they mean "separating", because they make no effort at linking. How is Marxist-Leninist theory to be linked with the practice of the Chinese revolution? To use a common expression, it is by "shooting the arrow at the target". As the arrow is to the target, so is Marxism-Leninism to the Chinese revolution. Some comrades, however, are "shooting without a target", shooting at random, and such people are liable to harm the revolution. Others merely stroke the arrow fondly, exclaiming, "What a fine arrow! What a fine arrow!", but never want to shoot it. These people are only connoisseurs of curios and have virtually nothing to do with the revolution. The arrow of Marxism-Leninism must be used to shoot at the target of the Chinese revolution. Unless this point is made clear, the theoretical level of our Party can never be raised and the Chinese revolution can never be victorious.

Our comrades must understand that we study Marxism-Leninism not for display, nor because there is any mystery about it, but solely because it is the science which leads the revolutionary cause of the proletariat to victory. Even now, there are not a few people who still regard odd quotations from Marxist-Leninist works as a ready-made panacea which, once acquired, can easily cure all maladies. These people show childish ignorance, and we should enlighten them. It is precisely such ignorant people who take Marxism-Leninism as a religious dogma. To them we should say bluntly, "Your dogma is worthless." Marx, Engels, Lenin and Stalin have repeatedly stated that our theory is not a dogma but a guide to action. But such people prefer to forget this statement which is of the greatest, indeed the utmost, importance. Chinese Communists can be regarded as linking theory with practice only when they become good at applying the Marxist-Leninist stand, viewpoint and method and the teachings of Lenin and Stalin concerning the Chinese revolution and when, further-more, through serious research into the realities of China's history and revolution, they do creative theoretical work to meet China's needs in different spheres. Merely talking about linking theory and practice without actually doing anything about it is of no use, even if one goes on talking for a hundred years. To oppose the subjectivist, one-sided approach to problems, we must demolish dogmatist sub-jectiveness and one-sidedness.

So much for today about combating subjectivism in order to rectify the style of study throughout the Party.

Let me now speak about the question of sectarianism.

Having been steeled for twenty years, our Party is no longer dominated by sectarianism. Remnants of sectarianism, however, are still found both in the Party's internal relations and in its external relations. Sectarian tendencies in internal relations lead to exclusiveness towards comrades inside the Party and hinder inner-Party unity and solidarity, while sectarian tendencies in external relations lead to ex-clusiveness towards people outside the Party and hinder the Party in its task of uniting the whole people. Only by uprooting this evil in both its aspects can the Party advance unimpeded in its great task of achieving unity among all Party comrades and among all the people of our country.

What are the remnants of inner-Party sectarianism? They are mainly as follows:

First, the assertion of "independence". Some comrades see only the interests of the part and not the whole; they always put undue

stress on that part of the work for which they themselves are responsible and always wish to subordinate the interests of the whole to
the interests of their own part. They do not understand the Party's
system of democratic centralism; they do not realize that the Communist Party not only needs democracy but needs centralization even
more. They forget the system of democratic centralism in which the
minority is subordinate to the majority, the lower level to the higher
level, the part to the whole and the entire membership to the Central
Committee. Chang Kuo-tao[5] asserted his "independence" of the
Central Committee of the Party and as a result "asserted" himself
into betraying the Party and became a Kuomintang agent. Although
the sectarianism we are now discussing is not of this extremely
serious kind, it must still be guarded against and we must do away
completely with all manifestations of disunity. We should encourage
comrades to take the interests of the whole into account. Every Party
member, every branch of work, every statement and every action
must proceed from the interests of the whole Party; it is absolutely
impermissible to violate this principle.

Those who assert this kind of "independence" are usually wedded
to the doctrine of "me first" and are generally wrong on the question
of the relationship between the individual and the Party. Although
in words they profess respect for the Party, in practice they put themselves first and the Party second. What are these people after? They
are after fame and position and want to be in the limelight. Whenever they are put in charge of a branch of work, they assert their
"independence". With this aim, they draw some people in, push others
out and resort to boasting, flattery and touting among the comrades,
thus importing the vulgar style of the bourgeois political parties into
the Communist Party. It is their dishonesty that causes them to
come to grief. I believe we should do things honestly, for without
an honest attitude it is absolutely impossible to accomplish anything
in this world. Which are the honest people? Marx, Engels, Lenin
and Stalin are honest, men of science are honest. Which are the
dishonest people? Trotsky, Bukharin, Chen Tu-hsiu and Chang
Kuo-tao are extremely dishonest; and those who assert "independence" out of personal or sectional interest are dishonest too. All sly
people, all those who do not have a scientific attitude in their work,
fancy themselves resourceful and clever, but in fact they are most
stupid and will come to no good. Students in our Party School must
pay attention to this problem. We must build a centralized, unified

Party and make a clean sweep of all unprincipled factional struggles. We must combat individualism and sectarianism so as to enable our whole Party to march in step and fight for one common goal.

Cadres from the outside and those from the locality must unite and combat sectarian tendencies. Very careful attention must be given to the relations between outside and local cadres because many anti-Japanese base areas were established only after the arrival of the Eighth Route Army or the New Fourth Army and much of the local work developed only after the arrival of outside cadres. Our comrades must understand that in these conditions it is possible for our base areas to be consolidated and for our Party to take root there only when the two kinds of cadres unite as one and when a large number of local cadres develop and are promoted; otherwise it is impossible. Both the outside and the local cadres have their strong and weak points, and to make any progress they must overcome their own weak points by learning from each other's strong points. The outside cadres are generally not up to the local cadres in familiarity with local conditions and links with the masses. Take me for instance. Although I have been in northern Shensi five or six years, I am far behind the local comrades in understanding local conditions and in links with the people here. Our comrades going to the anti-Japanese base areas in Shansi, Hopei, Shantung and other provinces must pay attention to this. Moreover, even within the same base area, owing to the fact that some districts develop earlier and others later, there is a difference between the local cadres of a district and those from outside it. Cadres who come from a more developed to a less developed district are also outside cadres in relation to that locality, and they, too, should pay great attention to fostering and helping local cadres. Generally speaking, in places where outside cadres are in charge, it is they who should bear the main responsibility if their relations with the local cadres are not good. And the chief comrades in charge should bear greater responsibility. The attention paid to this problem in some places is still very inadequate. Some people look down on the local cadres and ridicule them, saying, "What do these locals know? Clodhoppers!" Such people utterly fail to understand the importance of local cadres; they know neither the latter's strong points nor their own weaknesses and adopt an incorrect, sectarian attitude. All outside cadres must cherish the local cadres and give them constant help and must not be permitted to ridicule or attack them. Of course, the local cadres on their part must learn from the strong points of the outside cadres and rid themselves of inappropriate, narrow views so that they and the outside cadres become as one, with no distinction between "them" and "us", and thus avoid sectarian tendencies.

The same applies to the relationship between cadres in army service and other cadres working in the locality. They must be completely united and must oppose sectarian tendencies. The army cadres must help the local cadres, and vice versa. If there is friction between them, each should make allowance for the other and carry out proper self-criticism. Generally speaking, in places where army cadres are actually in positions of leadership, it is they who should bear the main responsibility if their relations with the local cadres are not good. Only when the army cadres understand their own responsibility and are modest in their attitude towards the local cadres can the conditions be created for the smooth progress of our war effort and our work of construction in the base areas.

The same applies to the relationship among different army units, different localities and different departments. We must oppose the tendency towards selfish departmentalism by which the interests of one's own unit are looked after to the exclusion of those of others. Whoever is indifferent to the difficulties of others, refuses to transfer cadres to other units on request, or releases only the inferior ones, "using the neighbour's field as an outlet for his overflow", and does not give the slightest consideration to other departments, localities or people — such a person is a selfish departmentalist who has entirely lost the spirit of communism. Lack of consideration for the whole and complete indifference to other departments, localities and people are characteristics of a selfish departmentalist. We must intensify our efforts to educate such persons and to make them understand that selfish departmentalism is a sectarian tendency which will become very dangerous, if allowed to develop.

Another problem is the relationship between old and new cadres. Since the beginning of the War of Resistance, our Party has grown enormously, and large numbers of new cadres have emerged; that is a very good thing. In his report to the Eighteenth Congress of the Communist Party of the Soviet Union (B.), Comrade Stalin said, ". . . there are never enough old cadres, there are far less than required, and they are already partly going out of commission owing to the operation of the laws of nature." Here he was discussing the cadres situation and not only the laws of nature. If our Party does not have a great many new cadres working in unity and co-operation with the old cadres, our cause will come to a stop. All old cadres, therefore, should welcome the new ones with the utmost enthusiasm and show them the warmest solicitude. True, new cadres have their shortcomings. They have not been long in the revolution and lack experience, and unavoidably some have brought with them vestiges of the unwholesome ideology of the old society, remnants of the ideology of petty-bourgeois individualism. But such shortcomings can be gradually eliminated through education and tempering in the revolution. The strong point of the new cadres, as Stalin has said, is that they are acutely sensitive to what is new and are therefore enthusiastic and active to a high degree — the very qualities which some of the old cadres lack.[6] Cadres, new and old, should respect each other, learn from each other and overcome their own shortcomings by learning from each other's strong points, so as to unite as one in the common cause and guard against sectarian tendencies. Generally speaking, in places where the old cadres are mainly in charge, it is they who should bear the chief responsibility if relations with the new cadres are not good.

All the above — relations between the part and the whole, relations between the individual and the Party, relations between outside and local cadres, relations between army cadres and other cadres working in the locality, relations between this and that army unit, between this and that locality, between this and that department and relations between old and new cadres — are relations within the Party. In all these relations it is necessary to enhance the spirit of communism and guard against sectarian tendencies, so that the ranks of our Party will be in good order, march in step and therefore fight well. This is a very important problem which we must solve thoroughly in rectifying the Party's style of work. Sectarianism is an expression of subjectivism in organizational relations; if we want to get rid of subjectivism and promote the Marxist-Leninist spirit of seeking truth from facts, we must sweep the remnants of sectarianism out of the Party and proceed from the principle that the Party's interests are above personal or sectional interests, so that the Party can attain complete solidarity and unity.

The remnants of sectarianism must be eliminated from the Party's external as well as its internal relations. The reason is this: we cannot defeat the enemy by merely uniting the comrades throughout the Party, we can defeat the enemy only by uniting the people throughout the country. For twenty years the Communist Party of China has done great and arduous work in the cause of uniting the people of the whole country, and the achievements in this work since the outbreak of the War of Resistance are even greater than in the past. This does not mean, however, that all our comrades already have a correct style in dealing with the masses and are free from sectarian tendencies. No. In fact, sectarian tendencies still exist among a number of comrades, and in some cases to a very serious degree. Many of our comrades tend to be overbearing in their relations with non-Party people, look down upon them, despise or refuse to respect them or appreciate their strong points. This is indeed a sectarian tendency. After reading a few Marxist books, such comrades become more arrogant instead of more modest, and invariably dismiss others as no good without realizing that in fact their own knowledge is only half-baked. Our comrades must realize the truth that Communist Party members are at all times a minority as compared with non-Party people. Supposing one out of every hundred persons were a Communist, then there would be 4,500,000 Communists among China's population of 450,000,000. Yet, even if our membership reached this huge figure, Communists would still form only one per cent of the whole population, while 99 per cent would be non-Party people. What reason can we then have for not co-operating with non-Party people? As regards all those who wish to co-operate with us or might co-operate with us, we have only the duty of co-operating and absolutely no right to shut them out. But some Party members do not understand this and look down upon, or even shut out, those who wish to co-operate with us. There are no grounds whatsoever for doing so. Have Marx, Engels, Lenin and Stalin given us any grounds? They have not. On the contrary, they have always earnestly enjoined us to form close ties with the masses and not divorce ourselves from them. Or has the Central Committee of the Communist Party of China given us any grounds? No. Among all its resolutions there is not a single one that says we may divorce ourselves from the masses and so isolate ourselves. On the contrary, the Central Committee has always told us to form close ties with the masses and not to divorce ourselves from them. Thus any action divorcing us from the masses has no justification at all and is simply the mischievous result of the sectarian ideas some of our comrades have themselves concocted. As such sectarianism remains very serious among some of our comrades and still obstructs the application of the Party line, we should carry out extensive education within the Party to meet this problem. Above all, we should make our cadres really understand how serious the problem is and how utterly impossible it is to overthrow the enemy and attain the goal of the revolution unless Party members unite with the non-Party cadres and with non-Party people.

All sectarian ideas are subjectivist and are incompatible with the real needs of the revolution; hence the struggle against sectarianism and the struggle against subjectivism should go on simultaneously.

There is no time today to talk about the question of stereotyped Party writing; I shall discuss it at another meeting. Stereotyped Party writing is a vehicle for filth, a form of expression for subjectivism and sectarianism. It does people harm and damages the revolution, and we must get rid of it completely.

To combat subjectivism we must propagate materialism and dialectics. However, there are many comrades in our Party who lay no stress on the propaganda either of materialism or of dialectics. Some tolerate subjectivist propaganda and regard it with equanimity. They think they believe in Marxism, but make no effort to propagate materialism and do not give it a thought or express any opinion when they hear or read subjectivist stuff. This is not the attitude of a Communist. It allows many of our comrades to be poisoned by subjectivist ideas, which numb their sensitivity. We should therefore launch a campaign of enlightenment within the Party to free the minds of our comrades from the fog of subjectivism and dogmatism and should call upon them to boycott subjectivism, sectarianism and stereotyped Party writing. Such evils are like Japanese goods, for only our enemy wishes us to preserve them and continue to befuddle ourselves with them; so we should advocate a boycott against them, just as we boycott Japanese goods.[7] We should boycott all the wares of subjectivism, sectarianism and stereotyped Party writing, make their sale difficult, and not allow their purveyors to ply their trade by exploiting the low theoretical level in the Party. Our comrades must develop a good nose for this purpose; they should take a sniff at everything and distinguish the good from the bad before they decide whether to welcome it or boycott it. Communists must always go into the whys and wherefores of anything, use their own heads and carefully think over whether or not it corresponds to reality and is really well founded; on no account should they follow blindly and encourage slavishness.

Finally, in opposing subjectivism, sectarianism and stereotyped Party writing we must have in mind two purposes: first, "learn from past mistakes to avoid future ones", and second, "cure the sickness to save the patient". The mistakes of the past must be exposed without sparing anyone's sensibilities; it is necessary to analyse and criticize what was bad in the past with a scientific attitude so that work in the future will be done more carefully and done better. This is what is meant by "learn from past mistakes to avoid future ones". But our aim in exposing errors and criticizing shortcomings, like that of a doctor curing a sickness, is solely to save the patient and not to doctor him to death. A person with appendicitis is saved when the surgeon removes his appendix. So long as a person who has made mistakes does not hide his sickness for fear of treatment or persist in his mistakes until he is beyond cure, so long as he honestly and sincerely wishes to be cured and to mend his ways, we should welcome him and cure his sickness so that he can become a good comrade. We can never succeed if we just let ourselves go, and lash out at him. In treating an ideological or a political malady, one must never be rough and rash but must adopt the approach of "curing the sickness to save the patient", which is the only correct and effective method.

I have taken this occasion of the opening of the Party School to speak at length, and I hope comrades will think over what I have said. (*Enthusiastic applause.*)

NOTES

¹ Stereotyped writing, or the "eight-legged essay", was the special form of essay prescribed in the imperial examinations under China's feudal dynasties from the 15th to the 19th centuries; it consisted in juggling with words, concentrated only on form and was devoid of content. Structurally the main body of the essay had eight parts — presentation, amplification, preliminary exposition, initial argument, inceptive paragraphs, middle paragraphs, rear paragraphs and concluding paragraphs, and the fifth to eighth parts each had to have two "legs", *i.e.*, two antithetical paragraphs, hence the name "eight-legged essay". The "eight-legged essay" became a byword in China denoting stereotyped formalism and triteness. Thus "stereotyped Party writing" characterizes the writings of certain people in the revolutionary ranks who piled up revolutionary phrases and terms higgledy-piggledy instead of analysing the facts. Like the "eight-legged essay", their writings were nothing but verbiage.

² This was the decision on recruiting intellectuals adopted by the Central Committee of the Communist Party of China in December 1939, which is printed under the title "Recruit Large Numbers of Intellectuals" in the *Selected Works of Mao Tse-tung*, Vol. II.

[3] See J. V. Stalin, "The Foundations of Leninism", *Problems of Leninism*, Eng. ed., FLPH, Moscow, 1954, p. 31.

[4] This is the opening sentence of the *Confucian Analects*, a record of the dialogues of Confucius and his disciples.

[5] Chang Kuo-tao was a renegade from the Chinese revolution. In early life, speculating on the revolution, he joined the Chinese Communist Party. In the Party he made many mistakes resulting in serious crimes. The most notorious of these was his opposition, in 1935, to the Red Army's northward march and his defeatism and liquidationism in advocating withdrawal by the Red Army to the minority-nationality areas on the Szechuan-Sikang borders; what is more, he openly carried out traitorous activities against the Party and the Central Committee, established his own bogus central committee, disrupted the unity of the Party and the Red Army, and caused heavy losses to the Fourth Front Army of the Red Army. But thanks to patient education by Comrade Mao Tse-tung and the Central Committee, the Fourth Front Army and its numerous cadres soon returned to the correct leadership of the Central Committee of the Party and played a glorious role in subsequent struggles. Chang Kuo-tao, however, proved incorrigible and in the spring of 1938 he slipped out of the Shensi-Kansu-Ningsia Border Region and joined the Kuomintang secret police.

[6] See J. V. Stalin, "Report to the Eighteenth Congress of the C.P.S.U. (B.) on the Work of the Central Committee", *Problems of Leninism*, Eng. ed., FLPH, Moscow, 1954, pp. 784-86.

[7] Boycotting Japanese goods was a method of struggle frequently used by the Chinese people against Japanese imperialist aggression in the first half of the 20th century, as in the patriotic May 4th Movement of 1919, after the September 18th Incident of 1931, and during the War of Resistance Against Japan.

OPPOSE STEREOTYPED PARTY WRITING

February 8, 1942

Comrade Kai-feng has just stated the purpose of today's meeting. I now want to discuss the ways subjectivism and sectarianism use stereotyped Party writing (or the Party "eight-legged essay")[1] as their instrument of propaganda or form of expression. We are fighting against subjectivism and sectarianism, but they will still have a hiding-place to lurk in if at the same time we do not get rid of stereotyped Party writing. If we destroy that too, we shall "checkmate" subjectivism and sectarianism and make both these monsters show themselves in their true colours, and then we shall easily be able to annihilate them, like "rats running across the street with everyone yelling: Kill them! Kill them!"

It does not matter much if a person produces stereotyped Party writings only for himself to read. If he passes them on to someone else, the number of readers is doubled, and already no small harm is done. If he has them posted up, mimeographed, printed in newspapers or published in book form, then the problem becomes indeed a big one, for they can influence many people. And those who produce stereotyped Party writing always seek large audiences. Thus it has become imperative to expose and destroy it.

Stereotyped Party writing is, moreover, one brand of the "foreign stereotype", which was attacked by Lu Hsun a long time ago.[2] Why then do we call it the Party "eight-legged essay"? Because, besides its foreign flavour, it has some smell of native soil. Perhaps it too can be counted as creative work of a sort! Who says our people have not produced any creative works? Here is one! (*Loud laughter.*)

Stereotyped Party writing has a long history in our Party; particularly during the Agrarian Revolution, it sometimes became quite rampant.

This speech was delivered by Comrade Mao Tse-tung at a cadres' meeting in Yenan.

Viewed historically, stereotyped Party writing is a reaction to the May 4th Movement.

During the May 4th Movement, modern-minded people opposed the use of the classical Chinese language and advocated vernacular Chinese, opposed the traditional dogmas and advocated science and democracy, all of which was quite right. The movement then was vigorous and lively, progressive and revolutionary. In those days the ruling classes indoctrinated students with Confucian teachings and compelled the people to venerate all the trappings of Confucianism as religious dogma, and all writers used the classical language. In short, what was written and taught by the ruling classes and their hangers-on was in the nature of stereotyped writing and dogma, both in content and in form. That was the old stereotype and the old dogma. A tremendous achievement of the May 4th Movement was its public exposure of the ugliness of the old stereotype and the old dogma and its call to the people to rise against them. Another great and related achievement was its fight against imperialism, but the struggle against the old stereotype and the old dogma remains one of the great achievements of the May 4th Movement. Later on, however, foreign stereotyped writing and foreign dogma came into being. Running counter to Marxism, certain people in our Party developed the foreign stereotype and dogma into subjectivism, sectarianism and stereotyped Party writing. These are the new stereotype and the new dogma. They have become so deeply ingrained in the minds of many comrades that today we still have a very strenuous job of remoulding to do. Thus we see that the lively, vigorous, progressive and revolutionary movement of the May 4th period which fought the old feudal stereotyped writing and dogma was later turned by some people into its very opposite, giving rise to the new stereotyped writing and dogma. The latter are not lively and vigorous but dead and stiff, not progressive but retrogressive, not revolutionary but obstacles to revolution. That is to say, the foreign stereotyped writing, or stereotyped Party writing, is a reaction to the original nature of the May 4th Movement. The May 4th Movement, however, had its own weaknesses. Many of the leaders lacked the critical spirit of Marxism, and the method they used was generally that of the bourgeoisie, that is, the formalist method. They were quite right in opposing the old stereotype and the old dogma and in advocating science and democracy. But in dealing with current conditions, with history, and with things foreign, they lacked the critical spirit of historical materialism and regarded what was bad as absolutely and wholly bad and what was good as absolutely and wholly good. This formalist approach to problems affected the subsequent course of the movement. In its development, the May 4th Movement divided into two currents. One section inherited its scientific and democratic spirit and transformed it on the basis of Marxism; this is what the Communists and some non-Party Marxists did. Another section took the road of the bourgeoisie; this was the development of formalism towards the Right. But within the Communist Party too the situation was not uniform; there, too, some members deviated and, lacking a firm grasp of Marxism, committed errors of formalism, namely, the errors of subjectivism, sectarianism and stereotyped Party writing. This was the development of formalism towards the "Left". So it can be seen that stereotyped Party writing is no accident, but is, on the one hand, a reaction to the positive elements of the May 4th Movement and, on the other, a legacy, a continuation or development of its negative elements. It is useful for us to understand this point. Just as it was revolutionary and necessary to fight the old stereotyped writing and the old dogmatism during the period of the May 4th Movement, so it is revolutionary and necessary today for us to use Marxism to criticize the new stereotyped writing and the new dogmatism. If there had been no fight against the old stereotype and the old dogmatism during the May 4th period, the minds of the Chinese people would not have been freed from bondage to them, and China would have no hope of freedom and independence. This task was merely begun in the period of the May 4th Movement, and a very great effort — a huge job of work on the road of revolutionary remoulding — is still necessary to enable the whole people to free themselves completely from the domination of the old stereotype and dogmatism. If today we do not oppose the new stereotyped writing and the new dogmatism, the minds of the Chinese people will be fettered by formalism of another kind. If we do not get rid of the poison of stereotyped Party writing and the error of dogmatism found among a section (only a section, of course) of Party comrades, then it will be impossible to arouse a vigorous and lively revolutionary spirit, to eradicate the bad habit of taking a wrong attitude towards Marxism and to disseminate and develop true Marxism; furthermore, it will be impossible to conduct an energetic struggle against the influence of the old stereotyped writing and dogma among the whole people, and against that of foreign stereotyped writing and dogma among many of the people, and impossible to attain the purpose of demolishing and sweeping away these influences.

Subjectivism, sectarianism and stereotyped Party writing — all three are anti-Marxist and meet the needs not of the proletariat but of the exploiting classes. They are a reflection of petty-bourgeois ideology in our Party. China is a country with a very large petty bourgeoisie and our Party is surrounded by this enormous class; a great number of our Party members come from this class, and when they join the Party they inevitably drag in with them a petty-bourgeois tail, be it long or short. Unless checked and transformed, the fanaticism and one-sidedness of petty-bourgeois revolutionaries can easily engender subjectivism and sectarianism, of which foreign stereotyped writing, or stereotyped Party writing, is one form of expression.

It is not easy to clean out these things and sweep them away. It must be done properly, that is, by taking pains to reason with people. If we reason earnestly and properly, it will be effective. The first thing to do in this reasoning process is to give the patient a good shake-up by shouting at him, "You are ill!" so as to administer a shock and make him break out in a sweat, and then to give him sincere advice on getting treatment.

Let us now analyse stereotyped Party writing and see where its evils lie. Using poison as an antidote to poison, we shall imitate the form of the stereotyped eight-section essay and set forth the following "eight legs", which might be called the eight major indictments.

The first indictment against stereotyped Party writing is that it fills endless pages with empty verbiage. Some of our comrades love to write long articles with no substance, very much like the "foot-bindings of a slattern, long as well as smelly". Why must they write such long and empty articles? There can be only one explanation; they are determined the masses shall not read them. Because the articles are long and empty, the masses shake their heads at the very sight of them. How can they be expected to read them? Such writings are good for nothing except to bluff the naive, among whom they spread bad influences and foster bad habits. On June 22 last year the Soviet Union began waging a gigantic war against aggression, and yet Stalin's speech on July 3 was only the length of an editorial in our *Liberation Daily*. Had any of our gentlemen written that speech, just imagine! It would have run to tens of thousands of words at a minimum. We are in the midst of a war, and we should learn how to write shorter and pithier articles. Although there is as yet no fighting here in Yenan, our troops at the front are daily engaged in battle, and the people in the rear are busy at work. If articles are too long, who will read them? Some comrades at the front, too, like to write long reports. They take pains over writing them and send them here for us to read. But who has the hardihood to read them? If long and empty articles are no good, are short and empty ones any better? They are no good either. We should forbid all empty talk. But the first and foremost task is to throw the long, smelly foot-bindings of the slattern into the dustbin. Some may ask, "Isn't *Capital* very long? What are we to do about that?" The answer is simple, just go on reading it. There is a proverb, "Sing different songs on different mountains"; another runs, "Fit the appetite to the dishes and the dress to the figure". Whatever we do must be done according to actual circumstances, and it is the same with writing articles and making speeches. What we oppose is long-winded and empty stereotyped writing, but we do not mean that everything must necessarily be short in order to be good. True, we need short articles in war time, but above all we need articles that have substance. Articles devoid of substance are the least justifiable and the most objectionable. The same applies to speech-making; we must put an end to all empty, long-winded speeches.

The second indictment against stereotyped Party writing is that it strikes a pose in order to intimidate people. Some stereotyped Party writing is not only long and empty, but also pretentious with the deliberate intention of intimidating people; it carries the worst kind of poison. Writing long-winded and empty articles may be set down to immaturity, but striking a pose to overawe people is not merely immature but downright knavish. Lu Hsun once said in criticism of such people, "Hurling insults and threats is certainly not fighting."[3] What is scientific never fears criticism, for science is truth and fears no refutation. But those who write subjectivist and sectarian articles and speeches in the form of Party stereotypes fear refutation, are very cowardly, and therefore rely on pretentiousness to overawe others, believing that they can thereby silence people and "win the day". Such pretentiousness cannot reflect truth but is an obstacle to truth. Truth does not strike a pose to overawe people but talks and acts honestly and sincerely. Two terms used to appear in the articles and speeches of many comrades, one being "ruthless struggle" and the other "merciless blows". Measures of that kind are entirely necessary against the enemy or against enemy ideology, but to use them

against our own comrades is wrong. It often happens that enemies
and enemy ideology infiltrate into the Party, as is discussed in Item
4 of the Conclusion of the *History of the Communist Party of the
Soviet Union (Bolsheviks), Short Course*. Against these enemies, we
must undoubtedly resort to ruthless struggle and merciless blows,
because the scoundrels use these very measures against the Party; if
we were tolerant of them, we should fall right into their trap. But
the same measures should not be used against comrades who occasionally make mistakes; to them we should apply the method of
criticism and self-criticism, the method indicated in Item 5 of the
Conclusion of the *History of the Communist Party of the Soviet Union
(Bolsheviks), Short Course*. The comrades who in the past loudly
advocated "ruthless struggle" and "merciless blows" against comrades who occasionally made mistakes did so because, for one thing,
they failed to make any analysis of the persons they were dealing
with and, for another, they were striking a pose in an effort to
intimidate. This method is no good, no matter whom you are dealing with. Against the enemy this tactic of intimidation is utterly useless, and with our own comrades it can only do harm. It is a tactic
which the exploiting classes and the *lumpen*-proletariat habitually
practise, but for which the proletariat has no use. For the proletariat
the sharpest and most effective weapon is a serious and militant
scientific attitude. The Communist Party lives by the truth of Marxism-
Leninism, by seeking truth from facts, by science, and not by intimidating people. Needless to say, the idea of attaining fame and
position for oneself by pretentiousness is even more contemptible.
In short, when organizations make decisions and issue instructions
and when comrades write articles and make speeches, they must
without exception depend on Marxist-Leninist truth and seek to
serve a useful purpose. This is the only basis on which victory in the
revolution can be achieved; all else is of no avail.

The third indictment against stereotyped Party writing is that
it shoots at random, without considering the audience. A few years
ago a slogan appeared on the Yenan city wall which read, "Working
men and peasants, unite and strive for victory in the War of Resistance
Against Japan!" The idea of the slogan was not at all bad, but the
character "工" [*kung*, meaning working] in "工人" [*kung jen*,
meaning working men], was written as "五", with its perpendicular
stroke twisted into a zigzag. How about the character "人" [*jen*,
meaning men]? It became "𠆢", with three slanting strokes added

to its right leg. The comrade who wrote this was no doubt a disciple of the ancient scholars, but it is rather baffling why he should have written such characters in such a place, on the Yenan city wall, at the time of the War of Resistance. Perhaps he had taken a vow that the common people should not read them; it is difficult to explain otherwise. Communists who really want to do propaganda must consider their audience and bear in mind those who will read their articles and slogans or listen to their speeches and their talk; otherwise they are in effect resolving not to be read or listened to by anyone. Many people often take it for granted that what they write and say can be easily understood by everybody, when it is not so at all. How can people understand them when they write and speak in Party stereotypes? The saying "to play the lute to a cow" implies a gibe at the audience. If we substitute the idea of respect for the audience, the gibe is turned against the player. Why should he strum away without considering his audience? What is worse, he is producing a Party stereotype as raucous as a crow, and yet he insists on cawing at the masses. When shooting an arrow, one must aim at the target; when playing the lute, one must consider the listener; how, then, can one write articles or make speeches without taking the reader or the audience into account? Suppose we want to make friends with a person, whoever he may be, can we become bosom friends if we do not understand each other's hearts, do not know each other's thoughts? It simply will not do for our propaganda workers to rattle on without investigating, studying and analysing their audience.

The fourth indictment against stereotyped Party writing is its drab language that reminds one of a *piehsan*. Like our stereotyped Party writing, the creatures known in Shanghai as "little *piehsan*" are wizened and ugly. If an article or a speech merely rings the changes on a few terms in a classroom tone without a shred of vigour or spirit, is it not rather like a *piehsan*, drab of speech and repulsive in appearance? If someone enters primary school at seven, goes to middle school in his teens, graduates from college in his twenties and never has contact with the masses of the people, he is not to blame if his language is poor and monotonous. But we are revolutionaries working for the masses, and if we do not learn the language of the masses, we cannot work well. At present many of our comrades doing propaganda work make no study of language. Their propaganda is very dull, and few people care to read their articles or listen to their talk.

Why do we need to study language and, what is more, spend much effort on it? Because the mastery of language is not easy and requires painstaking effort. First, let us learn language from the masses. The people's vocabulary is rich, vigorous, vivid and expressive of real life. It is because many of us have not mastered language that our articles and speeches contain few vigorous, vivid and effective expressions and resemble not a hale and healthy person, but an emaciated *piehsan*, a mere bag of bones. Secondly, let us absorb what we need from foreign languages. We should not import foreign expressions mechanically or use them indiscriminately, but should absorb what is good and suits our needs. Our current vocabulary has already incorporated many foreign expressions, because the old Chinese vocabulary was inadequate. For instance, today we are holding a meeting of *kanpu* [cadres], and the term *kanpu* is derived from a foreign word. We should continue to absorb many fresh things from abroad, not only progressive ideas but new expressions as well. Thirdly, let us also learn whatever is alive in the classical Chinese language. Since we have not studied classical Chinese hard enough, we have not made full and proper use of much that is still alive in it. Of course, we are resolutely opposed to the use of obsolete expressions or allusions, and that is final; but what is good and still useful should be taken over. Those who are badly infected by stereotyped Party writing do not take pains to study what is useful in the language of the people, in foreign languages, or in classical Chinese, so the masses do not welcome their dry and dull propaganda, and we too have no need for such poor and incompetent propagandists. Who are our propagandists? They include not only teachers, journalists, writers and artists, but all our cadres. Take the military commanders, for instance. Though they make no public statements, they have to talk to the soldiers and have dealings with the people. What is this if not propaganda? Whenever a man speaks to others, he is doing propaganda work. Unless he is dumb, he always has a few words to say. It is therefore imperative that our comrades should all study language.

The fifth indictment against stereotyped Party writing is that it arranges items under a complicated set of headings, as if starting a Chinese pharmacy. Go and take a look at any Chinese pharmacy, and you will see cabinets with numerous drawers, each bearing the name of a drug — toncal, foxglove, rhubarb, saltpetre . . . indeed, everything that should be there. This method has been picked up by our comrades. In their articles and speeches, their books and reports, they use first the big Chinese numerals, second the small Chinese numerals, third the characters for the ten celestial stems, fourth the characters for the twelve earthly branches, and then capital A, B, C, D, then small a, b, c, d, followed by the Arabic numerals, and what not! How fortunate that the ancients and the foreigners created all these symbols for us so that we can start a Chinese pharmacy without the slightest effort. For all its verbiage, an article that bristles with such symbols, that does not pose, analyse or solve problems and that does not take a stand for or against anything is devoid of real content and nothing but a Chinese pharmacy. I am not saying that such symbols as the ten celestial stems, etc., should not be used, but that this kind of approach to problems is wrong. The method borrowed from the Chinese pharmacy, which many of our comrades are very fond of, is really the most crude, infantile and philistine of all. It is a formalist method, classifying things according to their external features instead of their internal relations. If one takes a conglomeration of concepts that are not internally related and arranges them into an article, speech or report simply according to the external features of things, then one is juggling with concepts and may also lead others to indulge in the same sort of game, with the result that they do not use their brains to think over problems and probe into the essence of things, but are satisfied merely to list phenomena in ABCD order. What is a problem? A problem is the contradiction in a thing. Where one has an unresolved contradiction, there one has a problem. Since there is a problem, you have to be for one side and against the other, and you have to pose the problem. To pose the problem, you must first make a preliminary investigation and study of the two basic aspects of the problem or contradiction before you can understand the nature of the contradiction. This is the process of discovering the problem. Preliminary investigation and study can discover the problem, can pose the problem, but cannot as yet solve it. In order to solve the problem it is necessary to make a systematic and thorough investigation and study. This is the process of analysis. In posing the problem too, analysis is needed; otherwise, faced with a chaotic and bewildering mass of phenomena, you will not be able to discern where the problem or contradiction lies. But here, by the process of analysis we mean a process of systematic and thorough analysis. It often happens that although a problem has been posed it cannot be solved because the internal relations of things have not yet been revealed, because this process of systematic and thorough analysis has not yet been carried out; consequently we still cannot see the contours of the problem clearly, cannot make a synthesis and so cannot solve the problem well. If an article or speech is important and meant to give guidance, it ought to pose a particular problem, then analyse it and then make a synthesis pointing to the nature of the problem and providing the method for solving it; in all this, formalist methods are useless. Since infantile, crude, philistine and lazy-minded formalist methods are prevalent in our Party, we must expose them; only thus can everybody learn to use the Marxist method to observe, pose, analyse and solve problems; only thus can we do our work well and only thus can our revolutionary cause triumph.

The sixth indictment against stereotyped Party writing is that it is irresponsible and harms people wherever it appears. All the offences mentioned above are due partly to immaturity and partly to an insufficient sense of responsibility. Let us take washing the face to illustrate the point. We all wash our faces every day, many of us more than once, and inspect ourselves in the mirror afterwards by way of "investigation and study" (*loud laughter*), for fear that something may not be quite right. What a great sense of responsibility! If we wrote articles and made speeches with the same sense of responsibility, we would not be doing badly. Do not present what is not presentable. Always bear in mind that it may influence the thoughts and actions of others. If a man happens not to wash his face for a day or two, that of course is not good, and if after washing he leaves a smudge or two, that too is not so pleasing, but there is no serious danger. It is different with writing articles or making speeches; they are intended solely to influence others. Yet our comrades go about this task casually; this means putting the trivial above the important. Many people write articles and make speeches without prior study or preparation, and after writing an article, they do not bother to go over it several times in the same way as they would examine their faces in the mirror after washing, but instead offhandedly send it to be published. Often the result is "A thousand words from the pen in a stream, but ten thousand *li* away from the theme". Talented though these writers may appear, they actually harm people. This bad habit, this weak sense of responsibility, must be corrected.

The seventh indictment against stereotyped Party writing is that it poisons the whole Party and jeopardizes the revolution. The eighth indictment is that its spread would wreck the country and ruin the people. These two indictments are self-evident and require no elaboration. In other words, if stereotyped Party writing is not transformed but is allowed to develop unchecked, the consequences will be very serious indeed. The poison of subjectivism and sectarianism is hidden in stereotyped Party writing, and if this poison spreads it will endanger both the Party and the country.

The aforesaid eight counts are our call to arms against stereotyped Party writing.

As a form, the Party stereotype is not only unsuitable for expressing the revolutionary spirit but is apt to stifle it. To develop the revolutionary spirit it is necessary to discard stereotyped Party writing and instead to adopt the Marxist-Leninist style of writing, which is vigorous, lively, fresh and forceful. This style of writing has existed for a long time, but is yet to be enriched and spread widely among us. When we have destroyed foreign stereotyped writing and stereotyped Party writing, we can enrich our new style of writing and spread it widely, thereby advancing the Party's revolutionary cause.

The Party stereotype is not only confined to articles and speeches, but is also found in the conduct of meetings. "1. Opening announcement; 2. report; 3. discussion; 4. conclusions; and 5. adjournment." If this rigid procedure is followed at every meeting, large or small, everywhere and every time, is not that another Party stereotype? When "reports" are made at meetings they often go as follows: "1. the international situation; 2. the domestic situation; 3. the Border Region; and 4. our own department"; and the meetings often last from morning till night, with even those having nothing to say taking the floor, as though they would let the others down unless they spoke. In short, there is a disregard for actual conditions and deadly adherence to rigid old forms and habits. Should we not correct all these things too?

Nowadays many people are calling for a transformation to a national, scientific and mass style. That is very good. But "transformation" means thorough change, from top to bottom and inside out. Yet some people who have not made even a slight change are calling for a transformation. I would therefore advise these comrades to begin by making just a little change before they go on to "transform", or else they will remain entangled in dogmatism and stereotyped Party writing. This can be described as having grandiose aims but puny abilities, great ambition but little talent, and it will accomplish nothing. So whoever talks glibly about "transformation to a mass style" while in fact he is stuck fast in his own small circle had better watch out, or some day one of the masses may bump into him along the road and say, "What about all this 'transformation', sir? Can I see a bit of it, please?" and he will be in a fix. If he is not just prating but sincerely wants to transform to a mass style, he must really go among the common people and learn from them, otherwise his "transformation" will remain up in the air. There are some who keep clamouring for transformation to a mass style but cannot speak three sentences in the language of the common people. It shows they are not really determined to learn from the masses. Their minds are still confined to their own small circles.

At this meeting copies of *A Guide to Propaganda,* a pamphlet containing four articles, have been distributed, and I advise our comrades to read and re-read it.

The first piece, composed of excerpts from the *History of the Communist Party of the Soviet Union (Bolsheviks), Short Course,* deals with the way Lenin did propaganda work. It describes, among other things, how Lenin wrote leaflets:

> Under Lenin's guidance, the St. Petersburg League of Struggle for the Emancipation of the Working Class was the first body in Russia that began to *unite Socialism with the working-class movement.* When a strike broke out in some factory, the League of Struggle, which through the members of its circles was kept well posted on the state of affairs in the factories, immediately responded by issuing leaflets and Socialist proclamations. These leaflets exposed the oppression of the workers by the manufacturers, explained how the workers should fight for their interests, and set forth the workers' demands. The leaflets told the plain truth about the ulcers of capitalism, the poverty of the workers, their intolerably hard working day of 12 to 14 hours, and their utter lack of rights. They also put forward appropriate political demands.

Take note, "well posted" and "told the plain truth"! Again:

> With the collaboration of the worker Babushkin, Lenin at the end of 1894 wrote the first agitational leaflet of this kind and an appeal to the workers of the Semyannikov Works in St. Petersburg who were on strike.

To write a leaflet, you must consult with comrades who are well posted on the state of affairs. It was on the basis of such investigation and study that Lenin wrote and worked.

Every leaflet greatly helped to stiffen the spirit of the workers. They saw that the Socialists were helping and defending them.[4]

Do we agree with Lenin? If we do, we must work in the spirit of Lenin. That is, we must do as Lenin did and not fill endless pages with verbiage, or shoot at random without considering the audience, or become self-opinionated and bombastic.

The second piece is composed of excerpts from Dimitrov's statements at the Seventh World Congress of the Communist International. What did Dimitrov say? He said:

> We must learn to talk to the masses, not in the language of book formulas, but in the language of fighters for the cause of the masses, whose every word, whose every idea reflects the innermost thoughts and sentiments of millions.[5]

And again:

> . . . the masses cannot assimilate our decisions unless we learn to speak the language which the masses understand.
>
> We do not always know how to speak simply, concretely, in images which are familiar and intelligible to the masses. We are still unable to refrain from abstract formulas which we have learned by rote. As a matter of fact, if you look through our leaflets, newspapers, resolutions and theses, you will find that they are often written in a language and style so heavy that they are difficult for even our Party functionaries to understand, let alone the rank-and-file workers.[6]

Well? Does not Dimitrov put his finger on our weak spot? Apparently, stereotyped Party writing exists in foreign countries as well as in China, so you can see it is a common disease. (*Laughter.*) In any case, we should cure our own disease quickly in accordance with Comrade Dimitrov's injunction.

Every one of us must make this a law, a Bolshevik law, an elementary rule:

When writing or speaking always have in mind the rank-and-file worker who must understand you, must believe in your

*appeal and be ready to follow you! You must have in mind those
for whom you write, to whom you speak.*[7]

This is the prescription made out for us by the Communist International, a prescription that must be followed. Let it be a *law* for us!

The third article, selected from the *Complete Works of Lu Hsun*,
is the author's reply to the magazine *The Dipper*,[8] discussing how to
write. What did Lu Hsun say? Altogether he set forth eight rules of
writing, some of which I shall pick out for comment here.

Rule 1: "Pay close attention to all manner of things; observe
more, and if you have observed only a little, then do not write."

What he says is, "pay close attention to all manner of things",
not just to one thing or half a thing. He says "observe more", not
just take a look or half a look. How about us? Don't we often do
exactly the opposite and write after having observed only a little?

Rule 2: "Do not force yourself to write when you have nothing
to say."

What about us? Don't we often force ourselves to write a great
deal when it is all too clear that there is nothing in our heads? It is
sheer irresponsibility to pick up the pen and "force ourselves to write"
without investigation or study.

Rule 4: "After writing something, read it over twice at least,
and do your utmost to strike out non-essential words, sentences
and paragraphs, without the slightest compunction. Rather con-
dense the material for a novel into a sketch, never spin out the
material for a sketch into a novel."

Confucius advised, "Think twice",[9] and Han Yu said, "A deed
is accomplished through taking thought."[10] That was in ancient times.
Today matters have become very complicated, and sometimes it is
not even enough to think them over three or four times. Lu Hsun
said, "Read it over twice at least." And at most? He did not say,
but in my opinion it does no harm to go over an important article
more than ten times and to revise it conscientiously before it is
published. Articles are the reflection of objective reality, which is
intricate and complex and must be studied over and over again before
it can be properly reflected; to be slipshod in this respect is to be
ignorant of the rudiments of writing.

Rule 6: "Do not coin adjectives or other terms that are intelligible to nobody but yourself."

We have "coined" too many expressions that are "intelligible to nobody". Sometimes a single clause runs to forty or fifty words and is packed with "adjectives or other terms that are intelligible to nobody". Many who never tire of professing to follow Lu Hsun are the very ones who turn their backs on him!

The last piece is taken from the report on how to develop a national style of propaganda, which was adopted at the Sixth Plenary Session of the Sixth Central Committee of the Communist Party of China. At that session held in 1938, we said that "any talk about Marxism apart from China's specific characteristics is only Marxism in the abstract, Marxism in a vacuum". That is to say, we must oppose all empty talk about Marxism, and Communists living in China must study Marxism by linking it with the realities of the Chinese revolution.

The report said:

> Foreign stereotypes must be abolished, there must be less singing of empty, abstract tunes, and dogmatism must be laid to rest; they must be replaced by the fresh, lively Chinese style and spirit which the common people of China love. To separate internationalist content from national form is the practice of those who do not understand the first thing about internationalism. We, on the contrary, must link the two closely. In this matter there are serious errors in our ranks which should be conscientiously overcome.

The abolition of foreign stereotypes was demanded in that report, yet some comrades are still promoting them. Less singing of empty, abstract tunes was demanded, yet some comrades are obstinately singing more. The demand was made that dogmatism be laid to rest, yet some comrades are telling it to get out of bed. In short, many people have let this report which was adopted at the Sixth Plenary Session go in one ear and out of the other, as if wilfully opposed to it.

The Central Committee has now made the decision that we must discard stereotyped Party writing, dogmatism and the like once and for all, and that is why I have come and talked at some length. I hope that comrades will think over and analyse what I have said and that each comrade will also analyse his own particular case. Everyone should carefully examine himself, talk over with his close friends and the comrades around him whatever he has clarified and really get rid of his own defects.

NOTES

[1] For stereotyped Party writing, see "Rectify the Party's Style of Work", Note 1, p. 50 of this volume.

[2] Opposition to stereotyped writing, whether old or new, runs all through Lu Hsun's works. The foreign stereotype was developed after the May 4th Movement by some shallow bourgeois and petty-bourgeois intellectuals and, disseminated by them, existed for a long time among revolutionary cultural workers. In a number of essays, Lu Hsun fought against the foreign stereotype as found in their ranks and condemned it in these terms:

> A clean sweep should be made of all stereotyped writings, whether old or new. . . . For instance, it is also a kind of stereotype if all one can do is to "hurl insults", "threaten" or even "pass sentence" and merely copy old formulas and apply these indiscriminately to every fact, instead of specifically and concretely using formulas derived from science to interpret the new facts and phenomena which emerge every day. ("A Reply to Chu Hsiu-hsia's Letter", appended to "Giving the Show Away".)

[3] "Hurling Insults and Threats Is Certainly Not Fighting" was the title of an essay written in 1932 and included in the collection *Mixed Dialects* (Lu Hsun, *Complete Works*, Chin. ed., 1957, Vol. V).

[4] See *History of the Communist Party of the Soviet Union (Bolsheviks), Short Course*, Eng. ed., FLPH, Moscow, 1951, pp. 36-37.

[5] Georgi Dimitrov, "Unity of the Working Class Against Fascism", *Selected Articles and Speeches*, Eng. ed., Lawrence & Wishart, London, 1951, pp. 116-17.

[6] *Ibid.*, pp. 132-33.

[7] *Ibid.*, p. 135.

[8] *The Dipper* was a monthly published in 1931 and 1932 by the League of Chinese Left-Wing Writers. "In Reply to the Question Put by *The Dipper*" is included in the collection *Two Hearts* (Lu Hsun, *Complete Works*, Chin. ed., Vol. IV).

[9] From *Confucian Analects*, Book V, "Kungyeh Chang".

[10] Han Yu (768-824) was a famous Chinese writer of the Tang Dynasty. In his essay "The Scholar's Apologia" he wrote, "A deed is accomplished through taking thought and fails through lack of thought."

TALKS AT THE YENAN FORUM
ON LITERATURE AND ART

May 1942

INTRODUCTION
May 2, 1942

Comrades! You have been invited to this forum today to exchange ideas and examine the relationship between work in the literary and artistic fields and revolutionary work in general. Our aim is to ensure that revolutionary literature and art follow the correct path of development and provide better help to other revolutionary work in facilitating the overthrow of our national enemy and the accomplishment of the task of national liberation.

In our struggle for the liberation of the Chinese people there are various fronts, among which there are the fronts of the pen and of the gun, the cultural and the military fronts. To defeat the enemy we must rely primarily on the army with guns. But this army alone is not enough; we must also have a cultural army, which is absolutely indispensable for uniting our own ranks and defeating the enemy. Since the May 4th Movement such a cultural army has taken shape in China, and it has helped the Chinese revolution, gradually reduced the domain of China's feudal culture and of the comprador culture which serves imperialist aggression, and weakened their influence. To oppose the new culture the Chinese reactionaries can now only "pit quantity against quality". In other words, reactionaries have money, and though they can produce nothing good, they can go all out and produce in quantity. Literature and art have been an important and successful part of the cultural front since the May 4th Movement. During the ten years' civil war, the revolutionary literature and art movement grew greatly. That movement and the revolutionary war both headed in the same general direction, but

these two fraternal armies were not linked together in their practical
work because the reactionaries had cut them off from each other.
It is very good that since the outbreak of the War of Resistance
Against Japan, more and more revolutionary writers and artists
have been coming to Yenan and our other anti-Japanese base areas.
But it does not necessarily follow that, having come to the base areas,
they have already integrated themselves completely with the masses
of the people here. The two must be completely integrated if we
are to push ahead with our revolutionary work. The purpose of our
meeting today is precisely to ensure that literature and art fit well
into the whole revolutionary machine as a component part, that they
operate as powerful weapons for uniting and educating the people
and for attacking and destroying the enemy, and that they help the
people fight the enemy with one heart and one mind. What are the
problems that must be solved to achieve this objective? I think they
are the problems of the class stand of the writers and artists, their
attitude, their audience, their work and their study.

The problem of class stand. Our stand is that of the proletariat
and of the masses. For members of the Communist Party, this means
keeping to the stand of the Party, keeping to Party spirit and Party
policy. Are there any of our literary and art workers who are still
mistaken or not clear in their understanding of this problem? I think
there are. Many of our comrades have frequently departed from the
correct stand.

The problem of attitude. From one's stand there follow specific
attitudes towards specific matters. For instance, is one to extol or
to expose? This is a question of attitude. Which attitude is wanted?
I would say both. The question is, whom are you dealing with?
There are three kinds of persons, the enemy, our allies in the united
front and our own people; the last are the masses and their vanguard.
We need to adopt a different attitude towards each of the three. With
regard to the enemy, that is, Japanese imperialism and all the other
enemies of the people, the task of revolutionary writers and artists
is to expose their duplicity and cruelty and at the same time to point
out the inevitability of their defeat, so as to encourage the anti-
Japanese army and people to fight staunchly with one heart and one
mind for their overthrow. With regard to our different allies in the
united front, our attitude should be one of both alliance and criticism,
and there should be different kinds of alliance and different kinds
of criticism. We support them in their resistance to Japan and praise

them for any achievement. But if they are not active in the War of Resistance, we should criticize them. If anyone opposes the Communist Party and the people and keeps moving down the path of reaction, we will firmly oppose him. As for the masses of the people, their toil and their struggle, their army and their Party, we should certainly praise them. The people, too, have their shortcomings. Among the proletariat many retain petty-bourgeois ideas, while both the peasants and the urban petty bourgeoisie have backward ideas; these are burdens hampering them in their struggle. We should be patient and spend a long time in educating them and helping them to get these loads off their backs and combat their own shortcomings and errors, so that they can advance with great strides. They have remoulded themselves in struggle or are doing so, and our literature and art should depict this process. As long as they do not persist in their errors, we should not dwell on their negative side and consequently make the mistake of ridiculing them or, worse still, of being hostile to them. Our writings should help them to unite, to make progress, to press ahead with one heart and one mind, to discard what is backward and develop what is revolutionary, and should certainly not do the opposite.

The problem of audience, *i.e.*, the people for whom our works of literature and art are produced. In the Shensi-Kansu-Ningsia Border Region and the anti-Japanese base areas of northern and central China, this problem differs from that in the Kuomintang areas, and differs still more from that in Shanghai before the War of Resistance. In the Shanghai period, the audience for works of revolutionary literature and art consisted mainly of a section of the students, office workers and shop assistants. After the outbreak of the War of Resistance the audience in the Kuomintang areas became somewhat wider, but it still consisted mainly of the same kind of people because the government there prevented the workers, peasants and soldiers from having access to revolutionary literature and art. In our base areas the situation is entirely different. Here the audience for works of literature and art consists of workers, peasants, soldiers and revolutionary cadres. There are students in the base areas, too, but they are different from students of the old type; they are either former or future cadres. The cadres of all types, fighters in the army, workers in the factories and peasants in the villages all want to read books and newspapers once they become literate, and those who are illiterate want to see plays and operas, look at drawings and paintings, sing

songs and hear music; they are the audience for our works of literature and art. Take the cadres alone. Do not think they are few;
they far outnumber the readers of any book published in the Kuomintang areas. There, an edition usually runs to only 2,000 copies,
and even three editions add up to only 6,000; but as for the cadres
in the base areas, in Yenan alone there are more than 10,000 who
read books. Many of them, moreover, are tempered revolutionaries
of long standing, who have come from all parts of the country and
will go out to work in different places, so it is very important to do
educational work among them. Our literary and art workers must do
a good job in this respect.

Since the audience for our literature and art consists of workers,
peasants and soldiers and of their cadres, the problem arises of
understanding them and knowing them well. A great deal of work
has to be done in order to understand them and know them well, to
understand and know well all the different kinds of people and
phenomena in the Party and government organizations, in the villages
and factories and in the Eighth Route and New Fourth Armies. Our
writers and artists have their literary and art work to do, but their
primary task is to understand people and know them well. In this
regard, how have matters stood with our writers and artists? I would
say they have been lacking in knowledge and understanding; they
have been like "a hero with no place to display his prowess". What
does lacking in knowledge mean? Not knowing people well. The
writers and artists do not have a good knowledge either of those
whom they describe or of their audience; indeed they may hardly
know them at all. They do not know the workers or peasants or
soldiers well, and do not know the cadres well either. What does
lacking in understanding mean? Not understanding the language,
that is, not being familiar with the rich, lively language of the masses.
Since many writers and artists stand aloof from the masses and lead
empty lives, naturally they are unfamiliar with the language of the
people. Accordingly, their works are not only insipid in language but
often contain nondescript expressions of their own coining which run
counter to popular usage. Many comrades like to talk about "a mass
style". But what does it really mean? It means that the thoughts and
feelings of our writers and artists should be fused with those of the
masses of workers, peasants and soldiers. To achieve this fusion, they
should conscientiously learn the language of the masses. How can you
talk of literary and artistic creation if you find the very language of

the masses largely incomprehensible? By "a hero with no place to display his prowess", we mean that your collection of great truths is not appreciated by the masses. The more you put on the airs of a veteran before the masses and play the "hero", the more you try to peddle such stuff to the masses, the less likely they are to accept it. If you want the masses to understand you, if you want to be one with the masses, you must make up your mind to undergo a long and even painful process of tempering. Here I might mention the experience of how my own feelings changed. I began life as a student and at school acquired the ways of a student; I then used to feel it undignified to do even a little manual labour, such as carrying my own luggage in the presence of my fellow students, who were incapable of carrying anything, either on their shoulders or in their hands. At that time I felt that intellectuals were the only clean people in the world, while in comparison workers and peasants were dirty. I did not mind wearing the clothes of other intellectuals, believing them clean, but I would not put on clothes belonging to a worker or peasant, believing them dirty. But after I became a revolutionary and lived with workers and peasants and with soldiers of the revolutionary army, I gradually came to know them well, and they gradually came to know me well too. It was then, and only then, that I fundamentally changed the bourgeois and petty-bourgeois feelings implanted in me in the bourgeois schools. I came to feel that compared with the workers and peasants the unremoulded intellectuals were not clean and that, in the last analysis, the workers and peasants were the cleanest people and, even though their hands were soiled and their feet smeared with cow-dung, they were really cleaner than the bourgeois and petty-bourgeois intellectuals. That is what is meant by a change in feelings, a change from one class to another. If our writers and artists who come from the intelligentsia want their works to be well received by the masses, they must change and remould their thinking and their feelings. Without such a change, without such remoulding, they can do nothing well and will be misfits.

The last problem is study, by which I mean the study of Marxism-Leninism and of society. Anyone who considers himself a revolutionary Marxist writer, and especially any writer who is a member of the Communist Party, must have a knowledge of Marxism-Leninism. At present, however, some comrades are lacking in the basic concepts of Marxism. For instance, it is a basic Marxist concept that being determines consciousness, that the objective realities of class struggle and national struggle determine our thoughts and feelings. But some of our comrades turn this upside down and maintain that everything ought to start from "love". Now as for love, in a class society there can be only class love; but these comrades are seeking a love transcending classes, love in the abstract and also freedom in the abstract, truth in the abstract, human nature in the abstract, etc. This shows that they have been very deeply influenced by the bourgeoisie. They should thoroughly rid themselves of this influence and modestly study Marxism-Leninism. It is right for writers and artists to study literary and artistic creation, but the science of Marxism-Leninism must be studied by all revolutionaries, writers and artists not excepted. Writers and artists should study society, that is to say, should study the various classes in society, their mutual relations and respective conditions, their physiognomy and their psychology. Only when we grasp all this clearly can we have a literature and art that is rich in content and correct in orientation.

I am merely raising these problems today by way of introduction; I hope all of you will express your views on these and other relevant problems.

CONCLUSION

May 23, 1942

Comrades! Our forum has had three meetings this month. In the pursuit of truth we have carried on spirited debates in which scores of Party and non-Party comrades have spoken, laying bare the issues and making them more concrete. This, I believe, will very much benefit the whole literary and artistic movement.

In discussing a problem, we should start from reality and not from definitions. We would be following a wrong method if we first looked up definitions of literature and art in textbooks and then used them to determine the guiding principles for the present-day literary and artistic movement and to judge the different opinions and controversies that arise today. We are Marxists, and Marxism teaches that in our approach to a problem we should start from objective facts, not from abstract definitions, and that we should derive our guiding principles, policies and measures from an analysis of these facts. We should do the same in our present discussion of literary and artistic work.

What are the facts at present? The facts are: the War of Resistance Against Japan which China has been fighting for five years; the world-wide anti-fascist war; the vacillations of China's big landlord class and big bourgeoisie in the War of Resistance and their policy of high-handed oppression of the people; the revolutionary movement in literature and art since the May 4th Movement — its great contributions to the revolution during the last twenty-three years and its many shortcomings; the anti-Japanese democratic base areas of the Eighth Route and New Fourth Armies and the integration of large numbers of writers and artists with these armies and with the workers and peasants in these areas; the difference in both environment and tasks between the writers and artists in the base areas and those in the Kuomintang areas; and the controversial issues concerning literature and art which have arisen in Yenan and the other anti-Japanese base areas. These are the actual, undeniable facts in the light of which we have to consider our problems.

What then is the crux of the matter? In my opinion, it consists fundamentally of the problems of working for the masses and how to work for the masses. Unless these two problems are solved, or solved properly, our writers and artists will be ill-adapted to their environment and their tasks and will come up against a series of difficulties from without and within. My concluding remarks will centre on these two problems and also touch upon some related ones.

I

The first problem is: literature and art for whom?

This problem was solved long ago by Marxists, especially by Lenin. As far back as 1905 Lenin pointed out emphatically that our literature and art should "serve . . . the millions and tens of millions of working people".[1] For comrades engaged in literary and artistic work in the anti-Japanese base areas it might seem that this problem is already solved and needs no further discussion. Actually, that is not the case. Many comrades have not found a clear solution. Consequently their sentiments, their works, their actions and their views on the guiding principles for literature and art have inevitably been more or less at variance with the needs of the masses and of the practical struggle. Of course, among the numerous men of culture, writers, artists and other literary and artistic workers engaged in the great struggle for liberation together with the Communist Party and the Eighth Route and New Fourth Armies, a few may be careerists who are with us only temporarily, but the overwhelming majority are working energetically for the common cause. By relying on these comrades, we have achieved a great deal in our literature, drama, music and fine arts. Many of these writers and artists have begun their work since the outbreak of the War of Resistance; many others did much revolutionary work before the war, endured many hardships and influenced broad masses of the people by their activities and works. Why do we say, then, that even among these comrades there are some who have not reached a clear solution of the problem of whom literature and art are for? Is it conceivable that there are still some who maintain that revolutionary literature and art are not for the masses of the people but for the exploiters and oppressors?

Indeed literature and art exist which are for the exploiters and oppressors. Literature and art for the landlord class are feudal literature and art. Such were the literature and art of the ruling class in China's feudal era. To this day such literature and art still have considerable influence in China. Literature and art for the bourgeoisie are bourgeois literature and art. People like Liang Shih-chiu,[2] whom Lu Hsun criticized, talk about literature and art as transcending classes, but in fact they uphold bourgeois literature and art and oppose proletarian literature and art. Then literature and art exist which serve the imperialists — for example, the works of Chou Tso-jen, Chang Tzu-ping[3] and their like — which we call traitor literature and art. With us, literature and art are for the people, not for any of the above groups. We have said that China's new culture at the present stage is an anti-imperialist, anti-feudal culture of the masses of the people under the leadership of the proletariat. Today, anything that is truly of the masses must necessarily be led by the proletariat. Whatever is under the leadership of the bourgeoisie cannot possibly be of the masses. Naturally, the same applies to the new literature and art which are part of the new culture. We should take over the rich legacy and the good traditions in literature and art that have been handed down from past ages in China and foreign countries, but the aim must still be to serve the masses of the people. Nor do we refuse to utilize the literary and artistic forms of the past, but in our hands these old forms, remoulded and infused with new content, also become something revolutionary in the service of the people.

Who, then, are the masses of the people? The broadest sections of the people, constituting more than 90 per cent of our total population, are the workers, peasants, soldiers and urban petty bourgeoisie. Therefore, our literature and art are first for the workers, the class that leads the revolution. Secondly, they are for the peasants, the most numerous and most steadfast of our allies in the revolution. Thirdly, they are for the armed workers and peasants, namely, the Eighth Route and New Fourth Armies and the other armed units of the people, which are the main forces of the revolutionary war. Fourthly, they are for the labouring masses of the urban petty bourgeoisie and for the petty-bourgeois intellectuals, both of whom are also our allies in the revolution and capable of long-term co-operation with us. These four kinds of people constitute the overwhelming majority of the Chinese nation, the broadest masses of the people.

Our literature and art should be for the four kinds of people we have enumerated. To serve them, we must take the class stand of the proletariat and not that of the petty bourgeoisie. Today, writers who cling to an individualist, petty-bourgeois stand cannot truly serve the masses of revolutionary workers, peasants and soldiers. Their interest is mainly focused on the small number of petty-bourgeois intellectuals. This is the crucial reason why some of our comrades cannot correctly solve the problem of "for whom?" In saying this I am not referring to theory. In theory, or in words, no one in our ranks regards the masses of workers, peasants and soldiers as less important than the petty-bourgeois intellectuals. I am referring to practice, to action. In practice, in action, do they regard petty-bourgeois intellectuals as more important than workers, peasants and soldiers? I think they do. Many comrades concern themselves with studying the petty-bourgeois intellectuals and analysing their psychology, and they concentrate on portraying these intellectuals and excusing or defending their shortcomings, instead of guiding the intellectuals to join with them in getting closer to the masses of workers, peasants and soldiers, taking part in the practical struggles of the masses, portraying and educating the masses. Coming from the petty bourgeoisie and being themselves intellectuals, many comrades seek friends only among intellectuals and concentrate on studying and describing them. Such study and description are proper if done from a proletarian position. But that is not what they do, or not what they do fully. They take the petty-bourgeois stand and produce works that are the self-expression of the petty bourgeoisie, as can be seen in quite a number of literary and artistic products. Often they show heartfelt sympathy for intellectuals of petty-bourgeois origin, to the extent of sympathizing with or even praising their shortcomings. On the other hand, these comrades seldom come into contact with the masses of workers, peasants and soldiers, do not understand or study them, do not have intimate friends among them and are not good at portraying them; when they do depict them, the clothes are the clothes of working people but the faces are those of petty-bourgeois intellectuals. In certain respects they are fond of the workers, peasants and soldiers and the cadres stemming from them; but there are times when they do not like them and there are some respects in which they do not like them: they do not like their feelings or their manner or their nascent literature and art (the wall newspapers, murals, folk songs, folk tales, etc.). At times they are fond of these things too, but that is when they are hunting for novelty, for something with which to embellish their own works, or even for certain backward features. At other times they openly despise these things and are partial to what belongs to the petty-bourgeois intellectuals or even to the bourgeoisie. These comrades have their feet planted on the side of the petty-bourgeois intellectuals; or, to put it more elegantly, their innermost soul is still a kingdom of the petty-bourgeois intelligentsia. Thus they have not yet solved, or not yet clearly solved, the problem of "for whom?" This applies not only to newcomers to Yenan; even among comrades who have been to the front and worked for a number of years in our base areas and in the Eighth Route and New Fourth Armies, many have not completely solved this problem. It requires a long period of time, at least eight or ten years, to solve it thoroughly. But however long it takes, solve it we must and solve it unequivocally and thoroughly. Our literary and art workers must accomplish this task and shift their stand; they must gradually move their feet over to the side of the workers, peasants and soldiers, to the side of the proletariat, through the process of going into their very midst and into the thick of practical struggles and through the process of studying Marxism and society. Only in this way can we have a literature and art that are truly for the workers, peasants and soldiers, a truly proletarian literature and art.

This question of "for whom?" is fundamental; it is a question of principle. The controversies and divergences, the opposition and disunity arising among some comrades in the past were not on this fundamental question of principle but on secondary questions, or even on issues involving no principle. On this question of principle, however, there has been hardly any divergence between the two contending sides and they have shown almost complete agreement; to some extent, both tend to look down upon the workers, peasants and soldiers and divorce themselves from the masses. I say "to some extent" because, generally speaking, these comrades do not look down upon the workers, peasants and soldiers or divorce themselves from the masses in the same way as the Kuomintang does. Nevertheless, the tendency is there. Unless this fundamental problem is solved, many other problems will not be easy to solve. Take, for instance, the sectarianism in literary and art circles. This too is a question of principle, but sectarianism can only be eradicated by putting forward and faithfully applying the slogans, "For the workers and peasants!", "For the Eighth Route and New Fourth Armies!" and "Go among the masses!" Otherwise the problem of sectarianism can never be solved. Lu Hsun once said:

> A common aim is the prerequisite for a united front. . . . The fact that our front is not united shows that we have not been able to unify our aims, and that some people are working only for small groups or indeed only for themselves. If we all aim at serving the masses of workers and peasants, our front will of course be united.[4]

The problem existed then in Shanghai; now it exists in Chungking too. In such places the problem can hardly be solved thoroughly, because the rulers oppress the revolutionary writers and artists and deny them the freedom to go out among the masses of workers, peasants and soldiers. Here with us the situation is entirely different. We encourage revolutionary writers and artists to be active in forming intimate contacts with the workers, peasants and soldiers, giving them complete freedom to go among the masses and to create a genuinely revolutionary literature and art. Therefore, here among us the problem is nearing solution. But nearing solution is not the same as a complete and thorough solution. We must study Marxism and study society, as we have been saying, precisely in order to achieve a complete and thorough solution. By Marxism we mean living Marxism which plays an effective role in the life and struggle of the masses, not Marxism in words. With Marxism in words transformed into Marxism in real life, there will be no more sectarianism. Not only will the problem of sectarianism be solved, but many other problems as well.

II

Having settled the problem of whom to serve, we come to the
next problem, how to serve. To put it in the words of some of our
comrades: should we devote ourselves to raising standards, or should
we devote ourselves to popularization?

In the past, some comrades, to a certain or even a serious extent,
belittled and neglected popularization and laid undue stress on raising
standards. Stress should be laid on raising standards, but to do so
one-sidedly and exclusively, to do so excessively, is a mistake. The
lack of a clear solution to the problem of "for whom?", which I
referred to earlier, also manifests itself in this connection. As these
comrades are not clear on the problem of "for whom?", they have
no correct criteria for the "raising of standards" and the "popularization" they speak of, and are naturally still less able to find the
correct relationship between the two. Since our literature and art
are basically for the workers, peasants and soldiers, "popularization"
means to popularize among the workers, peasants and soldiers, and
"raising standards" means to advance from their present level. What
should we popularize among them? Popularize what is needed and
can be readily accepted by the feudal landlord class? Popularize what
is needed and can be readily accepted by the bourgeoisie? Popularize
what is needed and can be readily accepted by the petty-bourgeois
intellectuals? No, none of these will do. We must popularize only
what is needed and can be readily accepted by the workers, peasants
and soldiers themselves. Consequently, prior to the task of educating
the workers, peasants and soldiers, there is the task of learning from
them. This is even more true of raising standards. There must be a
basis from which to raise. Take a bucket of water, for instance; where
is it to be raised from if not from the ground? From mid-air? From
what basis, then, are literature and art to be raised? From the basis
of the feudal classes? From the basis of the bourgeoisie? From the
basis of the petty-bourgeois intellectuals? No, not from any of these;
only from the basis of the masses of workers, peasants and soldiers.
Nor does this mean raising the workers, peasants and soldiers to the
"heights" of the feudal classes, the bourgeoisie or the petty-bourgeois
intellectuals; it means raising the level of literature and art in the
direction in which the workers, peasants and soldiers are themselves
advancing, in the direction in which the proletariat is advancing.
Here again the task of learning from the workers, peasants and

soldiers comes in. Only by starting from the workers, peasants and soldiers can we have a correct understanding of popularization and of the raising of standards and find the proper relationship between the two.

In the last analysis, what is the source of all literature and art? Works of literature and art, as ideological forms, are products of the reflection in the human brain of the life of a given society. Revolutionary literature and art are the products of the reflection of the life of the people in the brains of revolutionary writers and artists. The life of the people is always a mine of the raw materials for literature and art, materials in their natural form, materials that are crude, but most vital, rich and fundamental; they make all literature and art seem pallid by comparison; they provide literature and art with an inexhaustible source, their only source. They are the only source, for there can be no other. Some may ask, is there not another source in books, in the literature and art of ancient times and of foreign countries? In fact, the literary and artistic works of the past are not a source but a stream; they were created by our predecessors and the foreigners out of the literary and artistic raw materials they found in the life of the people of their time and place. We must take over all the fine things in our literary and artistic heritage, critically assimilate whatever is beneficial, and use them as examples when we create works out of the literary and artistic raw materials in the life of the people of our own time and place. It makes a difference whether or not we have such examples, the difference between crudeness and refinement, between roughness and polish, between a low and a high level, and between slower and faster work. Therefore, we must on no account reject the legacies of the ancients and the foreigners or refuse to learn from them, even though they are the works of the feudal or bourgeois classes. But taking over legacies and using them as examples must never replace our own creative work; nothing can do that. Uncritical transplantation or copying from the ancients and the foreigners is the most sterile and harmful dogmatism in literature and art. China's revolutionary writers and artists, writers and artists of promise, must go among the masses; they must for a long period of time unreservedly and whole-heartedly go among the masses of workers, peasants and soldiers, go into the heat of the struggle, go to the only source, the broadest and richest source, in order to observe, experience, study and analyse all the different kinds of people, all the classes, all the masses, all the vivid patterns of life and struggle, all the raw materials of literature and art. Only then can they proceed to creative work. Otherwise, you will have nothing to work with and you will be nothing but a phoney writer or artist, the kind that Lu Hsun in his will so earnestly cautioned his son never to become.[5]

Although man's social life is the only source of literature and art and is incomparably livelier and richer in content, the people are not satisfied with life alone and demand literature and art as well. Why? Because, while both are beautiful, life as reflected in works of literature and art can and ought to be on a higher plane, more intense, more concentrated, more typical, nearer the ideal, and therefore more universal than actual everyday life. Revolutionary literature and art should create a variety of characters out of real life and help the masses to propel history forward. For example, there is suffering from hunger, cold and oppression on the one hand, and exploitation and oppression of man by man on the other. These facts exist everywhere and people look upon them as commonplace. Writers and artists concentrate such everyday phenomena, typify the contradictions and struggles within them and produce works which awaken the masses, fire them with enthusiasm and impel them to unite and struggle to transform their environment. Without such literature and art, this task could not be fulfilled, or at least not so effectively and speedily.

What is meant by popularizing and by raising standards in works of literature and art? What is the relationship between these two tasks? Popular works are simpler and plainer, and therefore more readily accepted by the broad masses of the people today. Works of a higher quality, being more polished, are more difficult to produce and in general do not circulate so easily and quickly among the masses at present. The problem facing the workers, peasants and soldiers is this: they are now engaged in a bitter and bloody struggle with the enemy but are illiterate and uneducated as a result of long years of rule by the feudal and bourgeois classes, and therefore they are eagerly demanding enlightenment, education and works of literature and art which meet their urgent needs and which are easy to absorb, in order to heighten their enthusiasm in struggle and confidence in victory, strengthen their unity and fight the enemy with one heart and one mind. For them the prime need is not "more flowers on the brocade" but "fuel in snowy weather". In present conditions, therefore, popularization is the more pressing task. It is wrong to belittle or neglect popularization.

Nevertheless, no hard and fast line can be drawn between popularization and the raising of standards. Not only is it possible to popularize some works of higher quality even now, but the cultural level of the broad masses is steadily rising. If popularization remains at the same level for ever, with the same stuff being supplied month after month and year after year, always the same "Little Cowherd"[6] and the same "man, hand, mouth, knife, cow, goat",[7] will not the educators and those being educated be six of one and half a dozen of the other? What would be the sense of such popularization? The people demand popularization and, following that, higher standards; they demand higher standards month by month and year by year. Here popularization means popularizing for the people and raising of standards means raising the level for the people. And such raising is not from mid-air, or behind closed doors, but is actually based on popularization. It is determined by and at the same time guides popularization. In China as a whole the development of the revolution and of revolutionary culture is uneven and their spread is gradual. While in one place there is popularization and then raising of standards on the basis of popularization, in other places popularization has not even begun. Hence good experience in popularization leading to higher standards in one locality can be applied in other localities and serve to guide popularization and the raising of standards there, saving many twists and turns along the road. Internationally, the good experience of foreign countries, and especially Soviet experience, can also serve to guide us. With us, therefore, the raising of standards is based on popularization, while popularization is guided by the raising of standards. Precisely for this reason, so far from being an obstacle to the raising of standards, the work of popularization we are speaking of supplies the basis for the work of raising standards which we are now doing on a limited scale, and prepares the necessary conditions for us to raise standards in the future on a much broader scale.

Besides such raising of standards as meets the needs of the masses directly, there is the kind which meets their needs indirectly, that is, the kind which is needed by the cadres. The cadres are the advanced elements of the masses and generally have received more education; literature and art of a higher level are entirely necessary for them. To ignore this would be a mistake. Whatever is done for the cadres is also entirely for the masses, because it is only through the cadres that we can educate and guide the masses. If we go against

this aim, if what we give the cadres cannot help them educate and
guide the masses, our work of raising standards will be like shooting
at random and will depart from the fundamental principle of serving
the masses of the people.

To sum up: through the creative labour of revolutionary writers
and artists, the raw materials found in the life of the people are
shaped into the ideological form of literature and art serving the
masses of the people. Included here are the more advanced literature
and art as developed on the basis of elementary literature and art
and as required by those sections of the masses whose level has been
raised, or, more immediately, by the cadres among the masses. Also
included here are elementary literature and art which, conversely,
are guided by more advanced literature and art and are needed
primarily by the overwhelming majority of the masses at present.
Whether more advanced or elementary, all our literature and art
are for the masses of the people, and in the first place for the workers,
peasants and soldiers; they are created for the workers, peasants
and soldiers and are for their use.

Now that we have settled the problem of the relationship between
the raising of standards and popularization, that of the relationship
between the specialists and the popularizers can also be settled. Our
specialists are not only for the cadres, but also, and indeed chiefly,
for the masses. Our specialists in literature should pay attention
to the wall newspapers of the masses and to the reportage written
in the army and the villages. Our specialists in drama should pay
attention to the small troupes in the army and the villages. Our
specialists in music should pay attention to the songs of the masses.
Our specialists in the fine arts should pay attention to the fine arts
of the masses. All these comrades should make close contact with
comrades engaged in the work of popularizing literature and art
among the masses. On the one hand, they should help and guide the
popularizers, and on the other, they should learn from these comrades
and, through them, draw nourishment from the masses to replenish
and enrich themselves so that their specialities do not become "ivory
towers", detached from the masses and from reality and devoid of
content or life. We should esteem the specialists, for they are very
valuable to our cause. But we should tell them that no revolutionary
writer or artist can do any meaningful work unless he is closely linked
with the masses, gives expression to their thoughts and feelings and
serves them as a loyal spokesman. Only by speaking for the masses

can he educate them and only by being their pupil can he be their teacher. If he regards himself as their master, as an aristocrat who lords it over the "lower orders", then, no matter how talented he may be, he will not be needed by the masses and his work will have no future.

Is this attitude of ours utilitarian? Materialists do not oppose utilitarianism in general but the utilitarianism of the feudal, bourgeois and petty-bourgeois classes; they oppose those hypocrites who attack utilitarianism in words but in deeds embrace the most selfish and short-sighted utilitarianism. There is no "ism" in the world that transcends utilitarian considerations; in class society there can be only the utilitarianism of this or that class. We are proletarian revolutionary utilitarians and take as our point of departure the unity of the present and future interests of the broadest masses, who constitute over 90 per cent of the population; hence we are revolutionary utilitarians aiming for the broadest and the most long-range objectives, not narrow utilitarians concerned only with the partial and the immediate. If, for instance, you reproach the masses for their utilitarianism and yet for your own utility, or that of a narrow clique, force on the market and propagandize among the masses a work which pleases only the few but is useless or even harmful to the majority, then you are not only insulting the masses but also revealing your own lack of self-knowledge. A thing is good only when it brings real benefit to the masses of the people. Your work may be as good as "The Spring Snow", but if for the time being it caters only to the few and the masses are still singing the "Song of the Rustic Poor",[8] you will get nowhere by simply scolding them instead of trying to raise their level. The question now is to bring about a unity between "The Spring Snow" and the "Song of the Rustic Poor", between higher standards and popularization. Without such a unity, the highest art of any expert cannot help being utilitarian in the narrowest sense; you may call this art "pure and lofty" but that is merely your own name for it which the masses will not endorse.

Once we have solved the problems of fundamental policy, of serving the workers, peasants and soldiers and of how to serve them, such other problems as whether to write about the bright or the dark side of life and the problem of unity will also be solved. If everyone agrees on the fundamental policy, it should be adhered to by all our workers, all our schools, publications and organizations in the field of literature and art and in all our literary and artistic activities. It is wrong to depart from this policy and anything at variance with it must be duly corrected.

III

Since our literature and art are for the masses of the people, we can proceed to discuss a problem of inner-Party relations, *i.e.*, the relation between the Party's work in literature and art and the Party's work as a whole, and in addition a problem of the Party's external relations, *i.e.*, the relation between the Party's work in literature and art and the work of non-Party people in this field, a problem of the united front in literary and art circles.

Let us consider the first problem. In the world today all culture, all literature and art belong to definite classes and are geared to definite political lines. There is in fact no such thing as art for art's sake, art that stands above classes or art that is detached from or independent of politics. Proletarian literature and art are part of the whole proletarian revolutionary cause; they are, as Lenin said, cogs and wheels[9] in the whole revolutionary machine. Therefore, Party work in literature and art occupies a definite and assigned position in Party revolutionary work as a whole and is subordinated to the revolutionary tasks set by the Party in a given revolutionary period. Opposition to this arrangement is certain to lead to dualism or pluralism, and in essence amounts to "politics — Marxist, art — bourgeois", as with Trotsky. We do not favour overstressing the importance of literature and art, but neither do we favour under-estimating their importance. Literature and art are subordinate to politics, but in their turn exert a great influence on politics. Revolu-tionary literature and art are part of the whole revolutionary cause, they are cogs and wheels in it, and though in comparison with certain other and more important parts they may be less significant and less urgent and may occupy a secondary position, nevertheless, they are indispensable cogs and wheels in the whole machine, an indispensable part of the entire revolutionary cause. If we had no literature and art even in the broadest and most ordinary sense, we could not carry on the revolutionary movement and win victory. Failure to recognize this is wrong. Furthermore, when we say that literature and art are subordinate to politics, we mean class politics, the politics of the masses, not the politics of a few so-called statesmen. Politics, whether revolutionary or counter-revolutionary, is the struggle of class against class, not the activity of a few individuals. The revolutionary struggle on the ideological and artistic fronts must be subordinate to the political struggle because only through politics can the needs of the class and the masses find expression in concentrated form. Revolutionary statesmen, the political specialists who know the science or art of revolutionary politics, are simply the leaders of millions upon millions of statesmen — the masses. Their task is to collect the opinions of these mass statesmen, sift and refine them, and return them to the masses, who then take them and put them into practice. They are therefore not the kind of aristocratic "statesmen" who work behind closed doors and fancy they have a monopoly of wisdom. Herein lies the difference in principle between proletarian statesmen and decadent bourgeois statesmen. This is precisely why there can be complete unity between the political character of our literary and artistic works and their truthfulness. It would be wrong to fail to realize this and to debase the politics and the statesmen of the proletariat.

Let us consider next the question of the united front in the world of literature and art. Since literature and art are subordinate to politics and since the fundamental problem in China's politics today is resistance to Japan, our Party writers and artists must in the first place unite on this issue of resistance to Japan with all non-Party writers and artists (ranging from Party sympathizers and petty-bourgeois writers and artists to all those writers and artists of the bourgeois and landlord classes who are in favour of resistance to Japan). Secondly, we should unite with them on the issue of democracy. On this issue there is a section of anti-Japanese writers and artists who do not agree with us, so the range of unity will unavoidably be somewhat more limited. Thirdly, we should unite with them on issues peculiar to the literary and artistic world, questions of method and style in literature and art; here again, as we are for socialist realism and some people do not agree, the range of unity will be narrower still. While on one issue there is unity, on another there is struggle, there is criticism. The issues are at once separate and interrelated, so that even on the very ones which give rise to unity, such as resistance to Japan, there are at the same time struggle and criticism. In a united front, "all unity and no struggle" and "all struggle and no unity" are both wrong policies — as with the Right capitulationism and tailism, or the "Left" exclusivism and sectarianism, practised by some comrades in the past. This is as true in literature and art as in politics.

The petty-bourgeois writers and artists constitute an important force among the forces of the united front in literary and art circles in China. There are many shortcomings in both their thinking and their works, but, comparatively speaking, they are inclined towards the revolution and are close to the working people. Therefore, it is an especially important task to help them overcome their short-comings and to win them over to the front which serves the working people.

IV

Literary and art criticism is one of the principal methods of struggle in the world of literature and art. It should be developed and, as comrades have rightly pointed out, our past work in this respect has been quite inadequate. Literary and art criticism is a complex question which requires a great deal of special study. Here I shall concentrate only on the basic problem of criteria in criticism. I shall also comment briefly on a few specific problems raised by some comrades and on certain incorrect views.

In literary and art criticism there are two criteria, the political and the artistic. According to the political criterion, everything is good that is helpful to unity and resistance to Japan, that encourages the masses to be of one heart and one mind, that opposes retrogression and promotes progress; on the other hand, everything is bad that is detrimental to unity and resistance to Japan, foments dissension and discord among the masses and opposes progress and drags people back. How can we tell the good from the bad — by the motive (the subjective intention) or by the effect (social practice)? Idealists stress motive and ignore effect, while mechanical materialists stress effect and ignore motive. In contradistinction to both, we dialectical ma-terialists insist on the unity of motive and effect. The motive of serving the masses is inseparably linked with the effect of winning their approval; the two must be united. The motive of serving the individual or a small clique is not good, nor is it good to have the motive of serving the masses without the effect of winning their approval and benefiting them. In examining the subjective intention of a writer or artist, that is, whether his motive is correct and good, we do not judge by his declarations but by the effect of his actions (mainly his works) on the masses in society. The criterion for judging subjective intention or motive is social practice and its effect. We want no sectarianism in our literary and art criticism and, subject to the general principle of unity for resistance to Japan, we should tolerate literary and art works with a variety of political attitudes. But at the same time, in our criticism we must adhere firmly to principle and severely criticize and repudiate all works of literature and art expressing views in opposition to the nation, to science, to the masses and to the Communist Party, because these so-called works of literature and art proceed from the motive and produce the effect of undermining unity for resistance to Japan. According to the artistic criterion, all works of a higher artistic quality are good or comparatively good, while those of a lower artistic quality are bad or comparatively bad. Here, too, of course, social effect must be taken into account. There is hardly a writer or artist who does not consider his own work beautiful, and our criticism ought to permit the free competition of all varieties of works of art; but it is also entirely necessary to subject these works to correct criticism according to the criteria of the science of aesthetics, so that art of a lower level can be gradually raised to a higher and art which does not meet the demands of the struggle of the broad masses can be transformed into art that does.

There is the political criterion and there is the artistic criterion; what is the relationship between the two? Politics cannot be equated with art, nor can a general world outlook be equated with a method of artistic creation and criticism. We deny not only that there is an abstract and absolutely unchangeable political criterion, but also that there is an abstract and absolutely unchangeable artistic criterion; each class in every class society has its own political and artistic criteria. But all classes in all class societies invariably put the political criterion first and the artistic criterion second. The bourgeoisie always shuts out proletarian literature and art, however great their artistic merit. The proletariat must similarly distinguish among the literary and art works of past ages and determine its attitude towards them only after examining their attitude to the people and whether or not they had any progressive significance historically. Some works which politically are downright reactionary may have a certain artistic quality. The more reactionary their content and the higher their artistic quality, the more poisonous they are to the people, and the more necessary it is to reject them. A common characteristic of the literature and art of all exploiting classes in their period of decline is the contradiction between their reactionary political content and their artistic form. What we demand is the unity of politics and art, the unity of content and form, the unity of revolutionary political content and the highest possible perfection of artistic form. Works of art which lack artistic quality have no force, however progressive they are politically. Therefore, we oppose both the tendency to produce works of art with a wrong political viewpoint and the tendency towards the "poster and slogan style" which is correct in political viewpoint but lacking in artistic power. On questions of literature and art we must carry on a struggle on two fronts.

Both these tendencies can be found in the thinking of many comrades. A good number of comrades tend to neglect artistic technique; it is therefore necessary to give attention to the raising of artistic standards. But as I see it, the political side is more of a problem at present. Some comrades lack elementary political knowledge and consequently have all sorts of muddled ideas. Let me cite a few examples from Yenan.

"The theory of human nature." Is there such a thing as human nature? Of course there is. But there is only human nature in the concrete, no human nature in the abstract. In class society there is only human nature of a class character; there is no human nature above classes. We uphold the human nature of the proletariat and of the masses of the people, while the landlord and bourgeois classes uphold the human nature of their own classes, only they do not say so but make it out to be the only human nature in existence. The human nature boosted by certain petty-bourgeois intellectuals is also divorced from or opposed to the masses; what they call human nature is in essence nothing but bourgeois individualism, and so, in their eyes, proletarian human nature is contrary to human nature. "The theory of human nature" which some people in Yenan advocate as the basis of their so-called theory of literature and art puts the matter in just this way and is wholly wrong.

"The fundamental point of departure for literature and art is love, love of humanity." Now love may serve as a point of departure, but there is a more basic one. Love as an idea is a product of objective practice. Fundamentally, we do not start from ideas but from objective practice. Our writers and artists who come from the ranks of the intellectuals love the proletariat because society has made them feel that they and the proletariat share a common fate. We hate Japanese imperialism because Japanese imperialism oppresses us. There is absolutely no such thing in the world as love or hatred without reason or cause. As for the so-called love of humanity, there has been no such all-inclusive love since humanity was divided into classes. All the ruling classes of the past were fond of advocating it, and so were many so-called sages and wise men, but nobody has ever really practised it, because it is impossible in class society. There will be genuine love of humanity — after classes are eliminated all over the world. Classes have split society into many antagonistic groupings; there will be love of all humanity when classes are eliminated, but not now. We cannot love enemies, we cannot love social evils, our aim is to destroy them. This is common sense; can it be that some of our writers and artists still do not understand this?

"Literary and artistic works have always laid equal stress on the bright and the dark, half and half." This statement contains many muddled ideas. It is not true that literature and art have always done this. Many petty-bourgeois writers have never discovered the bright side. Their works only expose the dark and are known as the "literature of exposure". Some of their works simply specialize in preaching pessimism and world-weariness. On the other hand, Soviet literature in the period of socialist construction portrays mainly the bright. It, too, describes shortcomings in work and portrays negative characters, but this only serves as a contrast to bring out the brightness of the whole picture and is not on a so-called half-and-half basis. The writers and artists of the bourgeoisie in its period of reaction depict the revolutionary masses as mobs and themselves as saints, thus reversing the bright and the dark. Only truly revolutionary writers and artists can correctly solve the problem of whether to extol or to expose. All the dark forces harming the masses of the people must be exposed and all the revolutionary struggles of the masses of the people must be extolled; this is the fundamental task of revolutionary writers and artists.

"The task of literature and art has always been to expose." This assertion, like the previous one, arises from ignorance of the science of history. Literature and art, as we have shown, have never been devoted solely to exposure. For revolutionary writers and artists the targets for exposure can never be the masses, but only the aggressors, exploiters and oppressors and the evil influence they have on the people. The masses too have shortcomings, which should be overcome by criticism and self-criticism within the people's own ranks, and such criticism and self-criticism is also one of the most important tasks of literature and art. But this should not be regarded as any sort of "exposure of the people". As for the people, the question is basically one of education and of raising their level. Only counter-revolutionary writers and artists describe the people as "born fools" and the revolutionary masses as "tyrannical mobs".

"This is still the period of the satirical essay, and Lu Hsun's style of writing is still needed." Living under the rule of the dark forces and deprived of freedom of speech, Lu Hsun used burning satire and freezing irony, cast in the form of essays, to do battle; and he was entirely right. We, too, must hold up to sharp ridicule the fascists, the Chinese reactionaries and everything that harms the people; but in the Shensi-Kansu-Ningsia Border Region and the anti-Japanese base areas behind the enemy lines, where democracy and freedom are granted in full to the revolutionary writers and artists and with-held only from the counter-revolutionaries, the style of the essay should not simply be like Lu Hsun's. Here we can shout at the top of our voices and have no need for veiled and roundabout expressions, which are hard for the people to understand. When dealing with the people and not with their enemies, Lu Hsun never ridiculed or attacked the revolutionary people and the revolutionary Party in his "satirical essay period", and these essays were entirely different in manner from those directed against the enemy. To criticize the people's short-comings is necessary, as we have already said, but in doing so we must truly take the stand of the people and speak out of whole-hearted eagerness to protect and educate them. To treat comrades like enemies is to go over to the stand of the enemy. Are we then to abolish satire? No. Satire is always necessary. But there are several kinds of satire, each with a different attitude, satire to deal with our enemies, satire to deal with our allies and satire to deal with our own ranks. We are not opposed to satire in general; what we must abolish is the abuse of satire.

"I am not given to praise and eulogy. The works of people who eulogize what is bright are not necessarily great and the works of those who depict the dark are not necessarily paltry." If you are a bourgeois writer or artist, you will eulogize not the proletariat but the bourgeoisie, and if you are a proletarian writer or artist, you will eulogize not the bourgeoisie but the proletariat and working people: it must be one or the other. The works of the eulogists of the bour-geoisie are not necessarily great, nor are the works of those who show that the bourgeoisie is dark necessarily paltry; the works of the eulogists of the proletariat are not necessarily not great, but the works of those who depict the so-called "darkness" of the proletariat are bound to be paltry — are these not facts of history as regards literature and art? Why should we not eulogize the people, the creators of the history of mankind? Why should we not eulogize the proletariat, the Communist Party, New Democracy and socialism? There is a type of person who has no enthusiasm for the people's cause and looks coldly from the side-lines at the struggles and victories of the proletariat and its vanguard; what he is interested in, and will never weary of eulogizing, is himself, plus perhaps a few figures in his small coterie. Of course, such petty-bourgeois individualists are unwilling to eulogize the deeds and virtues of the revolutionary people or heighten their courage in struggle and their confidence in victory. Persons of this type are merely termites in the revolutionary ranks; of course, the revolutionary people have no need for these "singers".

"It is not a question of stand; my class stand is correct, my intentions are good and I understand all right, but I am not good at expressing myself and so the effect turns out bad." I have already spoken about the dialectical materialist view of motive and effect. Now I want to ask, is not the question of effect one of stand? A person who acts solely by motive and does not inquire what effect his action will have is like a doctor who merely writes prescriptions but does not care how many patients die of them. Or take a political party which merely makes declarations but does not care whether they are carried out. It may well be asked, is this a correct stand? And is the intention here good? Of course, mistakes may occur even though the effect has been taken into account beforehand, but is the intention good when one continues in the same old rut after facts have proved that the effect is bad? In judging a party or a doctor, we must look at practice, at the effect. The same applies in judging a writer. A person with truly good intentions must take the effect into account, sum up experience and study the methods or, in creative work, study the technique of expression. A person with truly good intentions must criticize the shortcomings and mistakes in his own work with the utmost candour and resolve to correct them. This is precisely why Communists employ the method of self-criticism. This alone is the correct stand. Only in this process of serious and responsible practice is it possible gradually to understand what the correct stand is and gradually obtain a good grasp of it. If one does not move in this direction in practice, if there is simply the complacent assertion that one "understands all right", then in fact one has not understood at all.

"To call on us to study Marxism is to repeat the mistake of the dialectical materialist creative method, which will harm the creative mood." To study Marxism means to apply the dialectical materialist and historical materialist viewpoint in our observation of the world, of society and of literature and art; it does not mean writing philosophical lectures into our works of literature and art. Marxism embraces but cannot replace realism in literary and artistic creation, just as it embraces but cannot replace the atomic and electronic theories in physics. Empty, dry dogmatic formulas do indeed destroy the creative mood; not only that, they first destroy Marxism. Dogmatic "Marxism" is not Marxism, it is anti-Marxism. Then does not Marxism destroy the creative mood? Yes, it does. It definitely destroys creative moods that are feudal, bourgeois, petty-bourgeois, liberalistic, individualist, nihilist, art-for-art's sake, aristocratic, decadent or pessimistic, and every other creative mood that is alien to the masses of the people and to the proletariat. So far as proletarian writers and artists are concerned, should not these kinds of creative moods be destroyed? I think they should; they should be utterly destroyed. And while they are being destroyed, something new can be constructed.

V

The problems discussed here exist in our literary and art circles in Yenan. What does that show? It shows that wrong styles of work still exist to a serious extent in our literary and art circles and that there are still many defects among our comrades, such as idealism, dogmatism, empty illusions, empty talk, contempt for practice and aloofness from the masses, all of which call for an effective and serious campaign of rectification.

We have many comrades who are still not very clear on the difference between the proletariat and the petty bourgeoisie. There are many Party members who have joined the Communist Party organizationally but have not yet joined the Party wholly or at all ideologically. Those who have not joined the Party ideologically still carry a great deal of the muck of the exploiting classes in their heads, and have no idea at all of what proletarian ideology, or communism, or the Party is. "Proletarian ideology?" they think. "The same old stuff!" Little do they know that it is no easy matter to acquire this stuff. Some will never have the slightest Communist flavour about them as long as they live and can only end up by leaving the Party.

Therefore, though the majority in our Party and in our ranks are clean and honest, we must in all seriousness put things in order both ideologically and organizationally if we are to develop the revolutionary movement more effectively and bring it to speedier success. To put things in order organizationally requires our first doing so ideologically, our launching a struggle of proletarian ideology against non-proletarian ideology. An ideological struggle is already under way in literary and art circles in Yenan, and it is most necessary. Intellectuals of petty-bourgeois origin always stubbornly try in all sorts of ways, including literary and artistic ways, to project themselves and spread their views, and they want the Party and the world to be remoulded in their own image. In the circumstances it is our duty to jolt these "comrades" and tell them sharply, "That won't work! The proletariat cannot accommodate itself to you; to yield to you would actually be to yield to the big landlord class and the big bourgeoisie and to run the risk of undermining our Party and our country." Whom then must we yield to? We can mould the Party and the world only in the image of the proletarian vanguard. We hope our comrades in literary and art circles will realize the seriousness of this great debate and join actively in this struggle, so that every comrade may become sound and our entire ranks may become truly united and consolidated ideologically and organizationally.

Because of confusion in their thinking, many of our comrades are not quite able to draw a real distinction between our revolutionary base areas and the Kuomintang areas and they make many mistakes as a consequence. A good number of comrades have come here from the garrets of Shanghai, and in coming from those garrets to the revolutionary base areas, they have passed not only from one kind of place to another but from one historical epoch to another. One society is semi-feudal, semi-colonial, under the rule of the big landlords and big bourgeoisie, the other is a revolutionary new-democratic society under the leadership of the proletariat. To come to the revolutionary bases means to enter an epoch unprecedented in the thousands of years of Chinese history, an epoch in which the masses of the people wield state power. Here the people around us and the audience for our propaganda are totally different. The past epoch is gone, never to return. Therefore, we must integrate ourselves with the new masses without any hesitation. If, living among the new masses, some comrades, as I said before, are still "lacking in knowledge and understanding" and remain "heroes with no place to display their prowess", then difficulties will arise for them, and not only when they go out to the villages; right here in Yenan difficulties will arise for them. Some comrades may think, "Well, I had better continue writing for the readers in the Great Rear Area;[10] it is a job I know well and has 'national significance'." This idea is entirely wrong. The Great Rear Area is also changing. Readers there expect authors in the revolutionary base areas to tell about the new people and the new world and not to bore them with the same old tales. Therefore, the more a work is written for the masses in the revolutionary base areas, the more national significance will it have. Fadeyev in *The Debacle*[11] only told the story of a small guerrilla unit and had no intention of pandering to the palate of readers in the old world; yet the book has exerted world-wide influence. At any rate in China its influence is very great, as you know. China is moving forward, not back, and it is the revolutionary base areas, not any of the backward, retrogressive areas, that are leading China forward. This is a fundamental issue that, above all, comrades must come to understand in the rectification movement.

Since integration into the new epoch of the masses is essential, it is necessary thoroughly to solve the problem of the relationship between the individual and the masses. This couplet from a poem by Lu Hsun should be our motto:

Fierce-browed, I coolly defy a thousand pointing fingers,
Head-bowed, like a willing ox I serve the children.[12]

The "thousand pointing fingers" are our enemies, and we will never yield to them, no matter how ferocious. The "children" here symbolize the proletariat and the masses. All Communists, all revolutionaries, all revolutionary literary and art workers should learn from the example of Lu Hsun and be "oxen" for the proletariat and the masses, bending their backs to the task until their dying day. Intellectuals who want to integrate themselves with the masses, who want to serve the masses, must go through a process in which they and the masses come to know each other well. This process may, and certainly will, involve much pain and friction, but if you have the determination, you will be able to fulfil these requirements.

Today I have discussed only some of the problems of fundamental orientation for our literature and art movement; many specific problems remain which will require further study. I am confident that comrades here are determined to move in the direction indicated.

I believe that in the course of the rectification movement and in the long period of study and work to come, you will surely be able to bring about a transformation in yourselves and in your works, to create many fine works which will be warmly welcomed by the masses of the people, and to advance the literature and art movement in the revolutionary base areas and throughout China to a glorious new stage.

NOTES

[1] See V. I. Lenin, "Party Organisation and Party Literature", in which he described the characteristics of proletarian literature as follows:

It will be a free literature, because the idea of socialism and sympathy with the working people, and not greed or careerism, will bring ever new forces to its ranks. It will be a free literature, because it will serve, not some satiated heroine, not the bored "upper ten thousand" suffering from fatty degeneration, but the millions and tens of millions of working people — the flower of the country, its strength and its future. It will be a free literature, enriching the last word in the revolutionary thought of mankind with the experience and living work of the socialist proletariat, bringing about permanent interaction between the experience of the past (scientific socialism, the completion of the development of socialism from its primitive, utopian forms) and the experience of the present (the present struggle of the worker comrades). (*Collected Works*, Eng. ed., FLPH, Moscow, 1962, Vol. X, pp. 48-49.)

[2] Liang Shih-chiu, a member of the counter-revolutionary National Socialist Party, for a long time propagated reactionary American bourgeois ideas on literature and art. He stubbornly opposed the revolution and reviled revolutionary literature and art.

[3] Chou Tso-jen and Chang Tzu-ping capitulated to the Japanese aggressors after the Japanese occupied Peking and Shanghai in 1937.

[4] Lu Hsun, "My View on the League of Left-Wing Writers" in the collection *Two Hearts*, *Complete Works*, Chin. ed., Vol. IV.

[5] See Lu Hsun's essay, "Death", in the "Addenda", *The Last Collection of Essays Written in a Garret in the Quasi-Concession*, *Complete Works*, Chin. ed., Vol. VI.

[6] The "Little Cowherd" is a popular Chinese folk operetta with only two people acting in it, a cowherd and a village girl, who sing a question and answer duet. In the early days of the War of Resistance Against Japan, this form was used, with new words, for anti-Japanese propaganda and for a time found great favour with the public.

[7] The Chinese characters for these six words are written simply, with only a few strokes, and were usually included in the first lessons in old primers.

[8] "The Spring Snow" and the "Song of the Rustic Poor" were songs of the Kingdom of Chu in the 3rd century B.C. The music of the first was on a higher level than that of the second. As the story is told in "Sung Yu's Reply to the King

of Chu" in Prince Chao Ming's *Anthology of Prose and Poetry*, when someone sang "The Spring Snow" in the Chu capital, only a few dozen people joined in, but when the "Song of the Rustic Poor" was sung, thousands did so.

[9] See V. I. Lenin, "Party Organisation and Party Literature": "Literature must become *part* of the common cause of the proletariat, 'a cog and a screw' of one single great Social-Democratic mechanism set in motion by the entire politically-conscious vanguard of the entire working class." (*Collected Works*, Eng. ed., FLPH, Moscow, 1962, Vol. X, p. 45.)

[10] The Great Rear Area was the name given during the War of Resistance to the vast areas under Kuomintang control in southwestern and northwestern China which were not occupied by the Japanese invaders, as distinguished from the "small rear area", the anti-Japanese base areas behind the enemy lines under the leadership of the Communist Party.

[11] *The Debacle* by the famous Soviet writer Alexander Fadeyev was published in 1927 and translated into Chinese by Lu Hsun. The novel describes the struggle of a partisan detachment of workers, peasants and revolutionary intellectuals in Siberia against the counter-revolutionary brigands during the Soviet civil war.

[12] This couplet is from Lu Hsun's "In Mockery of Myself" in *The Collection Outside the Collection, Complete Works*, Chin. ed., Vol. VII.

A MOST IMPORTANT POLICY

September 7, 1942

Ever since the Central Committee of the Party put forward the policy of "better troops and simpler administration",[1] the Party organizations in many anti-Japanese base areas have been applying it, or making plans to apply it, in accordance with the directives of the Central Committee. The leading comrades of the Shansi-Hopei-Shantung-Honan border area have really taken this work in hand, setting an example of "better troops and simpler administration". In some base areas, however, the comrades have not tried to do so very seriously because of their incomplete comprehension of this policy. They still fail to understand how it is related to the current situation and to other Party policies, or fail to regard it as most important. This matter has been discussed several times before in the *Liberation Daily* and we now wish to explain it further.

All the Party's policies aim at the defeat of the Japanese invaders. From the fifth year onward, the War of Resistance has in fact entered the final stage of the struggle for victory. In this stage the situation is different from that in the first and second years of the war, and also from that in the third and fourth. A feature of the fifth and sixth years of the war is that while victory is drawing near, there are very great difficulties ahead; in other words, we are in the "darkness before the dawn". This situation prevails at the present stage in all the anti-fascist countries, and in the whole of China as well; it is not confined to the base areas of the Eighth Route Army and the New Fourth Army, although it is particularly acute here. We are striving to defeat the Japanese invaders in two years. They will be years of extreme difficulty, differing greatly from the first and second two years of the war. This particular point must be anticipated by

---

This editorial was written by Comrade Mao Tse-tung for the *Liberation Daily*, Yenan.

the leading personnel in the revolutionary party and revolutionary army. Should they fail to do so, they will simply drift with events and, no matter how hard they try, they will not be able to attain victory and may even jeopardize the cause of the revolution. Although the situation in the anti-Japanese base areas in the enemy rear is already several times as difficult as before, the difficulty is not yet extreme. If we do not have a correct policy now, then extreme difficulty will overtake us. People in general are liable to judge by past and present conditions and to be misled into thinking that the future will be much the same. They are unable to anticipate that the ship may encounter submerged rocks or to steer clear of these rocks with cool heads. What are the submerged rocks in the path of the ship of the War of Resistance? They are the extremely grave material difficulties of the final stage of the war. The Central Committee of the Party has pointed them out and called on us to be on the alert and steer clear of them. Many of our comrades already understand the point but some do not, and that is the first obstacle we must overcome. There is the need for unity in the War of Resistance, and unity involves difficulties. These difficulties are political; they have occurred in the past and may occur again in the future. For five years, our Party has been overcoming them gradually and with the utmost effort; our slogan is to strengthen unity, and we must keep on doing so. But there are difficulties of another kind, the material ones. They will grow more and more acute. Today some comrades are still taking it easy and are not alive to the situation, and we must therefore alert them. All comrades in all the anti-Japanese base areas must recognize that from now on the material difficulties are bound to grow graver, that we must overcome them and that one important way of doing so is "better troops and simpler administration".

Why is the policy of better troops and simpler administration important for overcoming the material difficulties? It is clear that the present, and still more the future, war situation in the base areas will not permit us to cling to our past views. Our enormous war apparatus is suited to past conditions. It was then permissible and necessary. But things are different now, the base areas have shrunk and may continue to shrink for a period, and undoubtedly we cannot maintain the same enormous war apparatus as before. There is already a contradiction, which we must resolve, between our war apparatus and the war situation. The enemy's objective is to aggravate this contradiction, hence his policy of "burn all, kill all, loot all". If we maintain our enormous apparatus, we shall fall right into his trap. If we reduce it and have better troops and simpler administration, our war apparatus, though reduced, will remain strong. By resolving the contradiction, which is that of "a big fish in shallow water", and by adapting our war apparatus to the war situation, we shall prove even stronger, and so far from being defeated by the enemy we shall finally defeat him. That is why we say that the policy of "better troops and simpler administration" put forward by the Central Committee of the Party is a most important policy.

But men's minds are liable to be fettered by circumstance and habit from which even revolutionaries cannot always escape. We created this enormous apparatus ourselves, little thinking that one day we ourselves would have to reduce it; and now that the time has come to do so, we feel reluctant and find it very difficult. The enemy is bearing down upon us with his enormous war apparatus, and how dare we reduce ours? If we do, we shall feel that our forces are too few to cope with him. Such misgivings are precisely the result of being fettered by circumstance and habit. When the weather changes, it becomes necessary to change one's clothing. Each year as spring turns into summer, summer into autumn, autumn into winter and winter into spring we have to make this change. But owing to the force of habit people sometimes fail to make it at the proper turn and they fall ill. Present conditions in the base areas already require us to shed our winter garments and put on summer clothing so that we can move about nimbly to fight the enemy, but we are still heavily padded and weighed down, and quite unfit for combat. As for the question of how to deal with the enemy's enormous apparatus, we can learn from the example of how the Monkey King dealt with Princess Iron Fan. The Princess was a formidable demon, but by changing himself into a tiny insect the Monkey King made his way into her stomach and overpowered her.[2] Liu Tsung-yuan's description of "The Donkey in Kweichow"[3] also contains a valuable lesson. A huge donkey was brought to Kweichow and the sight of him rather frightened a small tiger. But in the end this huge donkey was devoured by the small tiger. Our Eighth Route and New Fourth Armies are the Monkey King or the small tiger, and they are fully capable of dealing with the Japanese demon or donkey. Now it is imperative for us to do a little changing and make ourselves smaller but sturdier, and then we shall be invincible.

NOTES

[1] The phrase "better troops and simpler administration" is now widely used and is no longer confined to military matters. It suggests readjustment in organizations and their staff membership, and simplification of the administration and the work procedure.

[2] For the story of how Sun Wu-kung, the Monkey King, changed himself into a tiny insect and defeated Princess Iron Fan, see the Chinese novel, *Hsi Yu Chi (Pilgrimage to the West)*, Chapter 59.

[3] Liu Tsung-yuan (773-819), a great Chinese writer of the Tang Dynasty. His *Three Parables* includes "The Donkey in Kweichow", which tells how a tiger in Kweichow was scared when he saw a donkey for the first time. But discovering that all the donkey could do was to bray and kick, the tiger fell upon it and devoured it.

THE TURNING POINT IN WORLD WAR II

October 12, 1942

The Battle of Stalingrad has been compared by the British and American press to the Battle of Verdun, and the "Red Verdun" is now famous all over the world. This comparison is not altogether appropriate. The Battle of Stalingrad is different in nature from the Battle of Verdun in World War I. But they have this in common — now, as then, many people are misled by the German offensive into thinking that Germany can still win the war. In 1916 the German forces launched several attacks on the French fortress of Verdun, two years before World War I ended in the winter of 1918. The commander-in-chief at Verdun was the German Crown Prince and the forces thrown into the battle were the cream of the German army. The battle was of decisive significance. After the ferocious German assaults failed, the entire German-Austrian-Turkish-Bulgarian bloc had no future, and from then on its difficulties mounted, it was deserted by its followers, it disintegrated, and finally collapsed. But at the time, the Anglo-American-French bloc did not grasp this situation, believing that the German army was still very powerful, and they were unaware of their own approaching victory. Historically, all reactionary forces on the verge of extinction invariably conduct a last desperate struggle against the revolutionary forces, and some revolutionaries are apt to be deluded for a time by this phenomenon of outward strength but inner weakness, failing to grasp the essential fact that the enemy is nearing extinction while they themselves are approaching victory. The rise of the forces of fascism and the war of aggression they have been conducting for some years are precisely the expression of such a last desperate struggle; and in this present war the attack on Stalingrad is the expression of the last desperate

---

This editorial was written by Comrade Mao Tse-tung for the *Liberation Daily*, Yenan.

struggle of fascism itself. At this turning point in history, too, many people in the world anti-fascist front have been deluded by the ferocious appearance of fascism and have failed to discern its essence. For forty-eight days there raged an unprecedentedly bitter battle, unparalleled in the history of mankind — from August 23, when the entire German force crossed the bend of the River Don and began the all-out attack on Stalingrad, through September 15, when some German units broke into the industrial district in the northwestern section of the city, and right up to October 9, when the Soviet Information Bureau announced that the Red Army had breached the German line of encirclement in that district. Ultimately this battle was won by the Soviet forces. During those forty-eight days, the news of each setback or triumph from that city gripped the hearts of countless millions of people, now bringing them anxiety, now stirring them to elation. This battle is not only the turning point of the Soviet-German war, or even of the present anti-fascist world war, it is the turning point in the history of all mankind. Throughout these forty-eight days, the people of the world watched Stalingrad with even greater concern than they watched Moscow last October.

Until his victory on the western front, Hitler seems to have been cautious. When he attacked Poland, when he attacked Norway, when he attacked Holland, Belgium, and France, and when he attacked the Balkans, he concentrated all his strength on one objective at a time, not daring to disperse his attention. After his victory on the western front, he became dizzy with success and attempted to defeat the Soviet Union in three months. He launched an offensive against this huge and powerful socialist country along the whole front stretching from Murmansk in the north to the Crimea in the south, and in so doing dispersed his forces. The failure of his Moscow campaign last October marked the end of the first stage of the Soviet-German war, and Hitler's first strategic plan failed. The Red Army halted the German offensive last year and launched a counteroffensive on all fronts in the winter, which constituted the second stage of the Soviet-German war, with Hitler turning to retreat and the defensive. In this period, after dismissing Brauchitsch, his commander-in-chief, and taking over the command himself, he decided to abandon the plan for an all-out offensive, combed Europe for all available forces and prepared a final offensive which, though limited to the southern front, would, he imagined, strike at the vitals of the Soviet Union. Because it was in the nature of a final offensive on which the fate of fascism hung, Hitler concentrated the greatest possible forces and even moved in part of his aircraft and tanks from the North African battle front. With the German attack on Kerch and Sevastopol in May this year, the war entered its third stage. Massing an army of over 1,500,000, which was supported by the bulk of his air and tank forces, Hitler launched an offensive of unprecedented fury on Stalingrad and the Caucasus. He endeavoured to capture these two objectives at great speed for the twofold purpose of cutting the Volga and seizing Baku, intending subsequently to drive against Moscow to the north and break through to the Persian Gulf in the south; at the same time he directed the Japanese fascists to mass their troops in Manchuria in preparation for an attack on Siberia after the fall of Stalingrad. Hitler vainly hoped to weaken the Soviet Union to such an extent that he would be able to release the main forces of the German army from the Soviet theatre of war for dealing with an Anglo-American attack on the western front, and for seizing the resources of the Near East and effecting a junction with the Japanese; at the same time this would allow the main forces of the Japanese to be released from the north and, with their rear secure, to move west against China and south against Britain and the United States. That was how Hitler reckoned on winning victory for the fascist camp. But how did things turn out in this stage? Hitler came up against the Soviet tactics which sealed his fate. The Soviet Union adopted the policy of first luring the enemy in deep and then putting up a stubborn resistance. In five months of fighting the German army has failed either to penetrate to the Caucasian oil-fields or to seize Stalingrad, so that Hitler has been forced to halt his troops before high mountains and outside an impregnable city, unable to advance and unable to retreat, suffering immense losses and getting into an impasse. October is already here and winter is approaching; soon the third stage of the war will end and the fourth stage will begin. Not one of Hitler's strategic plans of attack against the Soviet Union has succeeded. In this period, bearing in mind his failure in the summer of last year when his forces were divided, Hitler concentrated his strength on the southern front. But as he still wanted to achieve the twofold purpose of cutting the Volga in the east and seizing the Caucasus in the south at a single stroke, he again divided his forces. He did not recognize that his strength did not match his ambitions, and he is now doomed — "when the carrying pole is not secured at both ends, the loads slip off". As for the Soviet Union,

the more she fights the stronger she grows. Stalin's brilliant strategic
direction has completely gained the initiative and is everywhere
drawing Hitler towards destruction. The fourth stage of the war,
beginning this winter, will mark the approach of Hitler's doom.

Comparing Hitler's position in the first and third stages of the
war, we can see that he is on the threshold of final defeat. Both at
Stalingrad and in the Caucasus the Red Army has now in fact stopped
the German offensive; Hitler is now nearing exhaustion, having
failed in his attacks on Stalingrad and the Caucasus. The forces
which he managed to assemble throughout the winter, from last
December to May of this year, have already been used up. In less
than a month winter will set in on the Soviet-German front, and
Hitler will have to turn hastily to the defensive. The whole belt west
and south of the Don is his most vulnerable area, and the Red Army
will go over to the counter-offensive there. This winter, goaded on
by the fear of his impending doom, Hitler will once again reorganize
his forces. To meet the dangers on both the eastern and western
fronts, he may perhaps be able to scrape together the remnants of
his forces, equip them and form them into a few new divisions and,
in addition, he will turn for help to his three fascist partners, Italy,
Rumania and Hungary, and extort some more cannon-fodder from
them. However, he will have to face the enormous losses of a winter
campaign in the east and be ready to deal with the second front in
the west, while Italy, Rumania and Hungary, becoming pessimistic
as they see that it is all up with Hitler, will increasingly fall away
from him. In short, after October 9 there is only one road open to
Hitler, the road to extinction.

The Red Army's defence of Stalingrad in these forty-eight days
has a certain similarity to the defence of Moscow last year. That
is to say, Hitler's plan for this year has been foiled just as was his
plan for last year. The difference, however, is that, although the
Soviet people followed up their defence of Moscow with a winter
counter-offensive, they had yet to face the summer offensive of the
German army this year, partly because Germany and her European
accomplices still had some fight left in them and partly because
Britain and the United States delayed the opening of the second
front. But now, following the battle for the defence of Stalingrad,
the situation will be totally different from that of last year. On the
one hand, the Soviet Union will launch a second winter counter-
offensive on a vast scale, Britain and the United States will no longer

be able to delay the opening of the second front (though the exact date cannot yet be foretold), and the people of Europe will be ready to rise up in response. On the other hand, Germany and her European accomplices no longer have the strength to mount large-scale offensives, and Hitler will have no alternative but to change his whole line of policy to the strategic defensive. Once Hitler is compelled to go over to the strategic defensive, the fate of fascism is as good as sealed. From its birth, a fascist state like Hitler's builds its political and military life on taking the offensive, and once its offensive stops its very life stops too. The Battle of Stalingrad will stop the offensive of fascism and is therefore a decisive battle. It is decisive for the whole world war.

There are three powerful foes confronting Hitler, the Soviet Union, Britain and the United States, and the people in the German-occupied territories. On the eastern front stands the Red Army, firm as a rock, whose counter-offensives will continue through the whole of the second winter and beyond; it is this force which will decide the outcome of the whole war and the destiny of mankind. On the western front, even if Britain and the United States continue their policy of looking on and stalling, the second front will eventually be opened, when the time comes to belabour the slain tiger. Then there is the internal front against Hitler, the great uprising of the people which is brewing in Germany, in France and in other parts of Europe; they will respond with a third front the moment the Soviet Union launches an all-out counter-offensive and the guns roar on the second front. Thus, an attack from three fronts will converge on Hitler — such is the great historical process that will follow the Battle of Stalingrad.

Napoleon's political life ended at Waterloo, but the decisive turning point was his defeat at Moscow. Hitler today is treading Napoleon's road, and it is the Battle of Stalingrad that has sealed his doom.

These developments will have a direct impact on the Far East. The coming year will not be propitious for Japanese fascism either. As time goes on its headaches will grow, until it descends into its grave.

All those who take a pessimistic view of the world situation should change their point of view.

IN CELEBRATION OF
THE TWENTY-FIFTH ANNIVERSARY OF
THE OCTOBER REVOLUTION

November 6, 1942

It is with the greatest optimism that we celebrate the anniversary of the October Revolution this year. I firmly believe that this anniversary marks the turning point not only of the Soviet-German war, but also of the victory of the world anti-fascist front over the fascist front.

Hitler was previously able to keep up the offensive without being defeated because the Red Army was alone in resisting fascist Germany and its accomplices in Europe. Now the Soviet Union has grown more powerful in the course of the war and Hitler's second summer offensive has failed. Henceforward the task of the world anti-fascist front is to take the offensive against the fascist front and inflict final defeat on fascism.

The warriors of the Red Army at Stalingrad have performed prodigies of heroism which will affect the destiny of mankind. They are the sons and daughters of the October Revolution. The banner of the October Revolution is invincible, and all the forces of fascism are doomed to extinction.

In celebrating the victory of the Red Army, we the Chinese people are also celebrating our own victory. Our War of Resistance Against Japan has been going on for more than five years, and although there are still difficulties ahead the dawn of victory is already in sight. Victory over the Japanese fascists is not only certain but is not far off.

It is the task of the Chinese people to concentrate every effort on beating the Japanese fascists.

IN CELEBRATION OF
THE TWENTY-FIFTH ANNIVERSARY OF
THE C. TOLBERT EDITION

ECONOMIC AND FINANCIAL PROBLEMS
IN THE ANTI-JAPANESE WAR

December 1942

The general policy guiding our economic and financial work is to develop the economy and ensure supplies. But many of our comrades place one-sided stress on public finance and do not understand the importance of the economy as a whole; engrossed in matters of revenue and expenditure as such, they cannot find solutions to any problem hard as they try. The reason is that an outmoded and conservative notion is doing mischief in their minds. They do not know that while a good or a bad financial policy affects the economy, it is the economy that determines finance. Without a well-based economy it is impossible to solve financial difficulties, and without a growing economy it is impossible to attain financial sufficiency. The financial problem in the Shensi-Kansu-Ningsia Border Region is that of supplying funds for the living and operating expenses of tens of thousands of troops and civilian personnel, in other words, the problem of supplying funds for waging the war. These funds come partly from taxes paid by the people and partly from production carried on by the tens of thousands of troops and civilian personnel themselves. We shall simply be resigning ourselves to extinction unless we develop both the private and the public sectors of the economy. Financial difficulties can be overcome only by down-to-earth and effective economic development. To neglect economic development and the

This article, originally entitled "A Basic Summing-Up of Our Past Work", was the first chapter of *Economic and Financial Problems*, a report delivered by Comrade Mao Tse-tung at a conference of senior cadres of the Shensi-Kansu-Ningsia Border Region. The years 1941 and 1942 were the hardest for the Liberated Areas in the War of Resistance Against Japan. The savage attacks by the Japanese invaders and the encirclement and blockade by the Kuomintang created enormous financial difficulties for the Liberated Areas. Comrade Mao Tse-tung pointed out that in order to overcome these difficulties it was necessary for the Party to exert

opening up of sources of finance, and instead to hope for the solution
of financial difficulties by curtailing indispensable expenditures, is a
conservative notion which cannot solve any problem.

In the last five years we have passed through several stages. Our
worst difficulties occurred in 1940 and 1941, when the Kuomintang
created friction by its two anti-Communist drives. For a time we had
a very acute scarcity of clothing, cooking oil, paper and vegetables,
of footwear for our soldiers and of winter bedding for our civilian
personnel. The Kuomintang tried to strangle us by cutting off the
funds due to us and imposing an economic blockade; we were indeed
in dire straits. But we pulled through. Not only did the people of
the Border Region provide us with grain but, in particular, we
resolutely built up the public sector of our economy with our own
hands. The government established many industries to meet the needs
of the Border Region, the troops engaged in an extensive production
campaign and expanded agriculture, industry and commerce to supply
their own needs, and the tens of thousands of people in the various
organizations and schools also developed similar economic activities
for their own support. This self-supporting economy, which has been
developed by the troops and the various organizations and schools,
is a special product of the special conditions of today. It would be
unreasonable and incomprehensible in other historical conditions, but
it is perfectly reasonable and necessary at present. It is by such means
that we have been overcoming our difficulties. Do not these indisputable
historical facts prove the truth that supplies can be ensured only through

---

itself in leading the people in developing agriculture and other branches of production, and he called upon the government and other organizations, the schools and
the army in the Liberated Areas to produce as much as possible for their own
support. Comrade Mao Tse-tung's *Economic and Financial Problems* and his articles
"Spread the Campaigns to Reduce Rent, Increase Production and 'Support the
Government and Cherish the People' in the Base Areas" and "Get Organized!"
formed the Party's basic programme for leading the production campaign in the
Liberated Areas. Comrade Mao Tse-tung here severely criticizes the mistaken notion
of concentrating on public revenue and expenditure to the neglect of economic
development, and the wrong working style of making demands on the people
without mobilizing and helping them to develop production and surmount difficulties, and he set forth the Party's correct policy of "developing the economy and
ensuring supplies". With this policy great successes were achieved in the production
campaign which was unfolded in the Shensi-Kansu-Ningsia Border Region and in
the Liberated Areas behind the enemy lines. It not only enabled the armed forces
and the people of the Liberated Areas successfully to tide over the most difficult
period of the war, but also provided the Party with a rich store of experience for
guiding economic construction in later years.

economic development? While we still face many difficulties, the foundation of the public sector of our economy has already been laid. In another year, by the end of 1943, this foundation will be even firmer.

Developing the economy is the correct line, but development does not mean reckless or ill-founded expansion. Some comrades who disregard the specific conditions here and now are setting up an empty clamour for development; for example, they are demanding the establishment of heavy industry and putting forward plans for huge salt and armament industries, all of which are unrealistic and unacceptable. The Party's line is the correct line for development; it opposes outmoded and conservative notions on the one hand and grandiose, empty and unrealistic plans on the other. This is the Party's struggle on two fronts in financial and economic work.

While we must develop the public sector of our economy, we should not forget the importance of help from the people. They have given us grain, 90,000 *tan* in 1940, 200,000 in 1941 and 160,000 in 1942,[1] thus ensuring food for our troops and civilian personnel. Up to the end of 1941, the grain output of the public sector of our agriculture was meagre and we relied on the people for grain. We must urge the army to produce more grain, but for a time we shall still have to rely mainly on the people. Although the Shensi-Kansu-Ningsia Border Region is in the rear and has not suffered direct war damage, it has only 1,500,000 inhabitants, a small population for so large an area, and the provision of such large quantities of grain is not easy. Besides, the people transport salt for us or pay a salt transport levy, and in 1941 they purchased five million yuan worth of government bonds; all of which represents no small burden. To meet the needs of the War of Resistance and national reconstruction, the people must shoulder such burdens, the necessity of which they very well realize. When the government is in very great difficulties, it is necessary to ask the people to bear a heavier burden, and they understand that too. But while taking from the people we must at the same time help them to replenish and expand their economy. That is to say, appropriate steps and methods must be adopted to help the people develop their agriculture, animal husbandry, handicrafts, salt industry and commerce, so that they gain at the same time as they give and, moreover, gain more than they give; only thus can we sustain a long war against Japan.

Disregarding the needs of the war, some comrades insist that the government should adopt a policy of "benevolence". This is a mistake.

For unless we win the war against Japan, such "benevolence" will mean nothing to the people and will benefit only the Japanese imperialists. Conversely, although the people have to carry rather heavy burdens for the time being, things will get better for them as the difficulties confronting the government and the troops are overcome, the War of Resistance is sustained and the enemy is defeated; and this is where the true benevolence of the revolutionary government lies.

Another mistake is "draining the pond to catch the fish", that is, making endless demands on the people, disregarding their hardships and considering only the needs of the government and the army. That is a Kuomintang mode of thinking which we must never adopt. Although we have temporarily added to the people's burden, we have immediately set to work building the public sector of our economy. In the years 1941 and 1942 the army, the government and other organizations and the schools met most of their needs by their own efforts. This is a wonderful achievement without precedent in Chinese history, and it contributes to the material basis of our invincibility. The greater our self-supporting economic activities, the more we shall be able to lighten the people's tax burdens. In the first stage, from 1937 to 1939, we took very little from them; during this stage they were able to build up considerable strength. In the second stage, from 1940 to 1942, the burden on the people was increased. The third stage will begin in 1943. In the next two years, 1943 and 1944, if the public sector of our economy continues to grow and if all or most of our troops in the Shensi-Kansu-Ningsia Border Region are in a position to engage in farming, then by the end of 1944 the people's burden will again be lightened, and they will again be able to build up strength. This is a possibility which we should prepare to turn into actuality.

We must refute all one-sided views and advance the correct slogan of our Party, "Develop the economy and ensure supplies". With regard to the relation between public and private interests, our slogans are "Give consideration to both public and private interests" and "Give consideration to both troops and civilians". We consider only such slogans to be correct. We can guarantee our financial needs only by expanding both the public and the private sectors of our economy in a realistic and practical way. Even in difficult times we must take care to set a limit to taxation so that the burdens, though heavy, will not hurt the people. And as soon as we can, we should lighten the burdens so that the people can build up strength.

The Kuomintang die-hards regard construction in the Border Region as a hopeless undertaking and the difficulties here as insurmountable; they are expecting the Border Region to collapse any day. It is not worth arguing with such people; they will never see the day of our "collapse" and we shall unquestionably grow more and more prosperous. They do not understand that under the leadership of the Communist Party and the Border Region revolutionary government the masses always give their support to the Party and government. And the Party and the government will always find ways to get over economic and financial difficulties, however serious. In fact we have already pulled through some of our recent difficulties and will soon overcome others. We encountered difficulties many times greater in the past and surmounted them all. With intense fighting going on every day, our base areas in northern and central China are now facing much greater difficulties than the Shensi-Kansu-Ningsia Border Region, but we have already held out for five and a half years in these areas and can certainly continue to do so till victory. For us, there is no ground for pessimism; we can conquer any difficulty.

After the present conference of senior cadres of the Shensi-Kansu-Ningsia Border Region we shall put into effect the policy of "better troops and simpler administration".[2] It must be carried out strictly, thoroughly and universally, and not perfunctorily, superficially or partially. In carrying it out, we must attain the five objectives of simplification, unification, efficiency, economy and opposition to bureaucracy. These five objectives have a very important bearing on our economic and financial work. Simplification will reduce nonproductive expenditures and increase our income from production; it will not only have a direct and healthy effect on our finances, but will lighten the people's burdens and benefit them economically. In our economic and financial set-up, we must overcome such evils as disunity, assertion of independence and lack of co-ordination, and must establish a working system which is unified and responsive to direction and which permits the full application of our policies and regulations. With the establishment of such a unified system working efficiency will rise. All our organizations, and particularly those engaged in economic and financial work, must pay attention to thrift. By practising thrift we can cut out a great deal of unnecessary and wasteful expenditure, which amounts possibly to tens of millions of yuan. Finally, people engaged in economic and financial work must overcome surviving bureaucratic practices, some of which, such as corruption and graft, over-elaborate organization, meaningless "stand-ardization" and red tape, are very serious. If we fully attain these five objectives in the Party, the government and the army, our policy of "better troops and simpler administration" will achieve its purpose, our difficulties will surely be overcome, and we shall silence the gibes about our approaching "collapse".

NOTES

[1] These figures are the totals paid in agricultural tax (public grain) by the peasants of the Shensi-Kansu-Ningsia Border Region from 1940 to 1942.

[2] For "better troops and simpler administration" see "A Most Important Policy", pp. 99-102 of this volume.

SOME QUESTIONS
CONCERNING METHODS OF LEADERSHIP

June 1, 1943

1. There are two methods which we Communists must employ in whatever work we do. One is to combine the general with the particular; the other is to combine the leadership with the masses.

2. In any task, if no general and widespread call is issued, the broad masses cannot be mobilized for action. But if persons in leading positions confine themselves to a general call — if they do not personally, in some of the organizations, go deeply and concretely into the work called for, make a break-through at some single point, gain experience and use this experience for guiding other units — then they will have no way of testing the correctness or of enriching the content of their general call, and there is the danger that nothing may come of it. In the rectification movement of 1942, for example, there were achievements wherever the method of combining the general call with particular and specific guidance was used, but there were no achievements wherever this method was not used. In the rectification movement of 1943, each bureau and sub-bureau of the Central Committee and each area and prefectural Party committee, in addition to making a general call (a rectification plan for the whole year), must do the following things, gaining experience in the process. Select two or three units (but not too many) from the organization itself and from other organizations, schools or army units in the vicinity. Make a thorough study of those units, acquire a detailed knowledge of the development of the rectification movement in them and a detailed knowledge of the political history, the ideological characteristics, the zeal in study and the strong and weak points in the work of some (again not too many) representative members of

This decision on methods of leadership was written by Comrade Mao Tse-tung for the Central Committee of the Communist Party of China.

their personnel. Furthermore, give personal guidance to those in charge to find concrete solutions for the practical problems facing those units. The leaders in every organization, school or army unit must do likewise, as each of these has a number of subordinate units. Moreover, this is the method by which the leaders combine leading and learning. No one in a leading position is competent to give general guidance to all the units unless he derives concrete experience from particular individuals and events in particular subordinate units. This method must be promoted everywhere so that leading cadres at all levels learn to apply it.

3. Experience in the 1942 rectification movement also proves it is essential for the success of the rectification that a leading group should be formed in each unit in the course of the movement, made up of a small number of activists and with the heads of the given unit as its nucleus, and that this leading group should link itself closely with the masses taking part in the movement. However active the leading group may be, its activity will amount to fruitless effort by a handful of people unless combined with the activity of the masses. On the other hand, if the masses alone are active without a strong leading group to organize their activity properly, such activity cannot be sustained for long, or carried forward in the right direction, or raised to a high level. The masses in any given place are generally composed of three parts, the relatively active, the intermediate and the relatively backward. The leaders must therefore be skilled in uniting the small number of active elements around the leadership and must rely on them to raise the level of the intermediate elements and to win over the backward elements. A leading group that is genuinely united and linked with the masses can be formed only gradually in the process of mass struggle, and not in isolation from it. In the process of a great struggle, the composition of the leading group in most cases should not and cannot remain entirely unchanged throughout the initial, middle and final stages; the activists who come forward in the course of the struggle must constantly be promoted to replace those original members of the leading group who are inferior by comparison or who have degenerated. One fundamental reason why the work in many places and many organizations cannot be pushed ahead is the lack of a leading group which is united, linked with the masses and kept constantly healthy. A school of a hundred people certainly cannot be run well if it does not have a leading group of several people, or a dozen or more, which is formed in accordance

with the actual circumstances (and not thrown together artificially) and is composed of the most active, upright and alert of the teachers, the other staff and the students. In every organization, school, army unit, factory or village, whether large or small, we should give effect to the ninth of Stalin's twelve conditions for the bolshevization of the Party, namely, that on the establishment of a nucleus of leadership.[1] The criteria for such a leading group should be the four which Dimitrov enumerated in his discussion of cadres policy — absolute devotion to the cause, contact with the masses, ability independently to find one's bearings and observance of discipline.[2] Whether in carrying out the central tasks — war, production, education (including rectification) — or in checking-up on work, examining the cadres' histories, or in other activities, it is necessary to adopt the method of linking the leading group with the masses, in addition to that of linking the general call with particular guidance.

4. In all the practical work of our Party, all correct leadership is necessarily "from the masses, to the masses". This means: take the ideas of the masses (scattered and unsystematic ideas) and concentrate them (through study turn them into concentrated and systematic ideas), then go to the masses and propagate and explain these ideas until the masses embrace them as their own, hold fast to them and translate them into action, and test the correctness of these ideas in such action. Then once again concentrate ideas from the masses and once again go to the masses so that the ideas are persevered in and carried through. And so on, over and over again in an endless spiral, with the ideas becoming more correct, more vital and richer each time. Such is the Marxist theory of knowledge.

5. The concept of a correct relationship between the leading group and the masses in an organization or in a struggle, the concept that correct ideas on the part of the leadership can only be "from the masses, to the masses", and the concept that the general call must be combined with particular guidance when the leadership's ideas are being put into practice — these concepts must be propagated everywhere during the present rectification movement in order to correct the mistaken viewpoints among our cadres on these questions. Many comrades do not see the importance of, or are not good at, drawing together the activists to form a nucleus of leadership, and they do not see the importance of, or are not good at, linking this nucleus of leadership closely with the masses, and so their leadership becomes bureaucratic and divorced from the masses. Many comrades do not

see the importance of, or are not good at, summing up the experience of mass struggles, but fancying themselves clever, are fond of voicing their subjectivist ideas, and so their ideas become empty and impractical. Many comrades rest content with making a general call with regard to a task and do not see the importance of, or are not good at, following it up immediately with particular and concrete guidance, and so their call remains on their lips, or on paper or in the conference room, and their leadership becomes bureaucratic. In the present rectification movement we must correct these defects and learn to use the methods of combining the leadership with the masses and the general with the particular in our study, in the check-up on work and in the examination of cadres' histories; and we must also apply these methods in all our future work.

6. Take the ideas of the masses and concentrate them, then go to the masses, persevere in the ideas and carry them through, so as to form correct ideas of leadership — such is the basic method of leadership. In the process of concentrating ideas and persevering in them, it is necessary to use the method of combining the general call with particular guidance, and this is a component part of the basic method. Formulate general ideas (general calls) out of the particular guidance given in a number of cases, and put them to the test in many different units (not only doing so yourself, but by telling others to do the same); then concentrate the new experience (sum it up) and draw up new directives for the guidance of the masses generally. Comrades should do this in the present rectification movement, and also in every other kind of work. Better leadership comes with greater skill in doing this.

7. In relaying to subordinate units any task (whether it concerns the revolutionary war, production or education; the rectification movement, check-up on work or the examination of cadres' histories; propaganda work, organizational work or anti-espionage, or other work), a higher organization and its departments should in all cases go through the leader of the lower organization concerned so that he may assume responsibility; in this way both division of labour and unified centralized leadership are achieved. A department at a higher level should not go solely to its counterpart at the lower level (for instance, a higher department concerned with organization, propaganda or anti-espionage should not go solely to the corresponding department at the lower level), leaving the person in over-all charge of the lower organization (such as the secretary, the chairman, the

director or the school principal) in ignorance or without responsibility. Both the person in over-all charge and the person with specific responsibility should be informed and given responsibility. This centralized method, combining division of labour with unified leadership, makes it possible, through the person with over-all responsibility, to mobilize a large number of cadres — on occasion even an organization's entire personnel — to carry out a particular task, and thus to overcome shortages of cadres in individual departments and turn a good number of people into active cadres for the work in hand. This, too, is a way of combining the leadership with the masses. Take, for instance, the examining of cadres' histories. If the job is done in isolation, if it is done only by the few people in the organization department in charge of such work, it certainly cannot be done well. But if it is done through the administrative head of a particular organization or school, who mobilizes many or even all of his staff, or many or even all of his students, to take part in the work, while at the same time the leading members of the organization department at the higher level give correct guidance, applying the principle of linking the leadership with the masses, then undoubtedly the task of examining the cadres' histories will be satisfactorily accomplished.

8. In any given place, there cannot be a number of central tasks at the same time. At any one time there can be only one central task, supplemented by other tasks of a second or third order of importance. Consequently, the person with over-all responsibility in the locality must take into account the history and circumstances of the struggle there and put the different tasks in their proper order; he should not act upon each instruction as it comes from the higher organization without any planning of his own, and thereby create a multitude of "central tasks" and a state of confusion and disorder. Nor should a higher organization simultaneously assign many tasks to a lower organization without indicating their relative importance and urgency or without specifying which is central, for that will lead to confusion in the steps to be taken by the lower organizations in their work and thus no definite results will be achieved. It is part of the art of leadership to take the whole situation into account and plan accordingly in the light of the historical conditions and existing circumstances of each locality, decide correctly on the centre of gravity and the sequence of the work for each period, steadfastly carry through the decision, and make sure that definite results are achieved. This is also a problem of method of leadership, and care must be taken to

solve it when applying the principles of combining the leadership with the masses and the general with the particular.

9. Details concerning methods of leadership are not dealt with here; it is hoped that comrades in all localities will themselves do some hard thinking and give full play to their own creativeness on the basis of the principles here set forth. The harder the struggle, the greater the need for Communists to link their leadership closely with the demands of the vast masses, and to combine general calls closely with particular guidance, so as to smash the subjectivist and bureaucratic methods of leadership completely. All the leading comrades of our Party must at all times counterpose scientific, Marxist methods of leadership to subjectivist, bureaucratic methods of leadership and use the former to overcome the latter. Subjectivists and bureaucrats do not understand the principles of combining the leadership with the masses and the general with the particular; they greatly impede the development of the work of the Party. To combat subjectivist and bureaucratic methods of leadership, we must promote scientific, Marxist methods of leadership both extensively and intensively.

NOTES

[1] See J. V. Stalin, "The Prospects of the Communist Party of Germany and the Question of Bolshevization", *Works*, Eng. ed., FLPH, Moscow, 1954, Vol. VII, p. 39.

[2] See Georgi Dimitrov, "Unity of the Working Class Against Fascism", *Selected Articles and Speeches*, Eng. ed., Lawrence & Wishart, London, 1951, pp. 138-39.

SOME POINTED QUESTIONS
FOR THE KUOMINTANG

July 12, 1943

The last few months have witnessed a most unusual and shocking event inside China's anti-Japanese camp, namely, the campaign launched by many Kuomintang-led party, government and army organizations to wreck unity and undermine the War of Resistance. It assumes the form of an attack on the Communist Party, but is in fact directed against the whole Chinese nation and people.

Consider first the Kuomintang armies. Of the Kuomintang-led armies throughout the country, as many as three group armies from the main forces are stationed in the Northwest — the 34th, 37th and 38th Group Armies, all under Hu Tsung-nan, Deputy Commander-in-Chief of the 8th War Zone. Of these, two have been used to encircle the Shensi-Kansu-Ningsia Border Region, while only one has been assigned defence duty along the Yellow River, from Yichuan to Tungkuan, against the Japanese invaders. This has been the situation for more than four years, and people became accustomed to it so long as there was no military clash. But in the last few days an unexpected change has taken place. Of the three army corps on defence duty along the river — the 1st, 16th and 90th Army Corps — two have been removed, the 1st Army Corps to the area of Pinchow and Chunhua and the 90th to the area of Lochuan, and both are actively preparing to attack the Border Region, while the greater part of the river defences is left unmanned against the Japanese invaders.

This inevitably makes people ask: What exactly are the relations between these Kuomintang people and the Japanese?

Day in day out many Kuomintang people have been brazenly spreading propaganda that the Communist Party is "sabotaging the

Comrade Mao Tse-tung wrote this editorial for the *Liberation Daily*, Yenan.

123

War of Resistance" and "wrecking unity". Can the withdrawal of
the main forces defending the river be called strengthening the War
of Resistance? Can attacks on the Border Region be called strengthening unity?

We should like to ask the Kuomintang people who are doing
all this: You are turning your backs on the Japanese while they are
still facing you. What is going to happen if the Japanese start advancing
on your heels?

What is the meaning of your abandonment of large sections of
the river defences while the Japanese quietly look on from the other
bank, without making any move other than to watch with glee
through their field-glasses the gradually receding view of your backs?
Why do the Japanese so greatly prefer seeing your backs? And what
makes you feel so much at ease after abandoning the river defences
and leaving large sections unmanned?

In a society based on private property, people usually bolt their
doors at night before going to bed. Everybody knows that this is
not fussiness but a precaution against burglars. Now, having left
the front door wide open, are you not afraid of burglars coming? And
if the front door is left wide open without the burglars coming, what
then is the reason?

According to you, in China it is the Communists who are "sabotaging the War of Resistance", while you yourselves are most
devoted to "the nation above all". Well now, what are you placing
"above all" when you turn your backs on the enemy?

According to you, it is also the Communists who are "wrecking
unity", while you are so very devoted to "unity in good faith". Well,
you have sent a huge force of three group armies (minus one army
corps), with fixed bayonets and heavy artillery, to march against the
people of the Border Region; can this be counted as "unity in
good faith"?

Or take another of your assertions — that you are very keen not
on "unity" but on "unification" — and you therefore want to wipe
out the Border Region, liquidate "feudal separatism" and kill off
every Communist. Very well! How is it then you are not afraid that
the Japanese will "unify" the Chinese nation, including you, out
of existence?

Supposing that while you triumphantly "unify" the Border Region
at one stroke and wipe out the Communists, you are able to keep
the Japanese stupefied by some "sleeping-draught" or by some "spell"

of yours, so that the nation and you yourselves both escape "unification" by them. Well, dear gentlemen of the Kuomintang, won't you give us some inkling of the secret of your sleeping-draught or spell?

But if you have no sleeping-draught or spell for dealing with the Japanese, and if you have not reached a secret understanding with them, then let us tell you plainly and formally: you should not and must not attack the Border Region. "When the snipe and the clam grapple, it is the fisherman who profits", "The mantis stalks the cicada, but behind them lurks the oriole" — there is truth in these two parables. The proper thing for you to do is to join forces with us to "unify" the territory occupied by the Japanese and drive the devils out. What is the reason for your anxiety and hurry to "unify" the span of land forming the Border Region? Though vast stretches of our beautiful country have fallen into the hands of the enemy, you are not anxious or in a hurry about this, but instead are anxious to attack the Border Region and in a hurry to crush the Communist Party. How painful! How disgraceful!

Next, consider the activities of the Kuomintang Party. To combat the Communist Party the Kuomintang has organized several hundred detachments of secret agents, into which it has recruited all kinds of scoundrels. For example, on July 6, 1943, in the 32nd year of the Chinese Republic, on the eve of the sixth anniversary of the War of Resistance, the Kuomintang Central News Agency released a news item stating that certain "cultural associations" in Sian, Shensi Province, had held a meeting and resolved to cable Mao Tse-tung, calling on him to use the opportunity of the dissolution of the Third International to "dissolve" the Communist Party of China and, in addition, to "abolish the separatist Border Region regime". The reader may well take this to be "news", but actually it is an old story.

It turns out that the whole thing was the handiwork of one of the several hundred detachments of secret agents. Acting on orders from headquarters (namely, "The Bureau of Investigation and Statistics of the Military Council of the National Government" and "The Bureau of Investigation and Statistics of the Central Executive Committee of the Kuomintang"), this detachment gave instructions to the Trotskyite and traitor Chang Ti-fei, who is now Director of Discipline in the Sian concentration camp and notorious for his anti-Communist writings in *Resistance and Culture*, a traitorous periodical financed by the Kuomintang; on June 12, that is, twenty-five days before the Central News Agency released its news item, he mustered together nine people in a ten-minute meeting which "endorsed" the text of the so-called telegram.

This telegram has not reached Yenan to this day but its contents are clear. It says, we are told, that since the Third International has been dissolved, the Communist Party of China should likewise be "dissolved", that "Marxism-Leninism has been discredited", and so on and so forth.

There it is. This is the sort of thing the Kuomintang are saying! We have always believed that anything may issue from the mouths of the likes of these Kuomintang creatures (and like attracts like), and as one would expect, they have now let out this gust of foul air!

There are now many political parties in China — there are even two Kuomintangs. One is the Wang Ching-wei brand of Kuomintang, set up in Nanking and elsewhere, which also has a flag with a white sun against a blue sky and a so-called Central Executive Committee, as well as a collection of secret police detachments. In addition, everywhere in the occupied areas there are the fascist parties created by the Japanese.

Dear gentlemen of the Kuomintang! Why is it that since the dissolution of the Third International you have been so terribly busy plotting the "dissolution" of the Communist Party but will not even lift a finger to dissolve a few of the traitorous and Japanese-sponsored parties? When you directed Chang Ti-fei to draft the telegram, why is it that, besides demanding the dissolution of the Communist Party, you did not deign to add that the traitorous and Japanese-sponsored parties, too, ought to be dissolved?

Is it possible that you think there is one Communist Party too many? In the whole of China there is only one Communist Party, while there are two Kuomintangs. After all, of which party is there one too many?

Gentlemen of the Kuomintang! Have you ever given the following matter a thought? Why is it that, in addition to yourselves, both the Japanese and Wang Ching-wei are making frantic efforts to overthrow the Communist Party, asserting that the Communist Party alone is one too many and must therefore be crushed? And why is it that they feel there are too few Kuomintangs and there never can be too many, and that they are everywhere grooming and fostering the Wang Ching-wei brand of Kuomintang?

Gentlemen of the Kuomintang! We don't mind taking the trouble to tell you that the Japanese and Wang Ching-wei have a special love for the Kuomintang and the Three People's Principles because they find something in both they can turn to good account. The only time since World War I that the imperialists and traitors had no love for the Kuomintang but bitterly hated it and tried their utmost to abolish it was in the period of 1924-27, when it was reorganized by Dr. Sun Yat-sen, admitted Communists into its ranks and became a national alliance in which the Kuomintang and the Communist Party co-operated. The only time that the imperialists and traitors had no love for the Three People's Principles but bitterly hated them and tried their utmost to abolish them was also in the same period, when these principles were transformed by Dr. Sun Yat-sen into the revolutionary Three People's Principles as set out in the Manifesto of the First National Congress of the Kuomintang. Save for that period, the Kuomintang has thrown out the Communists and the Three People's Principles have been emptied of Dr. Sun Yat-sen's revolutionary spirit, and both have therefore earned the love of all the imperialists and traitors and, for the same reasons, have earned the love of the Japanese fascists and the traitor Wang Ching-wei, who are grooming and fostering them like treasured possessions. There used to be a yellow patch in the upper left-hand corner of the flag of Wang Ching-wei's brand of Kuomintang to distinguish it from the other Kuomintang, but now even that has been removed and everything is made to look the same so as not to offend the eye. What great love!

Kuomintang specimens of the Wang Ching-wei brand are numerous in the Great Rear Area as well as in the occupied areas. Some are under cover, forming the enemy's fifth column. Others are in the open, depending for their food and keep upon the Kuomintang or upon their work as police agents, doing nothing at all to resist Japan but specializing in anti-communism. Though they do not wear Wang Ching-wei labels, these people are really his men. They, too, are enemy fifth-columnists, only they use a somewhat different guise in order to conceal their identity and fool people.

The whole thing is now perfectly clear. When you instructed Chang Ti-fei to draft the telegram demanding the "dissolution" of the Communist Party, the reason why you would in no circumstances trouble to add that the Japanese-sponsored parties and traitor parties should also be dissolved is that you have much in common with them in ideology, policy and organization, and that the fundamental feature of your common ideology is opposition to communism and to the people.

We want to ask you Kuomintang people yet another question. Is it true that the only "discredited" *ism* in China and indeed in the whole world is Marxism-Leninism and that all the others are great stuff? Apart from Wang Ching-wei's brand of the Three People's Principles which we have just mentioned, what about the fascism of Hitler, Mussolini and Hideki Tojo? What about the Trotskyism of Chang Ti-fei? What about the counter-revolutionary doctrines of the various brands of counter-revolutionary secret services in China?

Dear gentlemen of the Kuomintang! Why is it that when you instructed Chang Ti-fei to draft the telegram, you did not add a single phrase or proviso about all these so-called *isms* which are about as much good as the plague, or bedbugs, or dog's droppings? Is it possible that in your eyes all this counter-revolutionary rubbish is flawless and perfect, while Marxism-Leninism alone is completely discredited?

To be blunt, we strongly suspect that you are working in collusion with the Japanese-sponsored and traitorous parties, and that is why you and they "breathe through the same nostrils", that is why you and the enemy and traitors are so exactly alike, indeed, identical and indistinguishable both in your words and in your deeds. The Japanese and the traitors wanted the New Fourth Army disbanded, and you ordered it to be disbanded; they want to dissolve the Communist Party, and so do you; they want to abolish the Border Region, and so do you; they do not want you to defend the Yellow River, and so you abandon its defence; they attack the Border Region (for the last six years the enemy forces along the river bank opposite the counties of Suiteh, Michih, Chiahsien, Wupao and Chingchien have never ceased shelling the Eighth Route Army's river defences), and you too intend to attack it; they are anti-Communist, and so are you; they bitterly revile communism and liberal ideas, and so do you; when they seize a Communist, they force him to make a public recantation in the press, and so do you; they send counter-revolutionary agents to worm their way into the Communist Party and the Eighth Route and New Fourth Armies for disruptive purposes, and so do you. How is it that you and they are so remarkably alike, identical and indistinguishable? As you and the enemy and the traitors are exactly alike, identical and indistinguishable in so many words and deeds, how can people help suspecting that you are working hand in glove with them or have come to some secret understanding with them?

We hereby make this formal protest to the Central Executive Committee of the Kuomintang: Your action in withdrawing the main forces for river defence in preparation for attacking the Border Region and starting civil war is utterly wrong and impermissible. Your Central News Agency's publication of the news item of July 6, which is disruptive of unity and insulting to the Communist Party, is also utterly wrong and impermissible. Both these errors are towering crimes, indistinguishable from those committed by the enemy and the traitors. You must correct them.

We hereby make this formal demand to Mr. Chiang Kai-shek, Director-General of the Kuomintang: Please order Hu Tsung-nan's troops to return to the river defences, please discipline the Central News Agency and punish the traitor Chang Ti-fei.

We hereby appeal to all true patriots among the Kuomintang members who do not approve of the withdrawal of the river defence forces for the purpose of attacking the Border Region and do not approve of the demand for the dissolution of the Communist Party: please act now to avert the crisis of civil war. We are willing to co-operate with you to the very end to save the nation.

We believe that these are absolutely just demands.

SPREAD THE CAMPAIGNS
TO REDUCE RENT, INCREASE PRODUCTION
AND "SUPPORT THE GOVERNMENT
AND CHERISH THE PEOPLE"
IN THE BASE AREAS

October 1, 1943

1. As the time for autumn harvest is come, the leading bodies in the base areas must ask Party and government organizations at all levels to check up on the application of our policy of rent reduction. Wherever it has not been carried out in earnest, rents must be reduced this year without any exception. Wherever this work has not been thorough, it must be done thoroughly this year. Party committees should immediately issue directives based on the agrarian policy of the Central Committee and conforming to local conditions, and they should inspect a few villages at first hand, pick out good examples and so expedite the work in other places. At the same time, the press should carry editorials on rent reduction and reports of good examples. As rent reduction is a mass struggle by the peasants, Party directives and government decrees should guide and help it instead of trying to bestow favours on the masses. To bestow rent reduction as a favour instead of arousing the masses to achieve it by their own action is wrong, and the results will not be solid. Peasant organizations should be formed or reconstituted in the struggle for rent reduction. The government's position should be one of enforcing the decree on rent reduction and adjusting the relative interests of the landlords and the tenants. Now that the base areas have shrunk in size, it is of more immediate importance than at any time in the past six years for the Party to win the masses there by patient,

This inner-Party directive was written by Comrade Mao Tse-tung on behalf of the Central Committee of the Communist Party of China.

conscientious and thorough work, and to share weal and woe with them. If during this autumn we check on how far the policy has been carried out and perform the task of rent reduction thoroughly, we shall be able to arouse the initiative of the peasant masses and, in the coming year, intensify our struggle against the enemy and give impetus to the production campaign.

2. In the base areas behind the enemy lines most cadres have not yet learned how to get the personnel of the Party and government organizations, the troops and the people (including everyone, men and women, old and young, soldiers and civilians, and people in public and private employment) to undertake production on a wide scale. During this autumn and winter the Party committee, the government and the army in each base area must get ready to launch a big area-wide production campaign next year, covering both public and private farming, industry, handicrafts, transport, animal husbandry and commerce, with the main emphasis on farming — a campaign for overcoming difficulties by our own efforts (the slogan of "ample food and clothing" should not be raised for the time being except in the Shensi-Kansu-Ningsia Border Region). There should be planning household by household and mutual aid in labour (known as labour-exchange teams in northern Shensi and once known as ploughing teams or mutual-aid working groups in the former Red areas in Kiangsi), labour heroes should be rewarded, emulation in production should be practised and co-operatives serving the masses should be promoted. In the financial and economic field, the Party and government personnel at the county and district levels should devote nine-tenths of their energy to helping the peasants increase production, and only one-tenth to collecting taxes from them. If pains are taken with the first task, the second will be easy. In the present war conditions all organizations, schools and army units must make great efforts to grow vegetables, breed pigs, collect firewood, make charcoal, expand handicrafts and raise part of their own grain supply. Apart from the development of collective production in all units, whether big or small, every individual (except for those in the army) should also be encouraged to engage in some spare-time agricultural or handicraft production (but not in trade), the proceeds of which he can keep for himself. Seven to ten-day training courses should be given on vegetable-growing and pig-farming, and on the preparation of better food by the cooks. Thrift should be stressed, waste combated and corrupt practices forbidden in all Party, government

and army organizations. At all levels, the leading personnel in the Party, government and army organizations and in the schools should master all the skills involved in leading the masses in production. No one who fails to study production carefully can be considered a good leader. Any soldier or civilian who is not serious about production and who likes to eat but does not like to work cannot be considered a good soldier or a good citizen. Village Party members who are not diverted from production should realize that one of the qualifications for becoming a model among the masses is to work well in increasing production. In the campaign for production, it is wrong to take a conservative and purely financial point of view which concentrates on revenue and expenditure to the neglect of economic development. It is wrong to have a handful of government functionaries busying themselves with collecting grain and taxes, funds and food supplies to the neglect of organizing the enormous labour power of the rank and file of the Party, the government and the army, and that of the people, for a mass campaign of production. It is wrong simply to demand grain and money from the masses (as does the Kuomintang) without making every effort to help them to increase production. It is wrong to have a few economic departments organizing a small number of people for production and to neglect the launching of extensive mass campaigns for production. It is wrong to consider it dishonourable and selfish either for Communists in the countryside to engage in household production in order to support their families or for Communists in government organizations and schools to engage in private spare-time production in order to improve their own living conditions, for all such activity is in the interests of the revolutionary cause. It is wrong simply to exhort people in any base area to endure hardship in the bitter struggle without encouraging them to increase production and thereby try to improve their material conditions. It is wrong to regard the co-operatives as money-making concerns run for the benefit of the small number of functionaries or as stores run by the government and not as economic organizations run by and for the masses. It is wrong not to introduce the model methods of work used by some of the agricultural labour heroes of the Shensi-Kansu-Ningsia Border Region (*e.g.*, mutual aid in labour, repeated ploughing, frequent hoeing and ample manuring) on the pretext that these methods are not applicable in certain base areas. It is wrong, in production campaigns, to shift the task of production to the heads of the local departments in charge of economic development, the army supply chiefs or the administration chiefs in governmental and other bodies, instead of ensuring that the leading cadres themselves assume responsibility and participate personally, that the leading group links itself closely with the masses and general calls are combined with particular and specific guidance, that investigation and study are undertaken and priority is given to what is urgent and important, that efforts are made to bring everyone into production — men and women, young and old, and even the loafers — and that cadres are trained and the masses given education. In the present circumstances the organization of labour power is the key to increasing production. In each of the base areas, even under present war conditions, it is possible and altogether necessary to organize the labour power of tens of thousands of men and women in the Party, the government offices and the army, and hundreds of thousands of the people for production purposes (*i.e.*, to organize on a voluntary basis all people who are capable of performing part-time or full-time labour, using the forms of household-by-household planning, labour-exchange teams, transport teams, mutual-aid working groups or co-operatives, and keeping to the principle of exchange of equal values). Communist Party members must attain a full grasp of all the principles and methods of organizing labour power. Rent reduction carried out universally and thoroughly in all the base areas this year will stimulate a broad increase in production next year. And the great production campaign that will be carried on next year by Party and government, soldiers and civilians, men and women, and young and old, to increase the supply of grain and other necessities and to prepare against natural disasters, will lay the material foundation for the continued maintenance of the anti-Japanese base areas. Otherwise, we will encounter grave difficulties.

3. For the Party, the government and the army to be at one with the people in developing next year's anti-Japanese struggle and campaign for production, the Party committees and the leading army and government bodies in every single base area should prepare to launch a large-scale mass campaign in the first month of the coming lunar year to "support the government and cherish the people" and to "support the army and give preferential treatment to the families of soldiers who are fighting the Japanese". The troops should publicly renew their pledge to "support the government and cherish the people", hold meetings for self-criticism, arrange get-togethers with the local people (to which representatives of the local Party and govern-

ment organizations should also be invited), and apologize and give compensation for any past infringements upon the interests of the masses. Under the leadership of the local Party, government and mass organizations, the masses on their side should publicly renew their pledge to support the army and give preferential treatment to the families of the soldiers fighting the Japanese, and should set going an ardent campaign for greetings and gifts to the army units. In the course of these campaigns, the army on its side and the Party and the government on theirs should thoroughly examine the shortcomings and mistakes of 1943, and should resolutely correct them in 1944. From now on, such campaigns should be launched everywhere in the first month of every lunar year, and in the course of them the pledges to "support the government and cherish the people" and "support the army and give preferential treatment to the families of the soldiers who are fighting the Japanese" should be read out time and again, and there should be repeated self-criticism before the masses of any high-handed behaviour by the troops in the base areas towards the Party or government personnel or towards civilians, or of any lack of concern for the troops shown by the Party or government personnel or the civilians (each side criticizing itself and not the other) in order that these shortcomings and mistakes may be thoroughly corrected.

A COMMENT
ON THE SESSIONS OF THE KUOMINTANG CENTRAL EXECUTIVE COMMITTEE AND OF THE PEOPLE'S POLITICAL COUNCIL

October 5, 1943

The Kuomintang held the Eleventh Plenary Session of its Central Executive Committee from September 6 to 13, and the Kuomintang government held the Second Session of the Third People's Political Council from September 18 to 27. Now that all the documents of both these meetings are at hand, we can make a general comment.

The international situation is on the threshold of a great change, whose imminence is sensed on all sides. The European Axis Powers have sensed it, and Hitler is adopting a desperate last-ditch policy. In the main, it is the Soviet Union that is bringing this change about. The Soviet Union is now taking advantage of it — the Red Army has already fought its way to the Dnieper, sweeping all before it, and another winter offensive will bring it to the old, if not to the new, Soviet boundaries. Britain and the United States, too, are taking advantage of the change; Roosevelt and Churchill are waiting for the first sign of Hitler's downfall to thrust into France. In short, the German fascist war machine will soon fall apart, the problem of the anti-fascist war in Europe is on the eve of total solution, and the Soviet Union is the main force in annihilating fascism. As the world anti-fascist war has its pivot in Europe, once the problem there is solved, the fate of the two great world camps, the fascist and the anti-fascist camps, will be decided. The Japanese imperialists feel themselves cornered, and their policy, too, can only be to muster all possible strength for a desperate last-ditch struggle. In China, they

---

This editorial was written by Comrade Mao Tse-tung for the *Liberation Daily*, Yenan.

137

will try to "mop up" the Communists and entice the Kuomintang to capitulate.

The Kuomintang has also sensed the change. Faced with this situation it feels both joy and fear. Joy, because it imagines that with the war in Europe over, Britain and the United States will be left free to fight Japan on its behalf, and that it will be able to return to Nanking without any effort. Fear, because with the downfall of all three fascist powers the world will enter a great and unprecedented age of liberation, and the Kuomintang's comprador-feudal fascist dictatorship will become a small island in a vast ocean of freedom and democracy; it fears that its own brand of fascism with its "one party, one doctrine, one leader" will be buried beneath the waves.

Originally the Kuomintang hoped to have the Soviet Union fighting it out with Hitler single-handed and to instigate the Japanese to attack the Soviet Union, so that the land of socialism would be destroyed or at least badly mauled; it also hoped that Britain and the United States would shift all their forces to the East and first smash Japan and then wipe out the Chinese Communist Party, before bothering about any second or third front in Europe. It was for this ulterior purpose that the Kuomintang first clamoured for a strategy of "Asia before Europe" and then for "equal attention to Europe and Asia". In August this year, towards the end of the Quebec conference, when Roosevelt and Churchill summoned T. V. Soong, the foreign minister of the Kuomintang government, to Quebec and spoke a few words to him, the Kuomintang started shouting that "Roosevelt and Churchill are turning to the East", that "the 'Europe before Asia' plan is changed", that "Quebec is a conference of the three great powers, Britain, the United States and China", etc., and joyfully indulged in self-glorification. But this was the Kuomintang's last occasion to rejoice. Since then its mood has changed somewhat; "Asia before Europe" and "equal attention to Europe and Asia" have been consigned to the museum of history, and now the Kuomintang is probably cooking up new schemes. Perhaps the Eleventh Plenary Session of the Kuomintang Central Executive Committee and the Second Session of the Kuomintang-controlled People's Political Council mark the beginning of these new schemes.

The Eleventh Plenary Session of the Kuomintang CEC slanderously accused the Communist Party of "sabotaging the War of Resistance and endangering the state", and at the same time declared itself in favour of a "political solution" and of "preparations for constitutional government". Controlled and manipulated by its Kuomintang majority, the Second Session of the Third PPC passed resolutions against the Communist Party to roughly the same effect. In addition, the Eleventh Plenary Session of the Kuomintang CEC "elected" Chiang Kai-shek president of the Kuomintang government in order to strengthen its dictatorial machine.

What can the Kuomintang be planning to do now, following the Eleventh Plenary Session? There are only three possibilities:

(1) capitulation to Japanese imperialism;

(2) dragging along on the old road; and

(3) a change in its political line.

Serving the Japanese imperialists' purpose of "hitting the Communists and courting the Kuomintang", the defeatists and capitulationists within the Kuomintang have all along advocated surrender. They have constantly endeavoured to unleash an anti-Communist civil war which, once started, would naturally make resistance to Japan impossible, leaving capitulation as the only alternative. The Kuomintang has concentrated 400,000 to 500,000 troops in northwestern China and is stealthily diverting still more forces there from other fronts. It is said that the generals are in good fettle and are proclaiming, "Taking Yenan is no problem." This is how they have been talking since Mr. Chiang Kai-shek's speech at the Eleventh Plenary Session in which he described the Communist problem as "a political one and should be solved politically" and since the Session's resolutions to roughly the same effect. Similar resolutions were adopted last year at the Tenth Plenary Session of the Kuomintang CEC, and the ink was hardly dry before the generals were ordered to draw up military plans for liquidating the Border Region; in June and July this year forces were deployed in preparation for a blitz against the Border Region, and the scheme was temporarily shelved only because public opinion at home and abroad was against it. Now once again, no sooner have the resolutions of the Eleventh Plenary Session been put down in black and white than there are reports of the generals' braggadocio and of troop movements. "Taking Yenan is no problem" — what does this signify? It signifies a decision to capitulate to Japanese imperialism. Not all the Kuomintang members who favour "taking Yenan" are necessarily conscious and determined capitulationists. Some of them may think, "We shall still resist the Japanese while fighting the Communists." This is probably what many officers of the Whampoa clique[1] are thinking.

To these gentlemen we Communists would like to put the following questions. Have you forgotten the lessons of the ten years
of civil war? Once another civil war starts, will the determined
capitulationists allow you to continue the war against Japan? Will
the Japanese and Wang Ching-wei allow you to continue the war
against Japan? Are you really so strong that you can fight a civil
war and a war against the foreign foe at the same time? You claim
to have three million men, but your armies are so demoralized that
people have compared them to two baskets of eggs on the ends of a
carrying pole — one collision and they are finished. This is what has
happened in all the campaigns in the Chungtiao Mountains, the
Taihang Mountains, Chekiang and Kiangsi, western Hupeh and the
Tapieh Mountains. The simple reason is that you have followed the
fatal policy of being "active against the Communists" and "passive
against the Japanese". A national enemy has penetrated deep into
our country, and the more actively you fight the Communists and the
more passively you resist the Japanese, the lower will be the morale
of your troops. If you make such a poor show in fighting the foreign
aggressor, can you expect your troops suddenly to become tough in
fighting the Communists and the people? It is out of the question.
Once you start civil war, you will have to give it your undivided
attention and inevitably abandon all thought of "simultaneous resistance"; in the end you will inevitably find yourselves signing a treaty
of unconditional surrender to Japanese imperialism, with capitulation
as the only policy left to you. Those of you in the Kuomintang who
do not really wish to capitulate will inevitably end up as capitulationists if you take an active part in instigating or prosecuting civil
war. This will surely happen if you lend yourselves to the manoeuvres
of the capitulationist clique and use the resolutions of the Eleventh
Plenary Session and the People's Political Council as an instrument
for mobilizing public opinion and preparing for anti-Communist civil
war. Even if you do not want to capitulate in the first place, you will
end up by surrendering in the wake of the capitulationist clique if
you lend yourselves to their manoeuvres and take a wrong step. That
is the first possibility concerning the direction the Kuomintang may
take after the Eleventh Plenary Session, and there is an extremely
serious danger that it may materialize. From the standpoint of the
capitulationist clique, talk about a "political solution" and "preparations for constitutional government" is the best means of camouflaging
its preparations for civil war, i.e., for surrender; all Communists, all

patriotic members of the Kuomintang, all anti-Japanese parties, and all our fellow-countrymen who are opposed to Japan should be sharply on the alert against this extremely grave danger and should not be fooled by the camouflage. It must be recognized that the danger of civil war has never been so great as it is now after the Kuomintang's Eleventh Plenary Session.

There is another direction in which these resolutions may lead, that of "stalling for a while and starting the civil war later". This course, which differs somewhat from that of the capitulationist clique, may be taken by those people who still want to keep up the appearance of resistance to Japan while absolutely refusing to abandon anti-communism and dictatorial rule. They may move in this direction since they see that great changes in the international situation are inevitable and Japanese imperialism is doomed; that civil war would mean capitulation and the people throughout the country are for resistance and against civil war; that the Kuomintang is in a state of serious crisis, having alienated itself from the masses, lost popular support and become more isolated than ever; and that the United States, Britain and the Soviet Union are all opposed to the launching of civil war by the Chinese government. All this may force them to postpone their civil-war schemes and play for time with empty talk about a "political solution" and "preparations for constitutional government". These people are past masters in the tactics of deception and stalling. Even in their dreams they do not forget their desire to "take Yenan" and "liquidate the Communist Party". On this point they are entirely at one with the capitulationist clique. Nevertheless they do wish to keep up the pretence of resistance to Japan, they do not wish the Kuomintang to forfeit its international standing, and they sometimes fear the censure of domestic and foreign public opinion; therefore they may stall behind the smokescreen of a "political solution" and "preparations for constitutional government" while waiting for more favourable conditions. They have no sincere desire for a "political solution" or "constitutional government", at least certainly not at the moment. Last year, about the time of the Tenth Plenary Session of the Kuomintang CEC, Comrade Lin Piao was sent to Chungking by the Central Committee of the Communist Party to confer with Mr. Chiang Kai-shek. He waited in Chungking for ten long months, but Mr. Chiang Kai-shek and the Central Executive Committee of the Kuomintang had no desire to discuss a single concrete problem with him. In March this year, Mr. Chiang Kai-shek published his book

China's Destiny in which he emphasizes his opposition to communism and liberal ideas, shifts the blame for the ten years of civil war on to the Communist Party, slanders the Communist Party, the Eighth Route Army and the New Fourth Army as "warlords of a new type" and "separatists of a new type", and implies that he will finish off the Communists within two years. On June 28 this year, Mr. Chiang Kai-shek permitted Chou En-lai, Lin Piao and other comrades to return to Yenan, but at that very moment he ordered his defence forces on the Yellow River to march on the Border Region, and he also ordered the local authorities throughout the country to seize the opportunity of the dissolution of the Third International to demand, in the name of so-called people's organizations, that the Communist Party of China be dissolved. In these circumstances, we Communists were obliged to call on the Kuomintang and the whole nation to avert civil war, and we were obliged to expose all the Kuomintang's sinister schemes and conspiracies which were sabotaging the War of Resistance and endangering the state. Our patience has been taxed to the limit, as the historical facts show. Ever since the fall of Wuhan, there has been no end to the anti-Communist battles, large or small, in northern and central China. It is now two years since the Pacific war broke out, and throughout this time the Kuomintang has been attacking the Communists in central and northern China; apart from the troops originally stationed there, it has dispatched the group armies under Wang Chung-lien and Li Hsien-chou to attack the Communists in Kiangsu and Shantung. Pang Ping-hsun's group army in the area of the Taihang Mountains is under orders to concentrate exclusively on the Communists; so are the Kuomintang troops in Anhwei and Hupeh. For a long time, we did not make even these facts public. The Kuomintang newspapers and periodicals have never for a moment stopped vilifying the Communist Party, but for a long time we did not say a word in reply. Without any justification, the Kuomintang disbanded the New Fourth Army which was heroically fighting Japan, wiped out over nine thousand men of its contingents in southern Anhwei, arrested Yeh Ting, killed Hsiang Ying[2] and imprisoned hundreds of its cadres; although this was a monstrous betrayal of the people and the nation, we maintained our forbearance for the country's sake, simply lodging a protest and demanding redress. When Mr. Chiang Kai-shek met Comrade Chou En-lai, the representative of the Communist Party, at Lushan in June and July 1937, he promised that the Shensi-Kansu-Ningsia Border Region would be designated by decree as an administrative division under the direct jurisdiction of the Executive Yuan of the National Government and that its officials would receive formal appointments. Now Mr. Chiang Kai-shek has not only eaten his own words, he has gone so far as to encircle the Border Region with 400,000 to 500,000 men to enforce a military and economic blockade; he will not be happy with anything less than the destruction of the people of the Border Region as well as the rear headquarters of the Eighth Route Army. It is particularly notorious that promised supplies have been cut off from the Eighth Route Army and that the Communist Party is abused as the "traitor party", the New Fourth Army as the "rebel army", the Eighth Route Army as the "traitor army", etc. In short, all the Kuomintang people who are behaving in this way see the Communist Party as the enemy. To the Kuomintang, the Communist Party is ten times, nay, a hundred times more hateful than the Japanese. The Kuomintang concentrates its hatred on the Communist Party and has little, if any, to spare for the Japanese. This resembles the behaviour of the Japanese fascists, who treat the Kuomintang and the Communist Party differently. Concentrating their hatred on the Chinese Communist Party, the Japanese fascists have become more and more gentle with the Kuomintang; of their two slogans, "Oppose the Communists" and "Annihilate the Kuomintang", only the first now remains. The newspapers and periodicals controlled by the Japanese and Wang Ching-wei no longer print such slogans as "Down with the Kuomintang" and "Overthrow Chiang Kai-shek". Japan is bearing down on the Communist Party with 58 per cent of her forces in China and is just using 42 per cent to keep watch on the Kuomintang; she has recently relaxed this watch and withdrawn many of her troops from Chekiang and Hupeh in order to make it easier to inveigle the Kuomintang into capitulation. The Japanese imperialists have never dared utter a single word to persuade the Communist Party to capitulate, but they have no hesitation in directing an endless stream of words to persuade the Kuomintang to do so. The Kuomintang is fierce only towards the Communist Party and the people, but it drops all its ferocity in the face of the Japanese. Not only has it changed from being a participant to being a mere spectator in the war as far as fighting is concerned, but even in words it dares not offer as much as a single sharp rebuff to the insults and blandishments of Japanese imperialism. The Japanese say, "There is nothing wrong with the line of argument in Chiang Kai-shek's *China's Destiny*." Has Mr.

Chiang or any member of his party ever rebutted this? No, they have not and dare not. How can the Japanese help despising the Kuomintang when they see that Mr. Chiang Kai-shek and the Kuomintang use "military and governmental orders" and "discipline" only against the Communists, and neither desire nor dare to use them against the twenty members of the Kuomintang Central Executive Committee and the fifty-eight Kuomintang generals who have deserted to the enemy? The people throughout the country and the friendly nations throughout the world have seen Mr. Chiang Kai-shek and the Kuomintang disbanding the New Fourth Army and attacking the Eighth Route Army, encircling the Border Region, maligning them with such labels as "traitor party", "traitor army", "warlords of a new type", "a new type of separatist regime", "sabotaging the War of Resistance" and "endangering the state", and constantly invoking "military and governmental orders" and "discipline"; they have never seen Mr. Chiang and the Kuomintang enforcing any military orders, government decrees or disciplinary measures against the twenty members of the Kuomintang Central Executive Committee and the fifty-eight Kuomintang generals who went over to the enemy. Similarly, the resolutions recently passed at the Eleventh Plenary Session of the Kuomintang CEC and at the meeting of the People's Political Council are all directed against the Communist Party, while not a single one is directed against the many members of the Kuomintang CEC itself and the many army generals who have turned traitor and defected. What are the people throughout the country and the friendly nations throughout the world to think of the Kuomintang? As was to be expected, there was once again talk about a "political solution" and "preparations for constitutional government" at the Eleventh Plenary Session; well and good, we welcome such talk. But judging by the political line the Kuomintang has consistently followed all these years, we consider this talk to be just so many empty words designed to dupe the people, the real purpose being to gain time for preparing civil war so as to perpetuate its dictatorial rule over the people.

Is there a third direction in which the current situation may develop? Yes, there is. It is what a number of Kuomintang members, all the people and we Communists are hoping for. What is this third course? A just and reasonable political settlement of the relations between the Kuomintang and the Communist Party, a genuinely democratic and free constitutional government, the abolition of the fascist dictatorship with its "one party, one doctrine, one leader" and the convening during the War of Resistance of a national assembly genuinely elected by the people. We Communists have advocated this course from the very beginning. A number of Kuomintang members will also agree to it. For a long time we hoped that even Mr. Chiang Kai-shek and his own faction in the Kuomintang might pursue this course. But judging from what has happened in the last few years and what is happening now, there is nothing to show that Mr. Chiang and the majority of the Kuomintang personages in power are willing to do so.

A number of conditions, international and domestic, are needed before this course can be realized. At the present time (with fascism in Europe on the eve of complete collapse) the international conditions are favourable to China's War of Resistance, but it is at this very moment that the capitulators are especially eager to instigate civil war so that they can capitulate, and that the Japanese and Wang Ching-wei, too, are particularly keen on civil war, so as to inveigle them into capitulation. Wang Ching-wei said (according to the Domei News Agency, October 1): "Devoted brothers always remain brothers, and Chungking will certainly follow our road, the sooner the better, we hope." What affection, confidence and eagerness! Thus in the present situation the best that can be expected from the Kuomintang is stalling, while the danger of a sudden deterioration is very grave indeed. The conditions necessary for the third course are not all present yet, and patriots of all parties and the people throughout China must make many-sided efforts to bring them into being.

Mr. Chiang Kai-shek announced at the Eleventh Plenary Session:

> It should be stated clearly that the central authorities make no demands upon the Communist Party other than that it should give up its armed separatist regime and cease its surprise attacks on the National Army, which sabotage the War of Resistance; it is to be hoped that the Communist Party will carry out its declaration made in the 26th year of the Republic [1937] calling for united efforts to save the nation and will put into effect the four pledges given in that declaration.

Mr. Chiang's talk of "surprise attacks on the National Army, which sabotage the War of Resistance" ought to be applied to the Kuomintang itself, and it is a pity that he is so prejudiced and malicious as to slander the Communist Party in this way. Since the fall of Wuhan the Kuomintang has launched three anti-Communist onslaughts, in each of which, as the facts show, the Kuomintang troops sprang surprise attacks on the Communist forces. In the first campaign, from the winter of 1939 to the spring of 1940, the Kuomintang troops in their surprise attacks captured five county towns garrisoned by the Eighth Route Army in the Shensi-Kansu-Ningsia Border Region, Chunhua, Hsunyi, Chengning, Ninghsien and Chenyuan, even employing aircraft in these operations. In northern China, Chu Huai-ping's troops were dispatched to the Taihang Mountain region for a surprise attack on the Eighth Route Army forces, which only fought back in self-defence. The second campaign was launched in January 1941. Earlier, on October 19, 1940, Ho Ying-chin and Pai Chung-hsi had telegraphed a categorical order to Chu Teh, Peng Teh-huai, Yeh Ting and Hsiang Ying, commanding all units of the Eighth Route and New Fourth Armies south of the Yellow River to move north of the river within a month. We promised that our troops in southern Anhwei would move north; as for the others, while it was impossible for them to be shifted in the circumstances, we promised that they would move to the assigned positions after victory in the anti-Japanese war. Yet, before our 9,000 men in southern Anhwei began moving north on January 5 in compliance with the order, Mr. Chiang Kai-shek had already issued another order to "catch them all in a dragnet". Between January 6 and 14, the Kuomintang troops in southern Anhwei actually did catch these New Fourth Army units in a dragnet. Moreover, on January 17, Mr. Chiang Kai-shek ordered the whole New Fourth Army to be disbanded and Yeh Ting to be court-martialled. The Eighth Route and New Fourth Armies have since been attacked wherever there are Kuomintang troops in the anti-Japanese base areas in central and northern China, and they have only fought back in self-defence. The third campaign began in March of this year and is still going on. The Kuomintang forces have continued their assaults on the Eighth Route and New Fourth Armies in central and northern China. In addition, Mr. Chiang Kai-shek has published his *China's Destiny*, which is a diatribe against communism and against the people. He has diverted many of his Yellow River defence forces for a lightning attack on the Border Region. He has instigated so-called people's organizations all over the country to demand the dissolution of the Communist Party. He has mobilized the Kuomintang majority in the People's Political Council to endorse Ho Ying-chin's military report vilifying the Eighth Route Army and to adopt anti-Communist resolutions. He has thus turned the Council, which should be a symbol of anti-Japanese unity, into a private agency of the Kuomintang for manufacturing anti-Communist public opinion in preparation for civil war, with the result that Comrade Tung Pi-wu, the Communist member of the Council, had to walk out in protest. These three anti-Communist onslaughts were deliberately planned and launched by the Kuomintang. We may well ask, what are they if not actions which "sabotage the War of Resistance"?

On September 22 of the 26th year of the Republic (1937), the Central Committee of the Communist Party of China issued a declaration calling for united efforts to save the nation. In it we said:

> To strip the enemy of any pretext for his intrigues and to remove any misunderstanding among all well-intentioned doubters, the Central Committee of the Communist Party of China finds it necessary to proclaim its heartfelt devotion to the cause of national liberation. Therefore, it once again solemnly declares to the whole nation: (1) that Dr. Sun Yat-sen's Three People's Principles being what China needs today, our Party is ready to fight for their complete realization; (2) that we shall discontinue the policies of insurrection to overthrow the Kuomintang regime and of forcible confiscation of the land of the landlords; (3) that we shall reorganize the present Red government as the democratic government of a special region in the hope that state power will be unified throughout the country; and (4) that the Red Army will change its name and designation, will be reorganized as part of the National Revolutionary Army and placed under the Military Council of the National Government, and will be ready for orders to march to the anti-Japanese front and do its duty.

We have completely fulfilled these four pledges; neither Mr. Chiang Kai-shek nor anyone else in the Kuomintang can charge us with having defaulted on a single one of them. In the first place, the policies practised by the Communist Party in the Shensi-Kansu-Ningsia Border Region and in the anti-Japanese base areas behind the enemy lines are in keeping with Dr. Sun Yat-sen's Three People's Principles, and not a single one runs counter to them. In the second place, as long as the Kuomintang does not capitulate to the national enemy, disrupt Kuomintang-Communist co-operation or launch civil war against the Communists, we will always keep our promise not to overthrow the

Kuomintang regime or to confiscate the land of the landlords by force. We have kept this pledge in the past, are doing so now and will continue to do so in the future. That means that only when the Kuomintang capitulates to the enemy, disrupts co-operation and launches civil war will we be forced to cancel our pledge, for these are the only circumstances which would make it impossible for us to keep it. In the third place, the original Red government was reorganized in the very first year of the War of Resistance, and the "three thirds system" of democratic government has long been in operation, but to this day the Kuomintang has not fulfilled its promise to recognize the Shensi-Kansu-Ningsia Border Region and, what is more, it accuses us of "feudal separatism". Mr. Chiang Kai-shek and other members of the Kuomintang! You should know that what you call "separatism" — the state of affairs in which the Shensi-Kansu-Ningsia Border Region and other anti-Japanese base areas are not recognized by the Kuomintang government — is not of our seeking but has been entirely forced on us by yourselves. What reason do you have for accusing us of "separatism" while you go back on your own words, refuse the recognition you pledged to the Border Region and refuse to acknowledge its democratic government? Day in day out we ask for recognition and you refuse — who then is responsible? What reason does Mr. Chiang have for railing against "separatism" in his *China's Destiny*, without showing the slightest sense of his own responsibility in the matter, though he himself is Director-General of the Kuomintang and head of its government? Availing ourselves of the occasion of the Eleventh Plenary Session at which Mr. Chiang Kai-shek has again demanded that we fulfil our promise, we demand that he fulfil his promise to give legal recognition to the Shensi-Kansu-Ningsia Border Region, where the Principle of Democracy has long been in practice, and to the anti-Japanese democratic base areas behind the enemy's lines as well. If you persist in your policy of non-recognition, it will mean that you want us to continue with "separatism", and that, as in the past, the blame will fall entirely on you and not on us. In the fourth place, it is a long time since the Red Army changed its "name and designation", became "reorganized as part of the National Revolutionary Army" and was "placed under the Military Council of the National Government"; this pledge was fulfilled long ago. The only force directly under the Central Committee of the Communist Party and not under the Military Council of the National Government is the New Fourth Army of the National Revolutionary Army; the reason is that it was proscribed as a "rebel army" and "disbanded" on January 17, 1941 by the Military Council in a counter-revolutionary order sabotaging the War of Resistance and endangering the state, and was, moreover, subjected to daily attacks by the Kuomintang troops. Yet this army has consistently fought the Japanese in central China and fulfilled the first three of the four pledges; furthermore, it is willing to come "under the Military Council of the National Government" once again, and asks Mr. Chiang Kai-shek to repeal the order for its disbandment and restore its designation so as to enable it to fulfil the fourth pledge.

The document concerning the Communist Party adopted at the Eleventh Plenary Session also stated:

> As for the other problems, they can all be raised at the national assembly for discussion and solution, since the present session has resolved that a national assembly should be convened and a constitution drawn up and promulgated within one year after the conclusion of the war.

The "other problems" here referred to are the abolition of the Kuomintang dictatorship, the abolition of the fascist secret service, the establishment of democratic rule throughout the country, the abolition of economic controls, exorbitant taxes and miscellaneous levies harmful to the people, the application on a nation-wide scale of the agrarian policy of reducing rent and interest and of the economic policy of helping small and medium scale industries and improving the workers' livelihood. In its declaration of September 22, 1937 calling for united efforts to save the nation our Party stated:

> Democracy should be put into effect and a national assembly convened to frame and adopt a constitution and draw up a policy of national salvation. To enable the Chinese people to lead a happy and prosperous life, effective measures must first be taken to provide famine relief, ensure a stable livelihood, develop defence industries, deliver the people from suffering and improve their living conditions.

Since this declaration was accepted in its entirety by Mr. Chiang Kai-shek in a statement on the very next day (September 23), he should not merely ask the Communist Party to keep the four pledges it set forth, he should also ask himself, the Kuomintang and the Kuomintang government to carry out the provisions we have quoted.

Mr. Chiang Kai-shek is not only the Director-General of the Kuomintang, he has also become president of the Kuomintang government (nominally the National Government); he should therefore conscientiously carry out these provisions about democracy and the people's livelihood, honour the innumerable promises he himself has made to us Communists and to the people throughout the country, and should stop repudiating his promises and acting high-handedly, saying one thing and doing another. Together with the whole people, we Communists want deeds and not more empty, deceitful words. If deeds are forthcoming, we shall rejoice; empty words without deeds will not deceive the people for long. What we ask of Mr. Chiang Kai-shek and the Kuomintang is the following: Carry the War of Resistance through to the end, avert the danger of capitulation; continue co-operation, avert the crisis of civil war; recognize the democratic government in the Border Region and in the anti-Japanese base areas behind the enemy lines, reinstate the New Fourth Army, stop the anti-Communist campaign, withdraw the 400,000 to 500,000 troops now encircling the Shensi-Kansu-Ningsia Border Region; stop using the People's Political Council as a private agency of the Kuomintang for stirring up anti-Communist opinion, lift the ban on freedom of speech, assembly and association, abolish the one-party dictatorship of the Kuomintang; reduce rent and interest, improve the living and working conditions of the workers, help the small and medium scale industries; abolish the secret service, put an end to fascist education and introduce democratic education. You yourselves have promised to do most of these things. If you fulfil these demands and promises, we assure you that we shall continue to fulfil our promises. We are ready to resume the talks between the two parties at any time, if Mr. Chiang Kai-shek and the Kuomintang are ready.

In short, of the three possible directions which the Kuomintang may take, the first, capitulation and civil war, is the road of destruction for Mr. Chiang Kai-shek and the Kuomintang. The second, demagogic deception for the purpose of gaining time while clinging to fascist dictatorship and actively conducting secret preparations for civil war, likewise offers no salvation for Mr. Chiang and the Kuomintang. Only the third direction, the complete abandonment of the erroneous course of fascist dictatorship and civil war and the pursuit of the correct course of democracy and co-operation, can bring Mr. Chiang Kai-shek and the Kuomintang on to the road of salvation. However, Mr. Chiang and the Kuomintang have so far done nothing to convince the people that they intend to move in the third direction; hence, the people throughout the country must remain on guard against the extremely grave danger of capitulation and civil war.

Let all patriotic members of the Kuomintang unite and forbid the Kuomintang authorities to go in the first direction, prevent them from continuing in the second and demand that they take the third!

Let all patriotic anti-Japanese parties and people unite and forbid the Kuomintang authorities to go in the first direction, prevent them from continuing in the second and demand that they take the third!

An unparalleled change is imminent in the world. We hope that Mr. Chiang Kai-shek and the members of the Kuomintang will conduct themselves well at this great turning point of our era. We hope that all patriotic parties and patriotic people will conduct themselves well at this great turning point of our era.

NOTES

[1] The Whampoa clique refers to those Kuomintang generals and officers who had once been instructors or cadets at the Whampoa Military Academy. They were Chiang Kai-shek's closest followers in the Kuomintang army.

[2] Yeh Ting and Hsiang Ying were respectively Commander and Deputy Commander of the New Fourth Army.

GET ORGANIZED!

November 29, 1943

On behalf of the Central Committee of the Communist Party I would like to say a few words at this reception it is giving for the labour heroes and heroines and other model workers in production elected from the villages, the factories, the armed forces, the government and other organizations and the schools in the Shensi-Kansu-Ningsia Border Region. What I want to say can be summed up in the words, "Get organized!" This year the peasant masses and the people in the army, the government and other organizations, the schools and the factories of the Border Region have been conducting a production campaign in accordance with the resolutions of the meeting of senior cadres convened last winter by the Northwest Bureau of the Central Committee. Great achievements and advances have been scored in every field of production this year and the Border Region has taken on a new look. Facts have fully borne out the correctness of the policy adopted by the conference of senior cadres. The gist of this policy is to organize the masses, to mobilize and organize into a great army of labour all the available forces without exception — the people, the army, the government and other organizations and the schools — all men and women, young and old, who can contribute their labour power on a part-time or full-time basis. We have an army for fighting as well as an army for labour. For fighting we have the Eighth Route and New Fourth Armies; but even they do a dual job, warfare and production. With these two kinds of armies, and with a fighting army skilled in these two tasks and in mass work, we can overcome our difficulties and defeat Japanese imperialism. If the achievements of our production campaign in the Border Region in recent years were not great or remarkable enough to prove this

---

Comrade Mao Tse-tung made this speech at a reception in honour of the labour heroes of the Shensi-Kansu-Ningsia Border Region.

conclusively, our achievements this year have really done so, as we
have all seen with our own eyes.

In all the armed units of the Border Region that have been
allotted land this year, the soldiers have on the average cultivated
eighteen *mou* per person; and they can produce or make practically
everything — food (vegetables, meat and cooking oil), clothing (cotton-
padded clothes, woollen knitwear and footwear), shelter (cave-
dwellings, houses and meeting halls), articles of daily use (tables,
chairs, benches and stationery), and fuel (firewood, charcoal and coal).
By using our own hands we have attained the objective of "ample
food and clothing". Every soldier needs to spend only three months
of the year in production and can devote the remaining nine months
to training and fighting. Our troops depend for their pay neither on
the Kuomintang government, nor on the Border Region Government,
nor on the people, but can fully provide for themselves. What a vitally
important innovation for our cause of national liberation! During
the last six and a half years of the War of Resistance, the anti-Japanese
base areas have been subjected to the enemy's policy of "burn all,
kill all, loot all", the Shensi-Kansu-Ningsia Border Region has been
tightly blockaded by the Kuomintang and we were reduced to the
direst straits financially and economically; if our troops had been
able to do nothing except fight, we would never have solved our
problems. Now our troops in the Border Region have learned to
produce, and so have some of the troops at the front, while others
are learning. If every man in our heroic and combat-worthy Eighth
Route and New Fourth Armies becomes able not only to fight and
do mass work but also to produce, we need fear no difficulty and
shall be "invincible under heaven",[1] to use the words of Mencius.
Our organizations and schools have also taken a big step forward
this year. Only a small part of their expenditure has come from
the government, most of it being covered by their own production;
they have grown 100 per cent of the vegetables they consume as
compared with 50 per cent last year, considerably increased their
consumption of meat by raising pigs and sheep, and established many
workshops for making simple necessities. As the army, the organizations and the schools now meet their own material needs fully or
for the most part, less is taken in taxation from the people, who
can therefore enjoy more of the fruits of their labour. As soldiers
and civilians are alike increasing production, all have ample food
and clothing and are happy. In our factories, too, production has

been stepped up, secret agents have been combed out and productivity has risen greatly. Throughout the Border Region, labour heroes have come forward in great numbers in agriculture and industry, in the organizations and the schools, and also in the army; we can say that production in the Border Region has been set on the right path. All this comes from organizing the strength of the masses.

To organize the strength of the masses is one policy. Is there a contrary policy? Yes, there is. It is one that lacks the mass viewpoint, fails to rely on the masses or organize them, and gives exclusive attention to organizing the small number of people working in the financial, supply or trading organizations, while paying no attention to organizing the masses in the villages, the army, the government and other organizations, the schools and factories; it treats economic work not as a broad movement or as an extensive front, but only as an expedient for meeting financial deficits. That is the other policy, the wrong policy. Such a policy formerly existed in the Shensi-Kansu-Ningsia Border Region, but after the correct guidance given over these years, and especially after the senior cadres' conference last year and the mass movement this year, the number of people who still think this way is probably small. In the base areas in northern and central China, where fighting is intense and the leading bodies have not given it enough attention, the production campaign of the masses has not yet become widespread. However, since the Central Committee's directive of October 1[2] this year, preparations are being made everywhere for a production campaign next year. Conditions at the front are more difficult than in the Border Region; not only is there heavy fighting, but natural disasters have occurred in some places. Nevertheless, we must mobilize the entire Party, the government and the army and the civilian population both to fight against the enemy and to engage in production, in order to support the war, to cope with the enemy's policy of "burn all, kill all, loot all" and to provide disaster relief. With the experience already gained in the last few years in production at the front, and with the ideological, organizational and material preparations this winter, an extensive campaign can be and must be launched next year. In the front-line areas where fighting is going on, it is not yet possible to have "ample food and clothing" but quite possible and, indeed, imperative to "use our own hands and overcome difficulties".

The co-operatives are now the most important form of mass organization in the economic field. Although it is unnecessary to insist on attaching the label co-operative to the productive activities of the masses in our army, our government and other organizations and our schools, these activities are of a co-operative nature, being carried on under centralized leadership to meet the material needs of various departments, units and individuals through mutual help and joint labour. They are co-operatives of a sort.

Among the peasant masses a system of individual economy has prevailed for thousands of years, with each family or household forming a productive unit. This scattered, individual form of production is the economic foundation of feudal rule and keeps the peasants in perpetual poverty. The only way to change it is gradual collectivization, and the only way to bring about collectivization, according to Lenin, is through co-operatives.[3] We have already organized many peasant co-operatives in the Border Region, but at present they are only of a rudimentary type and must go through several stages of development before they can become co-operatives of the Soviet type known as collective farms. Ours is a new-democratic economy, and our co-operatives are still organizations for collective labour based on an individual economy (on private property). Furthermore, they are of several types. One type is the organization of agricultural labour for mutual aid, such as the "teams for the exchange of labour" and "teams for the exchange and hire of labour";[4] this kind of organization was known as the "mutual-aid working group" or "ploughing team"[5] in the Red areas in Kiangsi and is now called the "mutual-aid group" in some places at the front. So long as they are collective mutual-aid organizations which the people join voluntarily (compulsion must never be used), all of them are good, no matter how they are named, no matter whether they are each composed of a few, a few dozen or hundreds of people, or whether they are composed entirely or partly of people who can contribute full-time labour; no matter whether the members render each other mutual aid in terms of manpower, animal power or implements, or they live and eat together during the busy farming season; and no matter whether the organizations are temporary or permanent. These methods of collective mutual aid are the inventions of the masses themselves. In the past we summed up such experience among the masses in Kiangsi, and now we are summing it up in northern Shensi. In the Border Region mutual aid in labour has become much more systematic and better developed, after being encouraged by the meeting of senior cadres last year and put into practice all through the current year. Many labour-exchange teams in the Border Region have done their plough-ing, planting, weeding and reaping collectively, and the harvest this year is double that of last. Now that the masses have seen these substantial results, undoubtedly more and more people will adopt the practice next year. We do not expect to organize into co-operatives in one year all the hundreds of thousands of people in the Border Region who can contribute full-time or part-time labour, but this objective can be realized within a few years. All women, too, should be mobilized to do a certain amount of productive work. All loafers must be reformed into good citizens through participation in produc-tion. Such collective mutual-aid producers' co-operatives should be extensively and voluntarily organized in all the anti-Japanese base areas in northern and central China.

Besides the collective mutual-aid co-operative for agricultural production, there are three other varieties: the multi-purpose co-operative like the Southern District Co-operative of Yenan, which combines the functions of producers', consumers', transport (salt transport) and credit co-operatives; the transport co-operative (salt transport team); and the handicraft co-operative.

With these four kinds of co-operatives among the masses and the collective labour co-operatives in the army, the schools and the government and other organizations, we can organize all the forces of the people into a great army of labour. This is the only road to liberation for the people, the only road from poverty to prosperity and the only road to victory in the War of Resistance. Every Com-munist must learn to organize the labour of the masses. Communists with an intellectual background must also learn to do so; once they have set their minds on it, they can learn in six months or a year. They can help the masses to organize production and to sum up experience. When our comrades have learned, among other skills, to organize the labour of the masses — to help the peasants draw up their household production plans, to set up labour-exchange teams, salt transport teams and multi-purpose co-operatives, to organize production in the army, the schools and the government and other organizations, to organize production in the factories, develop emula-tion in production, encourage and reward labour heroes, and arrange production exhibitions — when our comrades have learned to bring the creative power and initiative of the masses into play, we shall certainly be able to drive out the Japanese imperialists and, together with the whole people, build up a new China.

We Communists must be able to integrate ourselves with the masses in all things. If our Party members spend their whole lives sitting indoors and never go out to face the world and brave the storm, what good will they be to the Chinese people? None at all, and we do not need such people as Party members. We Communists ought to face the world and brave the storm, the great world of mass struggle and the mighty storm of mass struggle. "Three cobblers with their wits combined equal Chukeh Liang the master mind."[6] In other words, the masses have great creative power. In fact there are thousands upon thousands of Chukeh Liangs among the Chinese people; every village, every town has its own. We should go to the masses and learn from them, synthesize their experience into better, articulated principles and methods, then do propaganda among the masses, and call upon them to put these principles and methods into practice so as to solve their problems and help them achieve liberation and happiness. If our comrades doing local work are isolated from the masses, fail to understand their feelings and to help them organize their production and improve their livelihood, and if they confine themselves to collecting "public grain for national salvation" without realizing that 10 per cent of their energy is quite enough for this purpose provided they first devote 90 per cent to helping the masses solve the problem of "private grain for the people's own salvation", then these comrades are contaminated with the Kuomintang style of work and covered with the dust of bureaucracy. The Kuomintang only demands things from the people and gives them nothing in return. If a member of our Party acts in this way, his style of work is that of the Kuomintang, and his face, caked with the dust of bureaucracy, needs a good wash in a basin of hot water. In my opinion, this bureaucratic style is to be found in local work in all our anti-Japanese base areas, and there are comrades who are isolated from the masses because they lack the mass viewpoint. We must firmly do away with this style of work before we can have close ties with the masses.

In addition, a kind of warlord style is to be found in our army work, a style also characteristic of the Kuomintang whose army is divorced from the masses. Our troops must observe the correct principles that govern relations between the army and the people, between the army and the government, between the army and the Party, between officers and men, and between military work and political work, and relations among the cadres, and must never commit the errors of warlordism. Officers must cherish their men and must not be indifferent to their well-being or resort to corporal punishment; the army must cherish the people and never encroach upon their interests; the army must respect the government and the Party and never "assert independence". Our Eighth Route and New Fourth Armies are the armed forces of the people; they have always been very good, and are indeed the best in the country. But it is true that in recent years errors of warlordism of a certain kind have arisen, and some comrades in the army have become arrogant and high-handed in their behaviour towards the soldiers, the people, the government and the Party, always blaming the comrades doing local work but never themselves, always seeing their own achievements but never their own shortcomings, and always welcoming flattery but never criticism. Such phenomena are to be found, for example, in the Shensi-Kansu-Ningsia Border Region. The tendency has been basically overcome as a result of the conference of senior cadres and the meeting of military and political cadres last year and of the campaigns to "support the government and cherish the people" and "support the army" during the Spring Festival[7] this year, but there is still a residue which we must make further efforts to eradicate. These faults are also to be found in the base areas in northern and central China, and the Party organizations and the army there must endeavour to eradicate them.

Whether it is the tendency towards bureaucracy in local work or towards warlordism in army work, the fault is of the same nature, namely, isolation from the masses. The overwhelming majority of our comrades are good comrades. Those who have this fault can correct it once they have been criticized and their mistakes pointed out. But self-criticism is imperative and wrong tendencies must be squarely faced and conscientiously corrected. If anyone fails to criticize the tendency towards bureaucracy in local work or towards warlordism in army work, it means that he wants to retain the Kuomintang style and keep the dust of bureaucracy or warlordism on his otherwise clean face, and he is not a good Communist. If these two tendencies are eliminated, all our work, including, of course, the production campaign, will proceed smoothly.

Our Border Region has taken on a totally different look because great results have been achieved here in production, whether among the peasant masses, or in the government and other organizations, the schools, the army or in the factories, and the relations between the army and the people have greatly improved. All this indicates that our comrades have a stronger mass viewpoint and have made great progress in becoming one with the masses. Nevertheless, we must not be complacent but continue our self-criticism and strive for further progress. We must strive for further progress in production, too. As our faces are apt to get dirty, we must wash them every day; as the floor is apt to gather dust, we must sweep it every day. Even though the tendencies towards bureaucracy in local work and warlordism in army work have been basically overcome, these bad tendencies may arise again. We are surrounded by the serried forces of Japanese imperialism and Chinese reaction, and we live in the midst of the undisciplined petty bourgeoisie, and hence great gusts of dirt of bureaucracy and warlordism blow in our faces daily. Therefore, we must not become complacent over every success. We should check our complacency and constantly criticize our shortcomings, just as we should wash our faces or sweep the floor every day to remove the dirt and keep them clean.

Labour heroes and model workers in production! You are leaders of the people, you have been very successful in your work, and I hope you, too, will not grow complacent. I hope that when you get back to the counties in the sub-regions of Kuanchung, Lungtung, Sanpien, Suiteh and Yenan,[8] when you get back to your organizations, schools, army units or factories, you will lead the people, lead the masses and work still better, and first of all get the masses organized on a voluntary basis into co-operatives, get them even better organized and in even greater numbers. I hope that, when you go back, you will do this work and propagate it, so that by next year's conference of labour heroes we shall have achieved still greater results.

NOTES

[1] From *Mencius*, Book III, "Kungsun Chou", Part I, Chapter 5.

[2] The Central Committee's directive of October 1 was "Spread the Campaigns to Reduce Rent, Increase Production and 'Support the Government and Cherish the People' in the Base Areas", pp. 131-35 of this volume.

[3] See V. I. Lenin, "On Cooperation", *Selected Works*, Eng. ed., FLPH, Moscow, 1952, Vol. II, Part 2, pp. 715-23.

[4] "Teams for the exchange of labour" and "teams for the exchange and hire of labour" were both labour organizations for collective mutual aid in agriculture

in the Shensi-Kansu-Ningsia Border Region. Labour-exchange is a means by which the peasants adjust labour power among themselves. Man-workdays were exchanged for man-workdays, ox-workdays for ox-workdays, man-workdays for ox-workdays, etc. Peasants who joined labour-exchange teams contributed their labour power or animal power to cultivate the land of each member-family collectively and in rotation. In settling accounts, the workday was taken as the unit of exchange; those who contributed more man-workdays or animal-workdays were paid for the difference by those who contributed less. "Teams for the exchange and hire of labour" were usually formed by peasants with insufficient land. Besides exchanging work among themselves for mutual aid, their members also hired themselves out collectively to families which were short of labour power.

[5] Mutual-aid working groups and ploughing teams, based on individual farming, were formed by peasants in the Red areas to facilitate production through a better organization of labour power. On the principle of voluntary participation and mutual benefit, the members did an equal amount of work for each other, or if one could not give another as much help as he received he made up the difference in cash. Apart from helping each other, the teams gave preferential treatment to the families of Red Army soldiers and worked for bereaved old folk without any pay except for meals during the work. As these measures of mutual aid were of great help to production and were carried out on a reasonable basis they won the warm support of the masses.

[6] Chukeh Liang was a statesman and strategist in the period of the Three Kingdoms (221-265), who became a symbol of resourcefulness and wisdom in Chinese folklore.

[7] The Spring Festival is New Year's Day in the Chinese lunar calendar.

[8] The Shensi-Kansu-Ningsia Border Region was divided into these five sub-regions.

OUR STUDY AND
THE CURRENT SITUATION

April 12, 1944

I

Since last winter, the senior cadres of our Party have been studying the question of the two lines that existed in the history of the Party. This has very greatly raised the political level of these numerous senior cadres. In the course of the study, comrades have brought up many questions, and the Political Bureau of the Central Committee has reached conclusions on some of the important ones. They are as follows:

1. On the question of what attitude to adopt in studying our historical experience. The Central Committee holds that we should enable the cadres to become perfectly clear ideologically on the questions which arose in the history of the Party and that at the same time we should adopt a lenient policy in arriving at decisions about comrades who formerly committed errors, so that on the one hand the cadres should thoroughly understand the historical experience of our Party and avoid repeating past errors, and on the other hand all comrades can be united for our common endeavour. In the history of our Party there were great struggles against the erroneous lines of Chen Tu-hsiu[1] and of Li Li-san, and they were absolutely necessary. But there were defects in the methods employed. For one thing, the cadres were not brought to a full ideological understanding of the

From 1942 to 1944 the central organ and senior cadres of the Communist Party of China held discussions on the history of the Party, especially of the period from the beginning of 1931 to the end of 1934. These discussions greatly helped in bringing about ideological unity in the Party on the basis of Marxism-Leninism. The enlarged meeting of the Political Bureau of the Central Committee at Tsunyi, Kweichow, in January 1935, had corrected the erroneous "Left" line pursued from early 1931 to late 1934, changed the composition of the central leading organ, established the leadership headed by Comrade Mao Tse-tung and set the Party line on the correct

163

causes of these errors, the circumstances in which they were committed and the detailed ways and means of correcting them, so that errors of a similar nature came to be repeated; and for another, too much stress was placed on the responsibility of individuals, so that we failed to unite as many people as we could have done for our common endeavour. We should take warning from these two defects. This time, in dealing with questions of Party history we should lay the stress not on the responsibility of certain individual comrades but on the analysis of the circumstances in which the errors were committed, on the content of the errors and on their social, historical and ideological roots, and this should be done in the spirit of "learning from past mistakes to avoid future ones" and "curing the sickness to save the patient", in order to achieve the twofold objective of clarity in ideology and unity among comrades. The adoption of a careful attitude in handling cases of individual comrades, neither glossing things over nor doing harm to comrades, is a sign that our Party is vigorous and flourishing.

2. Treat all questions analytically; do not negate everything. The question concerning the line of the central leadership during the period from the Fourth Plenary Session[2] to the Tsunyi Meeting,[3] for example, should be analysed from two aspects. It should be pointed out on the one hand that the political tactics, the military tactics and the cadres policy which the central leading body adopted during that period were wrong in their main aspects, but on the other hand that on such fundamental issues as opposing Chiang Kai-shek and carrying on the Agrarian Revolution and the struggle of the Red Army there was no dispute between ourselves and the comrades who committed errors. And even the tactical side needs to be analysed. On the land question, for instance, their error consisted in the ultra-Left policy of allotting no land to the landlords and poor land to the rich peasants, but these comrades were at one with us on con-

---

Marxist-Leninist track; nevertheless, many Party cadres had not yet reached a thorough understanding of the character of the erroneous lines of the past. In order to raise the Marxist-Leninist ideological level of Party cadres still higher, in 1942-43 the Political Bureau held several discussions on the history of the Party, and then led the senior cadres of the whole Party in holding similar discussions during 1943-44. These discussions were an important preparation for the Seventh National Congress of the Party in 1945, enabling it to attain an ideological and political unity without precedent in the history of the Communist Party of China. "Our Study and the Current Situation" was a speech made by Comrade Mao Tse-tung at a meeting of senior cadres in Yenan on April 12, 1944 on the subject of these discussions.

fiscating the land of the landlords for distribution among peasants who had little or no land. Concrete analysis of concrete conditions, Lenin said, is "the most essential thing in Marxism, the living soul of Marxism".[4] Lacking an analytical approach, many of our comrades do not want to go deeply into complex matters, to analyse and study them over and over again, but like to draw simple conclusions which are either absolutely affirmative or absolutely negative. The fact that our newspapers are lacking in analytical articles and that the habit of analysis is not yet fully cultivated in the Party shows that there are such shortcomings. From now on we should remedy this state of affairs.

3. On the discussion of the documents of the Sixth National Congress of the Party. It should be stated that the line of the Sixth National Congress was basically correct, since that Congress defined the character of the present revolution as bourgeois-democratic, defined the situation at that time as an interval between two revolutionary high tides, repudiated opportunism and putschism and promulgated the Ten-Point Programme.[5] All this was correct. The Congress also had its defects. For instance, among its other shortcomings or mistakes, it failed to point out the very protracted nature of the Chinese revolution and the very great importance of rural base areas in the revolution. Nonetheless, the Sixth National Congress played a progressive role in the history of our Party.

4. On the question of whether the provisional central leadership that was formed in Shanghai in 1931 and the Fifth Plenary Session[6] which it subsequently convened were legal or not. The Central Committee holds that both were legal, but it should be stated that the procedures for the election were inadequate and that this case should be taken as a historical lesson.

5. On the question of factions in the history of the Party. It should be stated that as a result of the series of changes since the Tsunyi Meeting the factions which formerly existed and played an unwholesome role in the history of our Party no longer exist. In our present study of the two lines within the Party, it is absolutely necessary to point out that these factions did exist and did play an unwholesome role. But it would be wrong to think that factions with the same erroneous political programmes and organizational forms still exist in the Party, after all the changes brought about by so many inner-Party struggles — the Tsunyi Meeting of January 1935, the Sixth Plenary Session of the Sixth Central Committee in October 1938, the

enlarged session of the Political Bureau in September 1941,[7] the Party-wide rectification movement in 1942 and the campaign begun in the winter of 1943 for the study of the past struggles between the two lines within the Party. The old factions are gone. What is left is only the remnants of dogmatist and empiricist ideology, which can be overcome by continuing and intensifying our rectification movement. But what still exists in our Party to a serious extent, and almost everywhere, is a more or less blind "mountain-stronghold" mentality.[8] For instance, there is a lack of mutual understanding, mutual respect and unity among comrades of different units, which arises from differences in their background of struggle, differences in the areas in which they work (as between one base area and another and as between the Japanese-occupied areas, the Kuomintang areas and the revolutionary base areas) and differences in their departments of work (as between one army unit and another and as between one kind of work and another); this phenomenon seems quite commonplace but in fact it seriously obstructs the unity of the Party and the growth of its fighting capacity. The social and historical roots of the mountain-stronghold mentality lie in the fact that the Chinese petty bourgeoisie is particularly large and that for a long period our rural base areas have been cut off from one another by the enemy, while the subjective cause is the insufficiency of inner-Party education. The important task now confronting us is to point out these causes, to persuade our comrades to get rid of their blindness and raise the level of their political awareness, to break down the ideological barriers that separate comrades and to promote mutual understanding and respect, so as to bring about unity throughout the Party.

A clear understanding of these questions by the whole Party will not only assure the success of our present course of study within the Party, but will also assure the victory of the Chinese revolution.

II

The present situation has two characteristics: one is that the anti-fascist front is growing stronger and the fascist front is declining, and the second is that within the anti-fascist front the people's forces are growing stronger and the anti-popular forces are declining. The first characteristic is quite obvious and can readily be seen. Hitler will be defeated before long, and the Japanese aggressors, too, are heading for defeat. The second characteristic is not so obvious and cannot readily be seen, but it is daily becoming more manifest in Europe, in Britain and the United States and in China.

The growth of the people's forces in China has to be explained with our Party as the centre of the picture.

The growth of our Party during the War of Resistance Against Japan can be divided into three stages. The first stage was from 1937 to 1940. In 1937 and 1938, the first two years of this stage, the Japanese militarists took the Kuomintang seriously and the Communist Party lightly; therefore they threw their main forces against the Kuomintang front, and, in their policy towards the Kuomintang, military attack was primary and political blandishments to bring about capitulation were supplementary; they did not take the Communist-led anti-Japanese base areas seriously, believing that these amounted to only a handful of Communists engaged in guerrilla actions. But after occupying Wuhan in October 1938, the Japanese imperialists began to change their policy and to take the Communist Party seriously and the Kuomintang lightly. In their policy towards the Kuomintang, political blandishments to bring about capitulation became primary and military attack supplementary, while at the same time they gradually shifted their main forces to deal with the Communists. For the Japanese imperialists now felt it was no longer the Kuomintang, but the Communist Party, that was to be feared. In 1937 and 1938, the Kuomintang put rather more effort into the War of Resistance, its relations with our Party were comparatively good and it permitted rather more freedom, although imposing many restrictions on the people's anti-Japanese movement. After the fall of Wuhan, however, because of its defeats in the war and its increasing hostility towards the Communist Party, the Kuomintang gradually became more reactionary, more active against the Communists and more passive in the war against Japan. In 1937, as a result of the setbacks in the civil war period, the Communist Party had only about 40,000 organized members and an army of 30,000 men; hence it was taken lightly by the Japanese militarists. But by 1940 the Party's membership had risen to 800,000, our army had grown to nearly 500,000, and the population of the base areas, including those paying grain tax only to us and those paying it both to us and to the Japanese and puppets,[9] totalled about 100,000,000. In the course of several years our Party had opened up such an extensive theatre of war, namely, the Liberated Areas,

that for no less than five and a half years we were able to prevent
any strategic offensive by the main forces of the Japanese invaders
against the Kuomintang front, draw these forces around ourselves,
extricate the Kuomintang from the crisis in its theatre of war and
maintain the protracted War of Resistance. But during that stage
some comrades in our Party committed an error; they underestimated
Japanese imperialism (and so did not see the protracted and ruthless
nature of the war, maintained that mobile warfare with large formations should be primary and belittled guerrilla warfare), placed reliance on the Kuomintang, and failed to pursue an independent policy
soberly (hence their capitulationism towards the Kuomintang and
their vacillation in applying the policy of boldly and freely arousing
the masses to establish anti-Japanese democratic base areas behind
the enemy lines and greatly expanding the armed forces led by our
Party). Meanwhile our Party had recruited large numbers of new
members who were still inexperienced, and all the base areas in the
enemy's rear were newly established and not yet consolidated. During
this stage, a kind of conceit appeared within the Party because of
the favourable development of the general situation and the growth
of our Party and armed forces, and many members became swelled-
headed. During this stage, however, we overcame the Right deviation
in the Party and carried out an independent policy; we not only hit
Japanese imperialism hard, created base areas and expanded the
Eighth Route and New Fourth Armies, but also repulsed the first
large-scale anti-Communist onslaught by the Kuomintang.

The years 1941 and 1942 formed the second stage. In order to prepare and prosecute the war against Britain and the United States,
the Japanese imperialists more actively pursued the policy to which
they had switched after the fall of Wuhan, the policy of concentrating
on the Communist Party and not on the Kuomintang. They massed
a still larger part of their main forces around all the Communist-led
base areas, conducted one "mopping-up" operation after another, and
executed the ruthless policy of "burn all, kill all, loot all", concentrating
their attacks on our Party. As a result, in the two years 1941-42, our
Party was placed in an extremely difficult position. During this stage
its base areas shrank in size, the population fell to under 50,000,000,
the Eighth Route Army was reduced to 300,000, the loss of cadres
was very great, and our finances and economy were very heavily
strained. Meanwhile, the Kuomintang, finding its hands free, moved
against our Party in a thousand and one ways, unleashed its second

large-scale anti-Communist onslaught and attacked us in co-ordination with the Japanese imperialists. But this difficult position served to educate us Communists and we learned many things. We learned how to combat the enemy's "mopping-up" operations, his policy of "nibbling" our territory, his "tighten public security" campaign,[10] his policy of "burn all, kill all, loot all" and his policy of extorting political recantations. We learned or began to learn how to carry out the "three thirds system" in the state organs of the united front, how to carry out the land policy, the rectification movement to correct our style of study, style in Party relations and style of writing, the policy of better troops and simpler administration, the policy of unified leadership, the movement for supporting the government and cherishing the people, and the development of production. And we overcame many shortcomings, including the conceit of many people that had arisen during the first stage. Although our losses in the second stage were very heavy, we held our ground; we repulsed the offensives of the Japanese invaders on the one hand and the second large-scale anti-Communist onslaught of the Kuomintang on the other. The Kuomintang's attacks on the Communist Party and the struggles we had to wage in self-defence gave rise to a kind of ultra-Left deviation in the Party, one example being the belief that Kuomintang-Communist co-operation would soon break down, with the result that excessive attacks were made on the landlords and unity with public figures outside the Party was neglected. But we overcame this deviation also. In the struggle to counter the friction created by the Kuomintang we affirmed the principle of waging struggles "on just grounds, to our advantage, and with restraint", and in united front work we pointed out the necessity of "unity, struggle, unity through struggle". Thus we maintained the Anti-Japanese National United Front throughout the country as well as in the base areas.

The third stage extends from 1943 to the present. Our various policies have become more effective and, in particular, the rectification movement and the development of production have yielded results of a fundamental nature, thereby making our Party invincible both ideologically and materially. Moreover, last year we learned, or began to learn, how to carry out our policy on the examination of the histories of cadres and our policy on combating secret agents. It is in these circumstances that our base areas have again expanded, that the population has risen to over 80,000,000, including those paying the grain tax only to us and those paying it both to us and to the Japanese and puppets, that our army has grown to 470,000 and our people's militia to 2,270,000, and that our Party membership has reached 900,000 and more.

In 1943 the Japanese militarists made no appreciable change in their policy towards China and continued to direct their main attacks at the Communist Party. For more than three years, from 1941 to the present, over 60 per cent of the Japanese troops in China have been pressing hard on the anti-Japanese base areas led by our Party. During these years the several hundred thousand Kuomintang troops who were left behind the enemy lines have been unable to withstand the blows of Japanese imperialism; about half surrendered, about half were wiped out, and only a small number survived and withdrew. Those Kuomintang troops who surrendered have turned and attacked our Party, which has consequently had to resist over 90 per cent of the puppet troops. The Kuomintang has only had to resist less than 40 per cent of the Japanese forces and less than 10 per cent of the puppet troops. For fully five and a half years since the fall of Wuhan in October 1938, the Japanese militarists have not launched a single strategic offensive on the Kuomintang front; there have been only a few relatively big operations (in Chekiang-Kiangsi, Changsha, western Hupeh, southern Honan and Changteh), and even these were mere raids, while they concentrated their main attention on the anti-Japanese base areas led by our Party. In this situation, the Kuomintang has pursued the policy of "retreating into the mountains" and "watching others fight", simply staving off blows when the enemy advanced and looking on with folded arms when he withdrew. In 1943 the Kuomintang became even more reactionary in its domestic policy and made its third large-scale anti-Communist onslaught, which we again repulsed.

From 1943 to the spring of this year, the Japanese aggressors have been steadily losing ground in the Pacific theatre, the United States has been intensifying its counter-offensive, and now, in the West, Hitler is tottering under the heavy blows of the Soviet Red Army. In an effort to avert their doom, the Japanese imperialists have conceived the idea of forcing the Peiping-Hankow and Hankow-Canton Railways open for through traffic and, since they have not yet succeeded in their policy of inducing the Kuomintang in Chungking to capitulate, they have found it necessary to deal it another blow; hence their plan for a large-scale offensive on the Kuomintang front this year. The Honan campaign[11] has been going on for over a month.

The enemy forces there amount to only a few divisions, yet several hundred thousand Kuomintang troops have collapsed without a battle, and only the troops of miscellaneous brands have been able to put up some sort of fight. In Tang En-po's command, utter disorder prevails, with the officers estranged from their men and the troops from the people, and more than two-thirds of his total forces have been lost. Likewise, the divisions which Hu Tsung-nan dispatched to Honan collapsed at their first encounter with the enemy. This is wholly the result of the reactionary policies which the Kuomintang has rigorously enforced for the past few years. During the five and a half years since the fall of Wuhan, the theatre of war of the Liberated Areas led by the Communist Party has borne the brunt of resisting the main forces of the Japanese and puppets; and although there may be some change in the future, it can only be temporary because the Kuomintang, rendered utterly degenerate by its reactionary policy of passive resistance to Japan and active opposition to the Communists, is bound to suffer serious reverses. When that happens, our Party's task in fighting the enemy and the puppets will become heavier still. What the Kuomintang has gained from looking on with folded arms for five and a half years is the loss of its fighting capacity. What the Communist Party has gained from fighting and struggling hard for five and a half years is the strengthening of its fighting capacity. This is what will decide China's destiny.

Comrades can see for themselves that in the seven years since July 1937 the people's democratic forces under the leadership of our Party have gone through three phases — a rise, a decline and a new rise. We have beaten back the ferocious attacks of the Japanese invaders, established extensive revolutionary base areas, greatly expanded the Party and the army, repulsed three large-scale anti-Communist onslaughts by the Kuomintang and overcome the erroneous Right and "Left" ideologies in the Party; and the whole Party has gained much valuable experience. This sums up our work over the past seven years.

Our present task is to prepare ourselves for a still greater responsibility. We must prepare to drive the Japanese invaders out of China, whatever the circumstances. To enable our Party to shoulder this responsibility, we must further expand and consolidate our Party, our army and base areas, pay attention to work in the big cities and along the main lines of communication and raise the work in the cities to a position of equal importance with that in the base areas.

As for our work in the base areas, during the first stage these areas were greatly expanded but not consolidated, and so in the second stage they contracted as soon as they came under the heavy blows of the enemy. In the second stage all the anti-Japanese base areas led by our Party went through a hard tempering process and improved greatly as compared with the first stage; the cadres and Party members considerably advanced their ideological and political level, and learned many things they did not know before. But it takes time to clarify thinking and to study policy, and we have still much to learn. Our Party is not yet sufficiently strong, not yet sufficiently united or consolidated, and so cannot yet take on greater responsibility than we now carry. From now on the problem is further to expand and consolidate our Party, our army and base areas in the continued prosecution of the War of Resistance; this is the first indispensable item in our ideological and material preparation for the gigantic work of the future. Without this preparation, we shall not be able to drive out the Japanese invaders and liberate the whole of China.

Our work in the big cities and along the main lines of communication has always been very inadequate. If now we do not strive to rally around our Party the tens of millions of the toiling masses and other people oppressed by the Japanese imperialists in the big cities and along the main lines of communication, and do not prepare armed mass insurrections, our army and rural base areas will face all sorts of difficulties for lack of co-ordination with the cities. For more than ten years we have been in the countryside and have had to encourage people to know the countryside well and to build the rural base areas. During these ten years and more the task of preparing insurrections in the cities, as decided by the Party's Sixth National Congress, was not and could not have been carried out. But now it is different, and the resolution of the Sixth National Congress will be carried out after the Seventh National Congress. This Congress will probably be held soon and will discuss the problems of strengthening our work in the cities and winning nation-wide victory.

The industrial conference of the Shensi-Kansu-Ningsia Border Region, now in session, is of great significance. In 1937 the number of factory workers in the Border Region was only 700, it increased to 7,000 by 1942 and is now 12,000. These figures are not to be treated lightly. While we are in the base areas, we must learn how to administer the industry, commerce and communications of big cities, or otherwise we shall not know what to do when the time comes.

Thus the second indispensable item in our ideological and material preparation for the future is to organize for armed insurrections in the big cities and along the main lines of communication and to learn how to administer industry and commerce. Without this preparation too, we shall not be able to drive out the Japanese invaders and liberate the whole of China.

III

In order to win new victories we must call on our Party cadres to get rid of the baggage and start up the machinery. "To get rid of the baggage" means to free our minds of many encumbrances. Many things may become baggage, may become encumbrances, if we cling to them blindly and uncritically. Let us take some illustrations. Having made mistakes, you may feel that, come what may, you are saddled with them and so become dispirited; if you have not made mistakes, you may feel that you are free from error and so become conceited. Lack of achievement in work may breed pessimism and depression, while achievement may breed pride and arrogance. A comrade with a short record of struggle may shirk responsibility on this account, while a veteran may become opinionated because of his long record of struggle. Worker and peasant comrades, because of pride in their class origin, may look down upon intellectuals, while intellectuals, because they have a certain amount of knowledge, may look down upon workers and peasants. Any specialized skill may be capitalized on and so may lead to arrogance and contempt of others. Even one's age may become ground for conceit. The young, because they are bright and capable, may look down upon the old; and the old, because they are rich in experience, may look down upon the young. All such things become encumbrances or baggage if there is no critical awareness. An important reason why some comrades are very lofty, isolating themselves from the masses and making repeated mistakes, is that they carry such baggage. Thus, a prerequisite for maintaining close links with the masses and making fewer mistakes is to examine one's baggage, to get rid of it and so emancipate the mind. There have been several occasions in the history of our Party when great conceit manifested itself and we suffered in consequence. The first was in the early half of 1927. The Northern Expeditionary Army had reached Wuhan, and some comrades became so proud and overweening as to forget that the Kuomintang was about to assault us. The result was the error of the Chen Tu-hsiu line, which brought defeat to the revolution. The second occasion was in 1930. Taking advantage of Chiang Kai-shek's large-scale war against Feng Yu-hsiang and Yen Hsi-shan,[12] the Red Army won a number of battles, and again some comrades became proud and overweening. The result was the error of the Li Li-san line, again causing some losses to the revolutionary forces. The third occasion was in 1931. The Red Army had smashed the Kuomintang's third "encirclement and suppression" campaign and, immediately afterwards, faced with the Japanese invasion, the people throughout the country started the stormy and heroic anti-Japanese movement; and again some comrades became proud and overweening. The result was an even more serious error in the political line, which cost us about 90 per cent of the revolutionary forces that we had built up with so much toil. The fourth occasion was in 1938. The War of Resistance had begun and the united front had been established; and once again some comrades became proud and overweening. As a result they committed an error somewhat similar to the Chen Tu-hsiu line. This time the revolutionary work suffered serious damage in those places where the effects of these comrades' erroneous ideas were more especially pronounced. Comrades throughout the Party should take warning from these instances of pride and error. Recently we have reprinted Kuo Mo-jo's essay on Li Tzu-cheng,[13] so that comrades may also take warning from this story and not repeat the error of becoming conceited at the moment of success.

"To start up the machinery" means to make good use of the organ of thought. Although some people carry no baggage and have the virtue of close contact with the masses, they fail to accomplish anything because they do not know how to think searchingly or are unwilling to use their brains to think much and think hard. Others refuse to use their brains because they are carrying baggage which cramps their intellect. Lenin and Stalin often advised people to use their brains, and we should give the same advice. This mechanism, the brain, has the special function of thinking. Mencius said, "The office of the mind is to think."[14] He defined the function of the brain correctly. We should always use our brains and think everything over carefully. A common saying goes, "Knit the brows and you will hit upon a stratagem." In other words, much thinking yields wisdom. In order to get rid of the practice of acting blindly which is so common in our Party, we must encourage our comrades to think, to learn the method of analysis and to cultivate the habit of analysis. There is all too little of this habit in our Party. If we get rid of our baggage and start up the machinery, if we march with light packs and know how to think hard, then we are sure to triumph.

NOTES

[1] Chen Tu-hsiu was originally a professor at Peking University and became famous as an editor of *New Youth*. He was one of the founders of the Communist Party of China. Because of his reputation at the time of the May 4th Movement and owing to the Party's immaturity in its initial period, he became General Secretary of the Party. In the last period of the revolution of 1924-27, the Rightist thinking in the Party represented by Chen Tu-hsiu developed into a line of capitulationism. Comrade Mao Tse-tung has observed that the capitulationists at that time "voluntarily gave up the Party's leadership of the peasant masses, urban petty bourgeoisie and middle bourgeoisie, and in particular gave up the Party's leadership of the armed forces, thus causing the defeat of the revolution" ("The Present Situation and Our Tasks", *Selected Works of Mao Tse-tung*, Eng. ed., FLP, Peking, 1961, Vol. IV, p. 171). After the defeat of 1927 Chen Tu-hsiu and a handful of other capitulationists lost faith in the future of the revolution and became liquidationists. They took the reactionary Trotskyist stand and together with the Trotskyites formed a small anti-Party group. Consequently Chen Tu-hsiu was expelled from the Party in November 1929. He died in 1942.

[2] The Fourth Plenary Session of the Sixth Central Committee of the Communist Party of China was held in January 1931.

[3] The Tsunyi Meeting was the enlarged meeting of the Political Bureau called by the Central Committee of the Communist Party of China at Tsunyi, Kweichow Province, in January 1935.

[4] See V. I. Lenin, " 'Communism' ", in which Lenin, criticizing the Hungarian Communist Bela Kun, said that he "gives up the most essential thing in Marxism, the living soul of Marxism, the concrete analysis of concrete conditions" (*Collected Works*, Russ. ed., Moscow, 1950, Vol. XXXI, p. 143).

[5] The Sixth National Congress of the Communist Party of China held in July 1928 adopted the following Ten-Point Programme: (1) overthrow imperialist rule; (2) confiscate foreign capitalist enterprises and banks; (3) unify China and recognize the right of the nationalities to self-determination; (4) overthrow the Kuomintang warlord government; (5) establish a government of councils of workers, peasants and soldiers; (6) institute the eight-hour day, increase wages, and establish unemployment relief and social insurance; (7) confiscate the land of all landlords and distribute the land among the peasants; (8) improve the living conditions of the soldiers, give land and jobs to ex-soldiers; (9) abolish all exorbitant taxes and miscellaneous levies and adopt a consolidated progressive tax; and (10) unite with the world proletariat, unite with the Soviet Union.

[6] The Fifth Plenary Session of the Sixth Central Committee of the Communist Party of China was held in January 1934.

⁷ This session of the Political Bureau in September 1941 reviewed the question of the political line in the past history of the Party, especially during the Second Revolutionary Civil War.

⁸ The "mountain-stronghold" mentality was a tendency to form cliques and arose mainly out of the circumstances of the protracted guerrilla war in which rural revolutionary bases were scattered and cut off from each other. Most of these bases were first established in mountain regions. Each tended to regard itself as a compact unit, like a single mountain stronghold, so this wrong tendency became known as mountain-stronghold mentality.

⁹ In the relatively stable parts of the base areas the people paid the regular grain tax only to the anti-Japanese democratic government. But in the outlying parts of the base areas and the guerrilla zones, which were constantly harassed by the enemy, the people were often forced to pay another grain levy to the enemy's puppet government.

¹⁰ In March 1941 the Japanese invaders and Chinese traitors in northern China proclaimed a "campaign for tightening public security", which included raiding the people's houses, establishing the neighbourhood guarantee system, making house-to-house check-ups and organizing puppet troops, all for the purpose of suppressing the anti-Japanese forces.

¹¹ In March 1944 the Japanese invaders launched their campaign in Honan Province with a force of 50,000 to 60,000 men. The 400,000 Kuomintang troops under Chiang Ting-wen, Tang En-po and Hu Tsung-nan melted away before the Japanese invaders. Thirty-eight counties, including Chengchow and Loyang, fell to the enemy one after another. Tang En-po lost 200,000 men.

¹² This large-scale war between the warlords, with Chiang Kai-shek on the one side and Feng Yu-hsiang and Yen Hsi-shan on the other, was fought along the Lunghai and Tientsin-Pukow Railways. It lasted six months, from May to October 1930. Casualties on both sides reached 300,000.

¹³ Kuo Mo-jo wrote the essay "The Tercentenary of the 1644 Uprising" in 1944 to commemorate the victory of the peasant uprising led by Li Tzu-cheng in the last years of the Ming Dynasty. He explained that the uprising met with defeat in 1645 because, after the entry of the peasant forces into Peking in 1644, some of their leaders were corrupted by luxurious living, and factional strife arose. The essay first appeared in *New China Daily* in Chungking and was later published as a pamphlet in Yenan and elsewhere in the Liberated Areas.

¹⁴ From *Mencius*, Book XI, "Kao Tzu", Part I.

SERVE THE PEOPLE

September 8, 1944

Our Communist Party and the Eighth Route and New Fourth Armies led by our Party are battalions of the revolution. These battalions of ours are wholly dedicated to the liberation of the people and work entirely in the people's interests. Comrade Chang Szu-teh[1] was in the ranks of these battalions.

All men must die, but death can vary in its significance. The ancient Chinese writer Szuma Chien said, "Though death befalls all men alike, it may be weightier than Mount Tai or lighter than a feather."[2] To die for the people is weightier than Mount Tai, but to work for the fascists and die for the exploiters and oppressors is lighter than a feather. Comrade Chang Szu-teh died for the people, and his death is indeed weightier than Mount Tai.

If we have shortcomings, we are not afraid to have them pointed out and criticized, because we serve the people. Anyone, no matter who, may point out our shortcomings. If he is right, we will correct them. If what he proposes will benefit the people, we will act upon it. The idea of "better troops and simpler administration" was put forward by Mr. Li Ting-ming,[3] who is not a Communist. He made a good suggestion which is of benefit to the people, and we have adopted it. If, in the interests of the people, we persist in doing what is right and correct what is wrong, our ranks will surely thrive.

We hail from all corners of the country and have joined together for a common revolutionary objective. And we need the vast majority of the people with us on the road to this objective. Today, we already lead base areas with a population of 91 million,[4] but this is not enough; to liberate the whole nation more are needed. In times of difficulty

---

This speech was delivered by Comrade Mao Tse-tung at a memorial meeting for Comrade Chang Szu-teh, held by departments directly under the Central Committee of the Communist Party of China.

we must not lose sight of our achievements, must see the bright future and must pluck up our courage. The Chinese people are suffering; it is our duty to save them and we must exert ourselves in struggle. Wherever there is struggle there is sacrifice, and death is a common occurrence. But we have the interests of the people and the sufferings of the great majority at heart, and when we die for the people it is a worthy death. Nevertheless, we should do our best to avoid unnecessary sacrifices. Our cadres must show concern for every soldier, and all people in the revolutionary ranks must care for each other, must love and help each other.

From now on, when anyone in our ranks who has done some useful work dies, be he soldier or cook, we should have a funeral ceremony and a memorial meeting in his honour. This should become the rule. And it should be introduced among the people as well. When someone dies in a village, let a memorial meeting be held. In this way we express our mourning for the dead and unite all the people.

NOTES

[1] Comrade Chang Szu-teh was a soldier in the Guards Regiment of the Central Committee of the Chinese Communist Party. A member of Communist Party who loyally served the interests of the people, he joined the revolution in 1933, took part in the Long March and was wounded in service. On September 5, 1944, when making charcoal in the mountains of Ansai County, northern Shensi, he was killed by the sudden collapse of a kiln.

[2] Szuma Chien, the famous Chinese historian of the 2nd century B.C., was the author of the *Historical Records*. The quotation comes from his "Reply to Jen Shao-ching's Letter".

[3] Li Ting-ming, an enlightened landlord of northern Shensi Province, was at one time elected Vice-Chairman of the Shensi-Kansu-Ningsia Border Region Government.

[4] This was the total population of the Shensi-Kansu-Ningsia Border Region and all other Liberated Areas in northern, central and southern China.

ON CHIANG KAI-SHEK'S SPEECH
ON THE DOUBLE TENTH FESTIVAL

October 11, 1944

One of the distinguishing features of Chiang Kai-shek's Double Tenth[1] speech is its utter lack of content and its failure to answer any of the questions about which the people are deeply concerned. Chiang Kai-shek declares that the enemy is not to be feared because there are still vast territories in the Great Rear Area. So far the autocratic Kuomintang leaders have shown neither the desire nor the ability to introduce political reforms or keep the enemy at bay, and territory is the only "capital" they can fall back upon for resisting the enemy. But it is plain to all that without a correct policy and without human effort this capital is not enough, for Japanese imperialism is daily threatening the remaining territories. In all probability Chiang Kai-shek has acutely felt this threat, as is shown by the very fact that he is repeatedly assuring the people that no such threat exists and even says, "In the twenty years since I founded the army at the Whampoa Military Academy,[2] the revolutionary situation has never been so stable as at present." He also keeps repeating, "We must not lose our self-confidence," which actually indicates loss of confidence among many people within the ranks of the Kuomintang and among many prominent public figures in the Kuomintang areas. Chiang Kai-shek has been casting about for some means to restore that confidence. But instead of looking for such means by examining his policy and work in the political, military, economic and cultural fields, he resorts to the rejection of criticisms and the whitewashing of his mistakes. He says that all "foreign observers" are "ignorant of the heart of the matter" and that the "babel of foreign criticism of our military and political affairs" is entirely due to credulous acceptance of "the rumours and tricks of the invaders and the Chinese collaborators".

Comrade Mao Tse-tung wrote this commentary for the Hsinhua News Agency.

Curiously enough, such foreigners as Franklin D. Roosevelt as well as
such Kuomintang members as Soong Ching Ling, many members
of the People's Political Council, and all Chinese who are not
devoid of conscience, disbelieve the plausible explanations offered
by Chiang Kai-shek and his trusted followers and are also raising
a "babel of criticism of our military and political affairs". Chiang
Kai-shek is annoyed, but not until this year's Double Tenth Festival
did he succeed in discovering what he regards as a compelling
argument, *i.e.*, that these people believe "the rumours and tricks of
the invaders and the Chinese collaborators". So in his speech Chiang
Kai-shek vehemently denounces these "rumours and tricks of the
invaders and the Chinese collaborators" at great length. He fancies
that, having made this denunciation, he can silence all the Chinese
and foreigners. And anyone who again raises a "babel of criticism"
of his military and political affairs will be put down as a willing
believer of "the rumours and tricks of the invaders and the Chinese
collaborators"! We consider Chiang Kai-shek's accusations ridiculous
in the extreme. For the invaders and the Chinese collaborators have
never criticized, but on the contrary have warmly applauded, the
Kuomintang for its autocracy, its half-hearted prosecution of the war,
its corruption and incompetence, and the fascist decrees and defeatist
military orders of its government. Chiang Kai-shek's *China's Destiny*,
a book which has met with general disapproval, has won sincere and
repeated praise from the Japanese imperialists. The invaders and the
Chinese collaborators have never said a word about reorganization
of the National Government and its supreme command, because it is
their cherished wish that this government and supreme command
which keep on oppressing the people and losing battles will be preserved. Is it not a fact that Chiang Kai-shek and his group have always
been the target of Japanese inducements to surrender? Is it not also a
fact that of the two slogans originally put forward by the Japanese
imperialists, one, "Annihilate the Kuomintang!" has been dropped
long ago and only the other, "Oppose the Communists!" remains?
To this very moment the Japanese imperialists have not declared war
on the Kuomintang government, and no state of war, so they say,
exists between Japan and the Kuomintang government! To this very
moment the invaders and the Chinese collaborators are taking good
care of the property of the Kuomintang bigwigs in Shanghai, Nanking,
Ningpo, etc. The enemy chieftain Shunroku Hata has sent his representatives to offer sacrifices at Chiang Kai-shek's ancestral tombs at

Fenghua. In Shanghai and elsewhere, emissaries secretly dispatched by Chiang Kai-shek's trusted followers are maintaining almost uninterrupted contact and carrying on clandestine negotiations with the Japanese invaders. These contacts and negotiations become more frequent whenever the Japanese intensify their offensives. Aren't all these things facts? Are those who raise a "babel of criticism" of the military and political affairs of Chiang Kai-shek and his group really "ignorant of the heart of the matter", or are they on the contrary only too well acquainted with it? After all, where is "the heart of the matter" to be found, in "the rumours and tricks of the invaders and the Chinese collaborators", or in Chiang Kai-shek himself and his own group?

In another statement in his speech, Chiang Kai-shek denies that civil war will break out in China. But he adds, "Certainly no one will ever again dare to rebel against the Republic and sabotage the War of Resistance, as Wang Ching-wei and his like have done." Here Chiang Kai-shek is seeking, and has in fact found, an excuse for civil war. Any Chinese whose memory is not too short will remember that in 1941, at the very moment when the betrayers of China were ordering the disbandment of the New Fourth Army and the Chinese people were rising to avert the crisis of civil war, Chiang Kai-shek made a speech in which he said that there would never be any war to "suppress the Communists" and that, should there be a war, it would only be a punitive one to put down rebels. Those who have read *China's Destiny* will also remember Chiang Kai-shek's remark that the Communist Party of China was "in league with" Wang Ching-wei in 1927 during the period of the Wuhan Government. In the resolutions of the Eleventh Plenary Session of the Kuomintang Central Executive Committee in 1943, an eight-word label was attached to the Chinese Communist Party: "Sabotaging the War of Resistance and endangering the state." After reading his present speech, one feels that the danger of civil war not only exists but is actually growing. From now on the Chinese people should firmly bear in mind that one fine morning Chiang Kai-shek will order a punitive expedition against so-called rebels and that the charge will be "rebellion against the Republic", "sabotaging the War of Resistance", and doing what "Wang Ching-wei and his like have done". Chiang is good at playing this game; he is no good at denouncing as rebels people like Pang Ping-hsun, Sun Liang-cheng and Chen Hsiao-chiang[3] or at launching punitive expeditions against them, but he is very good at denouncing as "rebels" the

New Fourth Army in central China and the Dare-to-Die Corps[4] in Shansi and is exceptionally good at launching punitive expeditions against them. The Chinese people must not forget that, while proclaiming that he will not fight a civil war, Chiang Kai-shek has already dispatched 775,000 troops who are now engaged exclusively in encircling or attacking the Eighth Route Army, the New Fourth Army and the people's guerrillas in southern China.

Chiang Kai-shek's speech has nothing to show on the positive side, and he has in no way met the Chinese people's eager desire to strengthen the anti-Japanese front. On the negative side, the speech is fraught with dangerous possibilities. His attitude is becoming more and more anomalous, as witness his stubborn opposition to the people's demand for political change, his bitter hatred of the Chinese Communist Party and his hint at a pretext for the anti-Communist civil war he is preparing. However, he will succeed in none of his schemes. Unless he is willing to mend his ways, he will be lifting a rock only to drop it on his own toes. We sincerely hope he will change his ways, because his present course of action will get him absolutely nowhere. Since he has proclaimed that "a greater latitude will be allowed to the voicing of opinions",[5] he should not stifle the "babel of criticism" by threatening people with the slander that they are willingly accepting "the rumours and tricks of the invaders and the Chinese collaborators". Since he has proclaimed that "the period of political tutelage will be shortened", he should not reject the demand for reorganizing the government and the supreme command. Since he has proclaimed that "the Communist problem should be solved politically", he should not again seek a pretext for preparing civil war.

NOTES

[1] The Double Tenth, October 10, is the anniversary of the armed uprising in Wuhan which set off the Revolution of 1911.

[2] The Whampoa Military Academy, located at Whampoa near Canton, was established by Dr. Sun Yat-sen in 1924 after the reorganization of the Kuomintang with the help of the Chinese Communist Party and the Soviet Union. Before Chiang Kai-shek's betrayal of the revolution in 1927, the academy was run jointly by the Kuomintang and the Communist Party. Comrades Chou En-lai, Yeh Chien-ying, Yun Tai-ying, Hsiao Chu-nu and others held responsible posts in the academy at one time or another. Many of the cadets were members of the Communist Party

or the Communist Youth League, and they formed the revolutionary core of the academy.

[3] Pang Ping-hsun, Sun Liang-cheng and Chen Hsiao-chiang were Kuomintang generals who openly deserted to the Japanese invaders.

[4] The Dare-to-Die Corps in Shansi was an anti-Japanese armed force of the people which developed under the leadership and influence of the Communist Party in the early days of the War of Resistance Against Japan.

[5] In April 1944 the Kuomintang announced that "a greater latitude will be allowed to the voicing of opinions". Its purpose was to fob off the people, because the demand that the Kuomintang dictatorship should be ended, democracy established, and freedom of speech guaranteed had become the general cry of the people in the Kuomintang areas from the beginning of the year. In May, the Twelfth Plenary Session of the Central Executive Committee of the Kuomintang again declared that it would "protect freedom of speech". But the Kuomintang never fulfilled any of the promises it had been compelled to make, and as the people's movement for democracy surged forward, it multiplied its measures for the suppression of popular opinion.

THE UNITED FRONT IN
CULTURAL WORK

October 30, 1944

The purpose of all our work is the overthrow of Japanese imperialism. Like Hitler, Japanese imperialism is approaching its doom.
But we must continue our efforts, for only so can we achieve its final
overthrow. In our work the war comes first, then production, then
cultural work. An army without culture is a dull-witted army, and a
dull-witted army cannot defeat the enemy.

The culture of the Liberated Areas already has its progressive side,
but it still has a backward side. The Liberated Areas already have a
new culture, a people's culture, but a good many vestiges of feudalism
survive. Among the 1,500,000 people of the Shensi-Kansu-Ningsia
Border Region there are more than 1,000,000 illiterates, there are
2,000 practitioners of witchcraft, and the broad masses are still
under the influence of superstition. These are enemies inside the
minds of the people. It is often more difficult to combat the enemies
inside people's minds than to fight Japanese imperialism. We must
call on the masses to arise in struggle against their own illiteracy,
superstitions and unhygienic habits. For this struggle a broad united
front is indispensable. And this united front has to be particularly
broad in a place like the Shensi-Kansu-Ningsia Border Region, which
has a sparse population, poor communications and a low cultural base
to start from and in addition is fighting a war. Hence, in our education we must have not only regular primary and secondary schools but
also scattered, irregular village schools, newspaper-reading groups and
literacy classes. Not only must we have schools of the modern type
but we must also utilize and transform the old-style village schools.

This speech was delivered by Comrade Mao Tse-tung at a conference of cultural
and educational workers of the Shensi-Kansu-Ningsia Border Region.

In the arts, we must have not only modern drama but also the Shensi opera and the *yangko* dance. Not only must we have new Shensi operas and new *yangko* dances, but we must also utilize and gradually transform the old opera companies and the old *yangko* troupes, which comprise 90 per cent of all *yangko* troupes. This approach is even more necessary in the field of medicine. In the Shensi-Kansu-Ningsia Border Region the human and animal mortality rates are both very high, and at the same time many people still believe in witchcraft. In such circumstances, to rely solely on modern doctors is no solution. Of course, modern doctors have advantages over doctors of the old type, but if they do not concern themselves with the sufferings of the people, do not train doctors for the people, do not unite with the thousand and more doctors and veterinarians of the old type in the Border Region and do not help them to make progress, then they will actually be helping the witch doctors and showing indifference to the high human and animal mortality rates. There are two principles for the united front: the first is to unite, and the second is to criticize, educate and transform. In the united front, capitulationism is wrong, and so is sectarianism with its exclusiveness and contempt for others. Our task is to unite with all intellectuals, artists and doctors of the old type who can be useful, to help them, convert them and transform them. In order to transform them, we must first unite with them. If we do it properly, they will welcome our help.

Our culture is a people's culture; our cultural workers must serve the people with great enthusiasm and devotion, and they must link themselves with the masses, not divorce themselves from the masses. In order to do so, they must act in accordance with the needs and wishes of the masses. All work done for the masses must start from their needs and not from the desire of any individual, however well-intentioned. It often happens that objectively the masses need a certain change, but subjectively they are not yet conscious of the need, not yet willing or determined to make the change. In such cases, we should wait patiently. We should not make the change until, through our work, most of the masses have become conscious of the need and are willing and determined to carry it out. Otherwise we shall isolate ourselves from the masses. Unless they are conscious and willing, any kind of work that requires their participation will turn out to be a mere formality and will fail. The saying "Haste does not bring success" does not mean that we should not make haste, but that we should not be impetuous; impetuosity leads only to failure. This is true in any kind of work, and particularly in the cultural and educational work the aim of which is to transform the thinking of the masses. There are two principles here: one is the actual needs of the masses rather than what we fancy they need, and the other is the wishes of the masses, who must make up their own minds instead of our making up their minds for them.

WE MUST LEARN TO DO ECONOMIC WORK

January 10, 1945

Heroes of Labour and Model Workers!

You have attended this conference and summed up your experience; we all welcome you and honour you. You have three good qualities and you play three roles. First, the role of initiators. In other words, by your outstanding efforts and your numerous innovations you have made your work a model for others, raising standards and inspiring others to learn from you. Second, the role of backbone. Most of you are not yet cadres, but you have become the backbone, the hard core of the masses; with you, it is easier to push our work forward. In the future you may become cadres; at present you are cadres in reserve. Third, the role of a bridge. You are a bridge between the leadership and the broad masses; through you the opinions of the masses are transmitted to the leadership and vice versa.

You have many good qualities and have rendered great service, but you must always remember not to become conceited. You are respected by all, and quite rightly, but this easily leads to conceit. If you become conceited, if you are not modest and cease to exert yourselves, and if you do not respect others, do not respect the cadres and the masses, then you will cease to be heroes and models. There have been such people in the past, and I hope you will not follow their example.

This conference has summed up your experience. The summary is a very good one and is applicable in the other Liberated Areas as well. However, I am not going to dwell upon that. I should just like to say a few words about our economic work.

In the past few years we have begun to learn how to do economic work and we have achieved substantial successes in this field, but it

Comrade Mao Tse-tung delivered this speech at a conference of labour heroes and model workers of the Shensi-Kansu-Ningsia Border Region.

is still only a beginning. We must see to it that within two or three years the Shensi-Kansu-Ningsia Border Region and the Liberated Areas in the enemy's rear are completely or largely self-supporting in grain and manufactured goods, and even have a surplus. We must achieve still greater successes in agriculture, industry and trade. Only then can we regard ourselves as having learned more about economic work and as having learned to do it better. In places where there is no improvement in the living conditions of the troops and the people, where the material foundations for the counter-offensive remain unstable and agriculture, industry and trade stagnate or even decline instead of expanding year by year, it is evident that the personnel of the Party, government and army have not learned how to do economic work, and great difficulties will undoubtedly be encountered.

There is one point I must again bring to everybody's attention, namely, that our ideas should be adapted to our immediate environment. Our immediate environment is rural; it would seem that nobody has any doubt on that score, for who does not know that we are living in the countryside? Yet actually, that is not the case. Many comrades do not understand the countryside at all, or at any rate not profoundly, although they live there and imagine they understand it. They do not proceed from the fact that our environment is the countryside, which is based on individual economy, cut up by the enemy and involved in guerrilla warfare, and the result is that their handling of political, military, economic and cultural problems, or of Party matters and the workers', peasants', youth and women's movements is often incorrect or only partially correct. They approach rural affairs from an urban viewpoint and often run their heads against a brick wall because they draw up many inappropriate plans subjectively and enforce them arbitrarily. In recent years our comrades have made much progress, thanks both to the rectification campaign and to the failures they have met with in their work. But we must still take care to adapt our ideas fully to our environment before we can obtain results in every field of work and do so quickly. If we truly understand the fact that the rural base areas in which we find ourselves are founded on individual economy, cut up by the enemy and involved in guerrilla warfare and make it the starting point in everything we do, then the pertinent question is, how do our results, which may seem slow and unspectacular, compare with the results of taking some other starting point, for instance, the urban viewpoint? Far from being slow, they are actually quite fast. For if we were to start from the urban viewpoint and depart from our present-day realities, the question would be not of getting fast or slow results, but of running into endless snags and getting no results at all.

Clear proof of this fact is provided by the great success of the present form of the army and civilian production drive we have promoted.

We want to hit the Japanese aggressors hard and make preparations for seizing the cities and recovering our lost territories. But how can we attain this aim, situated as we are in a countryside founded on individual economy, cut up by the enemy and involved in guerrilla warfare? We cannot imitate the Kuomintang, which does not lift a finger itself but depends entirely on foreigners even for such necessities as cotton cloth. We stand for self-reliance. We hope for foreign aid but cannot be dependent on it; we depend on our own efforts, on the creative power of the whole army and the entire people. But how do we go about it? By launching large-scale production campaigns simultaneously among the troops and the people.

Since we are in the countryside, where manpower and material resources are scattered, we have adopted the policy of "unified leadership and decentralized management" for production and supply.

Since we are in the countryside, where the peasants are scattered individual producers employing backward means of production and where most of the land is still owned by landlords and the peasants are subjected to feudal rent exploitation, we have adopted the policies of reducing rent and interest and of organizing mutual aid in labour to heighten the peasants' enthusiasm for production and to increase the productivity of agricultural labour. Rent reduction has heightened the peasants' enthusiasm in production and mutual aid has increased the productivity of agricultural labour. I have obtained data from various places in northern and central China, all of which show that after rent reduction the peasants take much greater interest in production and are willing to organize mutual-aid groups like our labour-exchange teams here, in which the productivity of three persons now equals that of four in the past. That being the case, 90 million people can do as much as 120 million. There are also instances of two persons doing what used to require the effort of three. If instead of coercion and commandism, which are self-defeating because of their quest for quick results, we adopt a policy of patiently persuading people by setting them good examples, then it will be possible for the majority of the peasants to be organized into mutual-aid groups for agricultural and handicraft production in the next few years. Once such production groups become the usual practice, not only will output increase and all kinds of innovations emerge, but there will also be political progress, a higher educational level, progress in hygiene, a remoulding of loafers and a change in social customs, and it will not take long before the implements of production will be improved, too. With all this happening, our rural society will gradually be rebuilt on new foundations.

If our cadres carefully study this sphere of work and most energetically help the rural people develop campaigns for production, there will be a plentiful supply of grain and other necessities in the countryside within a few years, and we shall be able not only to keep up the war and cope with crop failures but also to maintain a large reserve of grain and other necessities for future use.

We should organize the army units and the government and other organizations as well as the peasants for production.

Since we are in the countryside, which is constantly ravaged by the enemy and involved in protracted war, it is imperative for the army units and the government and other organizations to engage in production. And it is possible for them to do so because the guerrilla fighting is scattered over a wide area. Besides, the troops and government personnel in our Shensi-Kansu-Ningsia Border Region are very numerous in proportion to the total population, and they will go hungry if they themselves do not engage in production, while on the other hand the people will go hungry if too much is taken from them and the burden is too heavy for them to bear. These are the reasons why we are resolved to launch a large-scale production campaign. Take the Shensi-Kansu-Ningsia Border Region, for instance. The annual requirements of the army units and the government and other organizations total 260,000 *tan* (here 1 *tan* equals 300 *chin*) of husked grain (millet), of which they get 160,000 from the people and produce the rest themselves; if they did not engage in production themselves, either they or the people would go hungry. Thanks to our production campaigns, we are free from hunger, and in fact the troops and the people are quite well fed.

With the exception of grain, clothing and bedding, government and other organizations in the Border Region are self-supporting in most of their needs and some units are entirely self-supporting. Many units are partially self-supporting even in grain, clothing and bedding.

The achievements of the army units of the Border Region are even greater. Many are entirely self-supporting in grain, clothing, bedding and every other essential, that is, they are 100 per cent self-supporting and draw nothing from the government. This is the highest standard, the top grade, and it has been attained gradually over a period of several years.

This standard cannot be adopted at the front, where fighting has to be done. There a second and a third standard may be set up. The second standard requires that except for grain, clothing and bedding, which are supplied by the government, self-sufficiency through production should be achieved in the following items: cooking oil (0.5 *liang* per person per day), salt (0.5 *liang* per person per day), vegetables (1-1.5 *chin* per person per day), and meat (1-2 *chin* per person per month); the purchase of fuel, office supplies and miscellaneous items; subsidies for education and health; expenditures for the cleaning of weapons and for the provision of tobacco, shoes, socks, gloves, towels, tooth-brushes, etc.; these items amounting in all to some 50 per cent of the total expenditure. This standard can be gradually attained in two or three years. In some places it has already been attained. This standard may be adopted in the stable base areas.

The third standard applies to outlying districts and to the guerrilla zones where 50 per cent self-sufficiency is not possible but 15-25 per cent may be. Reaching this standard is good enough there.

In short, apart from those in exceptional circumstances, all army units and government and other organizations must engage in production in the intervals between fighting, training or work. In addition to using such intervals for collective production, they should organize some of their personnel specifically for production, assigning them to run farms, vegetable gardens, pastures, workshops, small factories, transport teams and co-operatives, or to grow grain and vegetables in partnership with the peasants. In our present circumstances, every organization or army unit should establish its own "domestic economy" to tide over the difficulties. Unwillingness to do so is a characteristic of loafers and is disgraceful. To stimulate production we should also institute a system of individual bonuses, graded according to the quality of the work, for all who participate in it directly. Further, as the effective way of pushing the work forward, the head of each organization must assume responsibility and personally take part, and must apply the method of linking the leading group with the masses and the general call with particular and specific guidance.

Some people say that if the army units go in for production, they will be unable to train or fight and that if the government and other organizations do so, they will be unable to do their own work. This is a false argument. In recent years our army units in the Border Region have undertaken production on a big scale to provide themselves with ample food and clothing and have simultaneously done their training and conducted their political studies and literacy and other courses much more successfully than before, and there is greater unity than ever within the army and between the army and the people. While there was a large-scale production campaign at the front last year, great successes were gained in the fighting and in addition an extensive training campaign was started. And thanks to production, the personnel of the government and other organizations live a better life and work with greater devotion and efficiency; this is the case both in the Border Region and at the front.

Thus it can be seen that in the context of guerrilla warfare in rural areas, those army units and government and other organizations which undertake production for self-support show greater energy and activity in their fighting, training and work, and improve their discipline and their unity both internally and with the civilians. Production for self-support is the outcome of our country's protracted guerrilla war and this is our glory. Once we master it, no material difficulty can daunt us. We shall grow in vigour and energy year by year and become stronger with every battle; we shall overwhelm the enemy and have no fear of his overwhelming us.

Here another point must be called to the attention of our comrades at the front. Some of our recently established areas are fairly rich in material resources and, counting on this, the cadres there are unwilling either to economize or to engage in production. This is very bad, and they are bound to suffer for it later. Wherever we happen to be, we must treasure our manpower and material resources, and must not take a short view and indulge in wastefulness and extravagance. Wherever we are, from the very first year of our work we must bear in mind the many years to come, the protracted war that must be maintained, the counter-offensive, and the work of reconstruction after the enemy's expulsion. On the one hand, never be wasteful or extravagant; on the other, actively expand production. Previously, in some places people suffered a great deal because they did not take the long view and neglected economy in manpower and material resources and the expansion of production. The lesson is there and attention must be called to it.

As regards manufactured goods, the Shensi-Kansu-Ningsia Border Region has decided to become completely self-supporting in cotton,

cotton yarn, cotton cloth, iron, paper and many other things within two years. We must grow, manufacture and supply whatever is not produced here or is produced only in small quantities, and must not depend on the outside at all. The whole task is to be accomplished by the public, private and co-operative enterprises. For all items, we demand not only quantity but also quality, that is, they must stand wear and tear. The Border Region Government, the Joint Defence Headquarters of the Eighth Route Army and the Northwest Bureau of the Central Committee of the Party are absolutely right in giving close attention to these matters. I hope that the same thing will be done in all places at the front. In many places it is already being done, and I wish them success.

In our Border Region and the other Liberated Areas, it will take another two or three years for us to learn every branch of economic work. The day when we grow all or most of our own grain, manufacture all or most of our own goods and thus are completely or mainly self-supporting and even have a surplus will also be the day when we have mastered every branch of economic work in the countryside. After we have cleared the cities of the enemy, we shall be able to take up new branches of economic work. We must exert ourselves and learn, because China depends on us for her reconstruction.

PRODUCTION IS ALSO POSSIBLE
IN THE GUERRILLA ZONES

January 31, 1945

It is already admitted and there is no longer any doubt that production campaigns can and must be conducted in the army and among the people in the relatively stable bases of the Liberated Areas behind the enemy lines. But whether they can be conducted in the guerrilla zones and in the furthermost areas behind the enemy lines has not yet been settled in many people's minds for want of proof.

But now we have proof. In 1944 production was undertaken on a considerable scale in many guerrilla zones and with excellent results, according to Comrade Chang Ping-kai's report on the production campaign of the guerrilla units in the Shansi-Chahar-Hopei border area, published in the *Liberation Daily* of January 28. The districts and units listed in his report are: in central Hopei, the sixth sub-region, the fourth district contingent of the second sub-region, the eighth district contingent of the fourth sub-region, the Hsushui-Tinghsien detachment, the Paoting-Mancheng detachment and the Yunpiao detachment; and in Shansi, the troops in the counties of Taihsien and Kuohsien. Conditions in those areas are most unfavourable:

> The place bristles with enemy and puppet strongpoints and blockhouses and is criss-crossed with ditches, walls and roads, and taking advantage of his military superiority and communication facilities, the enemy often launches surprise attacks and encirclement and "mopping-up" campaigns against us. Under such conditions the guerrilla units often have to shift their positions several times a day.

Nevertheless, the guerrilla units have managed to carry on production in the intervals between fighting. The results are:

Comrade Mao Tse-tung wrote this editorial for the *Liberation Daily*, Yenan.

Everybody is now better fed — each person has 0.5 *liang* of cooking oil and salt and 1 *chin* of vegetables per day, and 1.5 *chin* of meat per month. Furthermore, tooth-brushes, tooth-powder and reading primers, which for years were unavailable, are now all provided.

Just look! Who says that production is not possible in guerrilla zones? Many people claim that there is no spare land in the densely populated areas. Is there really no spare land? Again please look at the Shansi-Chahar-Hopei border area:

First, the land problem has been settled in accordance with the policy of giving primary attention to agriculture. They use nine methods in all: (1) razing walls and filling in ditches used by the enemy for blockade purposes; (2) destroying motor roads the enemy may use and planting crops along them; (3) making use of small pieces of waste land; (4) helping the people's militia by providing armed protection when, on moonlit nights, crops are planted in the fields around the blockhouses in defiance of the enemy; (5) ploughing the fields in partnership with peasants who are short of labour power; (6) ploughing the fields around the enemy's strongpoints or blockhouses more or less openly, using soldiers dressed as peasants; (7) making use of river banks by building dykes, removing the sand and turning the banks into fields; (8) helping peasants bring dry land under irrigation; and (9) helping in the farm work in every village in which they are active.

But if agriculture is possible, perhaps handicrafts and other production remain impossible? Is that actually the case? Please look at the Shansi-Chahar-Hopei border area:

The troops in the vicinity of the enemy's blockade lines or blockade ditches do not confine their production to agriculture but, as in the stable areas, have also developed handicrafts and transport. The fourth district contingent has set up a felt-cap workshop, an oil press and a flour mill, and in seven months has netted a profit of 500,000 yuan in local currency. Not only has it settled its own difficulties but it is satisfying the needs of the people in its guerrilla zone. The soldiers can now provide all their own woollen sweaters and socks.

Since military operations are so frequent in the guerrilla zones, perhaps fighting is affected if the troops engage in production? Is that really so? Please look at the Shansi-Chahar-Hopei border area:

> Applying the principle of integrating labour power and armed strength, they give equal importance to the tasks of production and fighting.

And

> Take, for instance, the fourth district contingent of the second sub-region. When they began their spring ploughing, they sent a special detachment to attack the enemy and at the same time launched a powerful political offensive. Precisely because of this, there was greater activity in the military sphere, too, and the combat effectiveness of the troops increased. From February to early September this small detachment fought 71 encounters, took the strongholds of Chutungsheh, Shangchuang, Yehchuang, Fengchiachai and Yaitou, inflicted 165 casualties on the enemy and puppet troops, and captured 91 puppet soldiers, 3 light machine-guns and 101 rifles and pistols.

And

> Co-ordinating military activity with propaganda for extensive production, they immediately launched a political offensive with the watchword: "Smash anyone who tries to wreck the great production drive!" In the county towns of Taihsien and Kuohsien the enemy asked the inhabitants: "Why has the Eighth Route Army become so tough recently?" They replied: "Because you are trying to wreck the great production drive in the border area." The puppet troops said to one another: "Better not go out while they are carrying out this great production drive."

Is it possible to get the people in the guerrilla zones to launch a production campaign too? Are the peasants interested in increasing production in such zones, where rents have perhaps not yet been reduced or the rent reduction has not been thorough? This has been answered in the affirmative in the Shansi-Chahar-Hopei border area:

> Furthermore, the troops in the vicinity of the enemy's blockade lines or blockade ditches give direct help to the local people by spreading the production campaign. On the one hand, they provide armed protection for the masses engaged in production and, on

the other, they render extensive help by their labour. Some units have made it a rule to assign 50 per cent of their manpower to provide free help for the masses during the busy farming seasons. Thus, the enthusiasm of the masses for production has become very much greater, the relations between the army and the people have become still more harmonious, and the masses have enough to eat. Hence the sympathy and support of the masses in the guerrilla zones for the Communist Party and the Eighth Route Army have grown.

All doubts have thus been answered as to whether the army and the people in the guerrilla zones can and must conduct large-scale production campaigns. We demand of all Party, government and army cadres in the Liberated Areas, and especially in the guerrilla zones, that they should attain full comprehension of this point, for once the "can" and the "must" are understood, production will be set going everywhere. It was precisely from this point that the start was made in the Shansi-Chahar-Hopei border area:

> In the production campaign the troops in the vicinity of the enemy's blockade lines or blockade ditches were not only able to fulfil their production plan on schedule in the short space of five months, but what is more, they introduced a number of practical innovations. This was because the cadres re-orientated their thinking, paid serious attention to production and to integrating labour power with armed strength, and brought forward labour heroes and model workers from among the masses (sixty-six labour heroes and model workers according to a preliminary summing-up).

In 1945, the Liberated Areas must carry out a bigger army and civilian production campaign than ever before through the united efforts of all, and in the coming winter we shall compare the achievements of all the areas.

War is not only a military and political contest but also an economic contest. In order to defeat the Japanese aggressors, in addition to all the other tasks we must apply ourselves to economic work and must master it within two or three years; in the present year, 1945, we must achieve greater results than ever before. This is what the Central Committee of the Chinese Communist Party eagerly expects of all our cadres and all the people throughout the Liberated Areas, and we hope this objective will be attained.

CHINA'S TWO POSSIBLE DESTINIES

April 23, 1945

Comrades! The Seventh National Congress of the Communist Party of China opens today.

What is the significance of our congress? It is a congress, it should be said, that affects the destiny of China's 450 million people. China can have one of two destinies. Someone has written a book about one of them;[1] our congress represents China's other destiny and we, too, shall write a book about it.[2] The aim of our congress is the overthrow of Japanese imperialism and the liberation of all the people of China. Ours is a congress for the defeat of the Japanese aggressors and the building of a new China, for final victory through the unity of all the Chinese people and of the peoples of the whole world.

The times are very favourable. In Europe, Hitler will soon be overthrown. The chief theatre of the world anti-fascist war is in the West, where the fighting will soon end in victory, thanks to the efforts of the Soviet Red Army. The guns of the Red Army can already be heard in Berlin, which will probably fall before long. In the East, too, victory in the war to overthrow Japanese imperialism is nigh. Our congress is meeting on the eve of final victory in the anti-fascist war.

Two roads lie before the Chinese people, the road of light and the road of darkness. Two possible destinies await China, a destiny of light and a destiny of darkness. Japanese imperialism has not yet been defeated. But even after its defeat, the two prospects will still confront us. Either a China which is independent, free, democratic, united, prosperous and strong, that is, a China full of light, a new China whose people have won liberation, or a China which is semi-colonial, semi-feudal, divided, poor and weak, that is, the old China. The

---

This was the opening speech at the Seventh National Congress of the Communist Party of China.

new China or the old China — these are the two prospects facing the Chinese people, the Communist Party of China and our present congress.

Since Japan is not yet defeated and since the two prospects will still face us even after its defeat, how should we set about our work? What is our task? Our sole task is boldly to mobilize the masses, expand the people's forces and unite all the forces of the nation capable of being united in order to struggle under our Party's leadership to defeat the Japanese aggressors and build a bright new China, a China that is independent, free, democratic, united, prosperous and strong. We must strive with all our might for a bright future, a destiny of light, and against a dark future, a destiny of darkness. This is our one and only task! Indeed, it is the task of our congress, of our whole Party, and of all the people of China.

Is it possible for our hopes to be realized? We believe it is. The possibility exists, because we already enjoy the following conditions:

(1) A powerful Communist Party with rich experience and a membership of 1,210,000.

(2) Powerful Liberated Areas with a population of 95,500,000, an army of 910,000 and a militia of 2,200,000.

(3) The support of the masses throughout the country.

(4) The support of the people of all countries, and especially of the Soviet Union.

With these conditions — a powerful Communist Party, powerful Liberated Areas, the support of the masses throughout the country and the support of the people of the world — can our hopes be realized? We believe they can. China has never enjoyed these conditions before. Some have been present for a number of years, but never so fully as today. Our Communist Party has never been so powerful, the revolutionary base areas have never had so large a population and so large an army, the prestige of the Communist Party is higher than ever among the people both in the Japanese-occupied and in the Kuomintang areas, and the revolutionary forces of the Soviet Union and the people of all countries are stronger than ever before. One must say that, with these conditions, it is entirely possible to defeat the aggressors and build a new China.

We must have a correct policy. The fundamental point of our policy is boldly to mobilize the masses and expand the people's forces so that, under the leadership of our Party, they will defeat the aggressors and build a new China.

In the twenty-four years of its existence since its birth in 1921 the Communist Party of China has gone through three historical periods of heroic struggle — the Northern Expedition, the Agrarian Revolutionary War and the War of Resistance Against Japan — and has accumulated a wealth of experience. Now our Party has become the centre of gravity of the Chinese people's struggle to resist Japan and save the nation, the centre of gravity of their struggle for liberation and of their struggle to defeat the aggressors and build a new China. China's centre of gravity lies right here where we are and nowhere else.

We should be modest and prudent, guard against arrogance and rashness, and serve the Chinese people heart and soul, in order to unite them for defeating the Japanese aggressors in the present and for building a new-democratic state in the future. Provided we do so, provided we have the correct policy and provided we make a united effort, we can definitely fulfil our task.

Down with Japanese imperialism!

Long live the liberation of the Chinese people!

Long live the Communist Party of China!

Long live the Seventh National Congress of the Communist Party of China!

NOTES

[1] This refers to Chiang Kai-shek's *China's Destiny* published in 1943.

[2] This refers to Comrade Mao Tse-tung's report "On Coalition Government" at the same congress.

ON COALITION GOVERNMENT

April 24, 1945

I. THE FUNDAMENTAL DEMANDS OF THE CHINESE PEOPLE

Our congress is being held in the following circumstances. A new situation has emerged after nearly eight years of resolute, heroic and indomitable struggle waged by the Chinese people with countless sacrifices and amid untold hardships against the Japanese aggressors; in the world as a whole, decisive victory has been gained in the just and sacred war against the fascist aggressors and the moment is near when the Japanese aggressors will be defeated by the Chinese people in co-ordination with the allied countries. But China remains disunited and is still confronted with a grave crisis. In these circumstances, what ought we to do? Beyond all doubt, the urgent need is to unite representatives of all political parties and groups and of people without any party affiliation and establish a provisional democratic coalition government for the purpose of instituting democratic re- forms, surmounting the present crisis, mobilizing and unifying all the anti-Japanese forces in the country to fight in effective co-ordination with the allied countries for the defeat of the Japanese aggressors, and thus enabling the Chinese people to liberate themselves from the latter's clutches. After that it will be necessary to convene a national assembly on a broad democratic basis and set up a formally constituted democratic government, which will also be in the nature of a coalition and will have a still wider representation of people from all parties and groups or without any party affiliation, and which will lead the liberated people of the whole country in building an independent, free, democratic, united, prosperous and powerful new China. In short, we

---

This was the political report made by Comrade Mao Tse-tung to the Seventh National Congress of the Communist Party of China.

must take the line of unity and democracy, defeat the aggressors and
build a new China.

We believe that this alone can give expression to the fundamental
demands of the Chinese people. Therefore, my report will deal
mainly with these demands. Whether or not a democratic coalition
government should be set up has become a matter of deep concern
for the Chinese people and for democratic public opinion in the allied
countries. My report will therefore lay particular stress on elucidating
this question.

In the eight years of the War of Resistance Against Japan, the
Communist Party of China has overcome many difficulties and achieved
great successes, but as things stand serious difficulties still confront
our Party and people. The present situation demands that our Party
should work still more solidly and intensively and that it should continue to overcome the difficulties and strive to fulfil the fundamental
demands of the Chinese people.

II. THE INTERNATIONAL AND
THE DOMESTIC SITUATION

Can the Chinese people translate these basic demands into reality?
This will depend on the level of their political consciousness, their
unity and their efforts. At the same time, the present international and
domestic situation offers extremely favourable opportunities. If the
Chinese people can make good use of these opportunities and continue
to fight on staunchly, vigorously and persistently, they will undoubtedly
defeat the aggressors and build a new China. They must redouble
their efforts in their struggle to accomplish their sacred tasks.

What is the present international situation?

The present military situation is that the Soviet Army is attacking
Berlin, and the allied forces of Britain, the United States and France
are attacking the Hitlerite remnants in co-ordination with this offensive, while the Italian people are launching uprisings. All this will
eliminate Hitler once and for all. After Hitler is wiped out, the defeat
of the Japanese aggressors will not be far distant. Contrary to the
predictions of the Chinese and foreign reactionaries, the forces of
fascist aggression will undoubtedly be overthrown and the people's
democratic forces will undoubtedly triumph. The world will unques-

tionably take the road of progress and not the road of reaction. Of course, we must remain very much on the alert and reckon with the possibility of certain temporary or perhaps even serious twists and turns in the course of events; in many countries there are still strong reactionary forces which begrudge the people at home and abroad their unity, progress and liberation. Anyone who loses sight of this possibility will make political mistakes. The general trend of history, however, is already clearly decided and will not change. This is bad only for the fascists and for the reactionaries of all countries who are in fact their helpers, but it is a blessing for the people and for the organized democratic forces in all countries. The people, and the people alone, are the motive force of world history. The Soviet people have built up great strength and become the main force in the defeat of fascism. It is their efforts, plus those of the people in the other anti-fascist allied countries, which are making the destruction of fascism possible. War has educated the people and it is the people who will win the war, win the peace and win progress.

This new situation is very different from that in World War I. The Soviet Union was not yet in existence then and the people were not politically awakened as they are in many countries today. The two world wars represent two entirely different epochs.

This does not mean that there will be no more struggles after the defeat of the fascist aggressor countries, the end of World War II and the establishment of international peace. The remnant forces of fascism which are still widespread will certainly continue to make trouble, while within the camp now fighting fascist aggression there are forces which oppose democracy and oppress other nations, and they will continue to oppress the people in various countries and in the colonies and semi-colonies. Therefore, after international peace is established, there will still be numerous struggles over the greater part of the world — between the anti-fascist masses and the remnants of fascism, between democracy and anti-democracy, between national liberation and national oppression. The people will achieve the most extensive victory only through long and sustained efforts, when the remaining forces of fascism, the anti-democratic forces and all the imperialist forces are overcome. To be sure, that day will not come very quickly or easily, but come it surely will. Victory in the anti-fascist Second World War will pave the way for the victory of the people in their post-war struggles. A stable and lasting peace will be ensured only when victory is won in these struggles.

What is the present domestic situation?

China's protracted war has exacted and will continue to exact great sacrifices from the Chinese people, but at the same time this very war has tempered them. It has awakened and united the Chinese people to a greater degree than all their great struggles in the last hundred years. The Chinese people face not only a formidable national enemy but also powerful domestic reactionary forces which are in fact helping the enemy; this is one side of the picture. But the other side is that the Chinese people are not only more politically conscious than ever before but have built powerful Liberated Areas and a nation-wide democratic movement that is growing day by day. These constitute favourable domestic conditions. If the defeats and setbacks in the Chinese people's struggles of the last hundred years were due to the absence of certain necessary international and domestic conditions, then today the situation is different — all the necessary conditions are present. There is every possibility of avoiding defeat and winning victory. We shall be victorious if we can unite the whole people in resolute struggle and give them proper leadership.

The Chinese people now have much greater confidence that they can unite to defeat the aggressors and build a new China. The time has come for them to conquer all difficulties and achieve their fundamental demands, their great historic aspirations. Is there any doubt about it? I think not.

Such is the general international and domestic situation today.

III.   TWO LINES IN THE ANTI-JAPANESE WAR

THE KEY TO CHINA'S PROBLEMS

In speaking of the domestic situation, we have also to make a specific analysis of China's War of Resistance.

China is one of the five biggest countries taking part in the war against fascism and it is the principal country fighting the Japanese aggressors on the continent of Asia. Not only have the Chinese people played a very great role in the war against Japan, but they will also play a very great role in safeguarding peace in the post-war world and the decisive one in safeguarding peace in the East. China has made very great efforts to liberate herself and to help the allied countries during the eight years of the War of Resistance Against Japan. These efforts have been made primarily by the people of China. Vast numbers of officers and men in China's armies have fought and shed their blood at the front; the workers, peasants, intellectuals and industrialists of China have worked hard in the rear; the Chinese overseas have made donations to support the war; and all the anti-Japanese political parties, except for such of their members as are opposed to the people, have played their part in the war. In short, with their blood and sweat, the Chinese people have heroically fought the Japanese aggressors for eight long years. But for a number of years the Chinese reactionaries have been spreading rumours and misleading public opinion in order to prevent the world from knowing the truth about the role played by the Chinese people in the war. Besides, there has as yet been no comprehensive summing-up of the varied experience gained by China during these eight years of war. Therefore, this congress should make a proper summing-up of all this experience in order to educate the people and provide our Party with a basis for the formulation of policy.

When it comes to such summing up, it is plain to all that there are two different guiding lines in China. One leads to the defeat of the Japanese aggressors, while the other not only makes their defeat impossible but in some respects actually helps them and undermines our War of Resistance.

The Kuomintang government's policy of passive resistance to Japan and its reactionary domestic policy of active repression of the people have resulted in military setbacks, enormous territorial losses, financial and economic crisis, oppression and hardship for the people and the disruption of national unity. This reactionary policy has been an obstruction to mobilizing and uniting all the anti-Japanese forces of the Chinese people for the effective prosecution of the war, and has hindered the awakening and unity of the people. Yet this political awakening and this unity have never ceased to develop, but have moved forward along a tortuous course, under the twofold repression of the Japanese aggressors and the Kuomintang government. Clearly, there have been two lines in China for a long time, the Kuomintang government's line of oppression of the people and of passive resistance, and the Chinese people's line of enhancing their own consciousness and unity for the waging of a people's war. Herein lies the key to all China's problems.

HISTORY FOLLOWS A TORTUOUS COURSE

To help people understand why this question of the two lines is the key to all of China's problems, it is necessary to trace the history of our War of Resistance Against Japan.

The Chinese people's War of Resistance has followed a tortuous course. It began as far back as 1931. On September 18 of that year, the Japanese aggressors occupied Shenyang, and within a few months they seized the three northeastern provinces. The Kuomintang government adopted a policy of non-resistance. But against the will of the Kuomintang government and led or assisted by the Chinese Communist Party, the people and a patriotic section of the troops of these provinces organized the Anti-Japanese Volunteers and the Anti-Japanese United Army and engaged in heroic guerrilla warfare. At one time this heroic guerrilla warfare grew to great dimensions and, despite many difficulties and setbacks, it has never been put down by the enemy. When the Japanese aggressors attacked Shanghai in 1932, a group of patriots in the Kuomintang once again defied the will of the Kuomintang government and led the 19th Route Army in resisting the Japanese aggressors. In 1933 the Japanese aggressors invaded Jehol and Chahar Provinces, and for the third time a group of patriots in the Kuomintang defied the will of the Kuomintang government and co-operated with the Communist Party in organizing the Anti-Japanese Allied Army to resist the enemy. But in all this fighting against Japan support came entirely from the Chinese people, the Chinese Communist Party, other democratic groups and the patriotic Chinese overseas, while the Kuomintang government with its policy of non-resistance contributed nothing. On the contrary, the anti-Japanese actions in Shanghai and Chahar were both wrecked by the Kuomintang government itself. In 1933 it also destroyed the people's government which had been established in Fukien by the 19th Route Army.

Why did the Kuomintang government of that day adopt a policy of non-resistance? The main reason was that it had wrecked Kuomintang-Communist co-operation and the unity of the Chinese people in 1927.

In 1924 Dr. Sun Yat-sen, accepting the proposals of the Chinese Communist Party, called the First National Congress of the Kuomintang in which Communists took part, adopted the Three Great Policies of alliance with Russia, co-operation with the Communist Party and assistance to the peasants and workers, established the

Whampoa Military Academy and formed the national united front of the Kuomintang, the Communist Party and all sections of the people. As a result, the reactionary forces in Kwangtung Province were destroyed in 1924-25, the triumphant Northern Expedition was carried out during 1926-27, most of the areas along the Yangtse and Yellow Rivers were taken over, the Northern warlord government was defeated, and the people's struggle for liberation was unfolded on a scale never before seen in Chinese history. But at a critical moment in the progress of the Northern Expedition, in the late spring and early summer of 1927, the treacherous and reactionary policies of "party purge" and massacre adopted by the Kuomintang authorities wrecked this national united front — the united front of the Kuomintang, the Communist Party and all sections of the people, which embodied the Chinese people's cause of liberation — and all its revolutionary policies. Yesterday's allies, the Chinese Communist Party and the Chinese people, were now regarded as enemies, and yesterday's enemies, the imperialists and feudalists, were now regarded as allies. So it came about that a sudden attack was perfidiously launched against the Chinese Communist Party and the people, and the great, dynamic and vigorous revolution was crushed. Thereupon unity was replaced by civil war, democracy by dictatorship, and a China full of brightness by a China covered in darkness. But the Chinese Communist Party and the Chinese people were neither cowed nor conquered nor exterminated. They picked themselves up, wiped off the blood, buried their fallen comrades and went into battle again. Holding high the great standard of revolution, they rose in armed resistance and over a vast territory in China they set up people's governments, carried out land reform, built up a people's army — the Chinese Red Army — and preserved and expanded the revolutionary forces of the Chinese people. Dr. Sun Yat-sen's revolutionary Three People's Principles, which the Kuomintang reactionaries had discarded, were carried forward by the people, the Communist Party and other democrats.

After the invasion of the three northeastern provinces by the Japanese aggressors, the Chinese Communist Party in 1933 proposed to all the Kuomintang forces then attacking the revolutionary base areas and the Red Army that an armistice agreement be concluded to facilitate united resistance to Japan; this proposal was made with three conditions — that the attacks should stop, that the people should be granted democratic rights, and that the people should be armed. But the Kuomintang authorities rejected it.

From then on the Kuomintang government's policy of civil war became increasingly vicious, while the voice of the Chinese people grew increasingly powerful in its demand for an end to civil war and for united resistance to Japan. All kinds of popular patriotic organizations were formed in Shanghai and many other places. Between 1934 and 1936, under the leadership of the Central Committee of our Party, the main forces of the Red Army north and south of the Yangtse River went through untold hardships and moved to northwestern China, joining forces with the Red Army units there. It was in those two years that the Chinese Communist Party decided on, and carried out, a new and comprehensive political line in keeping with the new situation — the line of the National United Front Against Japan, with united resistance to Japan and the establishment of a new-democratic republic as the goal of struggle. On December 9, 1935, the student masses in Peiping launched a heroic patriotic movement under our Party's leadership; they formed the Chinese National Liberation Vanguard Corps[1] and spread this movement to all the big cities in China. On December 12, 1936, two patriotic Kuomintang groups which favoured resistance to Japan, the Northeastern Army and the 17th Route Army, together staged the famous Sian Incident in courageous opposition to the reactionary Kuomintang policy of compromising with Japan and massacring the people at home. Other patriots in the Kuomintang were likewise dissatisfied with the policy of the Kuomintang authorities at the time. These were the circumstances in which the Kuomintang authorities were forced to abandon their policy of civil war and to acknowledge the demands of the people. The peaceful settlement of the Sian Incident became the turning point; under the new circumstances internal co-operation took shape and the nation-wide War of Resistance Against Japan began. In May 1937, shortly before the Lukouchiao Incident,[2] our Party called the historic national conference at which the new political line followed by the Central Committee of the Party since 1935 was endorsed.

From the Lukouchiao Incident of July 7, 1937 to the fall of Wuhan in October 1938, the Kuomintang government was relatively active in the war against Japan. During that period the large-scale Japanese attacks and the mounting patriotic indignation of the whole people compelled the Kuomintang government to make resistance to the Japanese aggressors the centre of gravity of its policy, which made it easier to bring about an upsurge in the struggle of the whole army and people against Japan, and for a time there was a new and dynamic atmosphere. All the people, including the Communists and other democrats, earnestly hoped that the Kuomintang government would seize the opportunity, at a time when the nation was in peril and the people were filled with enthusiasm, to institute democratic reforms and put Dr. Sun Yat-sen's revolutionary Three People's Principles into practice. But their hopes came to nought. Even in those two years of relatively active resistance, the Kuomintang authorities continued to oppose the mobilization of the masses for a people's war and to place restrictions on the people's spontaneous efforts to unite for anti-Japanese and democratic action. While the Kuomintang government had somewhat changed its previous attitude to the Chinese Communist Party and the other anti-Japanese parties, it continued to deny them equal status and restrict their activities in many ways. Patriotic political prisoners were still kept in jail in large numbers. Above all, the Kuomintang government still maintained the oligarchic dictatorship it had established after launching the civil war in 1927, so that it was impossible to set up a democratic coalition government representing the unanimous will of the nation.

At the very beginning of this period we Communists pointed out that there were two alternative lines for China's War of Resistance Against Japan, an all-embracing people's war leading to victory, or a partial war in which the people remained oppressed, leading to defeat. We also pointed out that the war would be protracted and would inevitably involve many obstacles and hardships, but that by their exertions the Chinese people were sure to win the final victory.

THE PEOPLE'S WAR

During the same period the main forces of the Communist-led Red Army, which had moved to northwestern China, were redesignated as the Eighth Route Army of the Chinese National Revolutionary Army, while the Chinese Red Army's guerrilla units, which had remained in various places on both sides of the Yangtse River, were redesignated as the New Fourth Army of the Chinese National Revolutionary Army. The former went to fight on the northern China front and the latter on the central China front. During the civil war period, the Chinese Red Army, which had preserved and developed the democratic tradition of the Whampoa Military Academy and of the National Revolutionary Army of the Northern Expedition days, had at one time grown to several hundred thousand men. But by the

beginning of the War of Resistance Against Japan it had been reduced
to a few tens of thousands as a result of the ruthless destruction wrought
in our southern base areas by the Kuomintang government, our losses
during the Long March, and other causes. Consequently there were
some who looked down on this army and thought that the main
reliance for resistance to Japan should be placed on the Kuomintang.
But the people are the best judges. The people knew that despite
their small number at the time, the Eighth Route and New Fourth
Armies were of high quality, that they alone could wage a real people's war and that boundless prospects would open up before them
once they reached the anti-Japanese fronts and joined with the broad
masses there. And the people were right. By now, as I make this report,
our army has already expanded to 910,000 men, and the number of
our rural militia, who are not withdrawn from normal productive
work, has grown to more than 2,200,000. Despite the fact that our
regular army is still numerically much smaller than that of the Kuomintang (counting the Kuomintang units under local as well as central
control), it has already become the main force in China's War of
Resistance, judging by the number of Japanese and puppet forces it
is engaging and the extent of its battle fronts, by its combat effectiveness, by the mass support it enjoys in its operations, and by its political
quality, cohesion and unity.

This army is powerful because all its members have a discipline
based on political consciousness; they have come together and they
fight not for the private interests of a few individuals or a narrow
clique, but for the interests of the broad masses and of the whole nation.
The sole purpose of this army is to stand firmly with the Chinese
people and to serve them whole-heartedly.

Guided by this purpose, this army has an indomitable spirit and
is determined to vanquish all enemies and never to yield. No matter
what the difficulties and hardships, so long as a single man remains,
he will fight on.

Guided by this purpose, this army has achieved remarkable unity
in its own ranks and with those outside its ranks. Internally, there is
unity between officers and men, between the higher and lower ranks,
and between military work, political work and rear service work;
and externally, there is unity between the army and the people,
between the army and government organizations, and between our
army and the friendly armies. It is imperative to overcome anything
that impairs this unity.

Guided by this purpose, this army has a correct policy for winning over enemy officers and men and for dealing with prisoners of war. Without exception all members of the enemy forces who surrender, who come over to our side or who, after laying down their arms, wish to join in fighting the common foe, are welcomed and given proper education. It is forbidden to kill, maltreat or insult any prisoner of war.

Guided by this purpose, this army has built up a system of strategy and tactics which is essential for the people's war. It is skilled in flexible guerrilla warfare conducted in accordance with the changing concrete conditions and is also skilled in mobile warfare.

Guided by this purpose, this army has built up a system of political work which is essential for the people's war and is aimed at promoting unity in its own ranks, unity with the friendly armies and unity with the people, and at disintegrating the enemy forces and ensuring victory in battle.

Guided by this purpose, the entire army, operating under conditions of guerrilla warfare, is able to utilize, and has in fact utilized, the intervals between battles and between training periods to produce grain and other necessities, thus becoming wholly, half or at least partly self-supporting, so that economic difficulties are overcome, living conditions improved and the burden on the people lightened. Every possibility has been exploited to establish a number of small-scale armament works in various military base areas.

Furthermore, this army is powerful because it has the people's self-defence corps and the militia — the vast armed organizations of the masses — fighting in co-ordination with it. In the Liberated Areas of China all men and women, from youth to middle age, are organized in the people's anti-Japanese self-defence corps on a voluntary and democratic basis and without giving up their work in production. The cream of the self-defence corps, except for those who join the army or the guerrilla units, is brought into the militia. Without the co-operation of these armed forces of the masses it would be impossible to defeat the enemy.

Finally, this army is powerful because of its division into two parts, the main forces and the regional forces, with the former available for operations in any region whenever necessary and the latter concentrating on defending their own localities and attacking the enemy there in co-operation with the local militia and the self-defence corps. This division of labour has won the whole-hearted support of the people. Without this correct division of labour — if, for example, attention were paid only to the role of the main forces while that of the regional forces were neglected — it would likewise be impossible to defeat the enemy in the conditions obtaining in China's Liberated Areas. Under the regional forces, numerous armed working teams have been organized, which are well trained and hence better qualified for military, political and mass work; they penetrate into the rearmost areas behind the enemy lines, strike at the enemy and arouse the masses to anti-Japanese struggle, thus giving support to the frontal military operations of the various Liberated Areas. In all this they have achieved great success.

Under the leadership of their democratic governments, all the anti-Japanese people in the Liberated Areas of China are called upon to join organizations of workers, peasants, youth and women, and cultural, professional and other organizations, which will wholeheartedly perform various tasks in support of the armed forces. These tasks are not limited to rallying the people to join the army, transporting grain for it, caring for soldiers' families and helping the troops in meeting their material needs. They also include mobilizing the guerrilla units, militia and self-defence corps to make widespread raids and lay land mines against the enemy, gather intelligence about him, comb out traitors and spies, transport and protect the wounded and take direct part in the army's operations. At the same time, the people in all the Liberated Areas are enthusiastically taking up various kinds of political, economic, cultural and health work. The most important thing in this connection is to mobilize everybody for the production of grain and other necessities and to ensure that all government institutions and schools, except in special cases, devote their free time to production for their own support in order to supplement the self-sufficiency production campaigns of the army and the people and thus help to create a great upsurge of production to sustain the protracted War of Resistance. In China's Liberated Areas, the enemy has wrought great havoc, and floods, droughts and damage by insect pests have been frequent. However, the democratic governments there have been leading the people in overcoming these difficulties in an organized way, and unprecedented results have been achieved by the great mass campaigns for pest extermination, flood control and disaster relief, thus making it possible to persevere in the protracted War of Resistance. In a word, everything for the front, everything for the defeat of the Japanese aggressors and for the liberation of the Chinese people — this is the general slogan, the general policy for the whole army and the whole people in the Liberated Areas of China.

Such is a real people's war. Only by waging such a people's war can we defeat the national enemy. The Kuomintang has failed precisely because of its desperate opposition to a people's war.

Once it is equipped with modern weapons, the army of China's Liberated Areas will become still more powerful and will be able to accomplish the final defeat of the Japanese aggressors.

TWO BATTLE FRONTS

From the very beginning there have been two fronts in China's War of Resistance, the Kuomintang front and the front of the Liberated Areas.

After the fall of Wuhan in October 1938, the Japanese aggressors stopped their strategic offensive against the Kuomintang front and gradually shifted their main forces to the front of the Liberated Areas; at the same time, taking advantage of the defeatist sentiments of the Kuomintang government, they declared their willingness to arrive at a compromise peace with it, and, adopting a policy designed to deceive the Chinese nation, they induced the traitor Wang Ching-wei to leave Chungking and establish a puppet government in Nanking. The Kuomintang government then began to change its policy, gradually shifting the emphasis from resistance to Japan to opposition to the Communist Party and the people. This shift first made itself apparent in the military sphere. To conserve its own military strength, the Kuomintang government adopted the policy of passive resistance to Japan; it threw the burden of fighting onto the front of the Liberated Areas by letting the Japanese invaders attack the Liberated Areas in force, while itself "sitting on top of the mountain to watch the tigers fight".

In 1939, the Kuomintang government adopted the reactionary "Measures for Restricting the Activities of Alien Parties" and completely deprived the people and the anti-Japanese parties of whatever rights they had won during the early period of the War of Resistance. From then on, in the Kuomintang areas, all the democratic parties, and first and foremost the Communist Party of China, have been driven underground by the Kuomintang government. In every province in these areas the prisons and concentration camps are packed with Communists, young patriots and other fighters for democracy. In the five years from 1939 to the autumn of 1943, the Kuomintang government launched three large-scale anti-Communist onslaughts[3] to split national unity, and thus created serious danger of civil war. It was in this period that the "disbanding" of the New Fourth Army was ordered and more than nine thousand of its troops in southern Anhwei were annihilated — an event which shocked the world. To this very moment the attacks by Kuomintang troops on the forces of the Liberated Areas have not ceased, nor is there any sign that they will. At the same time, the Kuomintang reactionaries have been pouring out slanders and calumnies of all sorts. It is they who have fabricated such labels and expressions as "traitor party", "traitor army", "traitor areas", and "sabotaging the War of Resistance and endangering the state", for the purpose of maligning the Communist Party, the Eighth Route and New Fourth Armies and the Liberated Areas. To meet the crisis, on July 7, 1939 the Central Committee of the Chinese Communist Party issued a manifesto setting forth the following slogans, "Persist in resistance and oppose capitulation! Persist in unity and oppose a split! Persist in progress and oppose retrogression!" In these five years, our Party, acting on these timely slogans, vigorously repulsed the three reactionary and anti-popular anti-Communist onslaughts and overcame the crisis on each occasion.

There was actually no serious fighting on the Kuomintang front during those years. The sword-edge of Japanese aggression was mainly directed against the Liberated Areas. By 1943, the army and the people of the Liberated Areas were pinning down 64 per cent of the Japanese forces invading China and 95 per cent of the puppet troops, while the Kuomintang front faced only 36 per cent of the former and 5 per cent of the latter.

In 1944 the Japanese aggressors launched operations to force China's north-south trunk railways open for through traffic;[4] panic-stricken, the Kuomintang forces were totally incapable of offering resistance. Within a few months extensive areas in Honan, Hunan, Kwangsi and Kwangtung Provinces had fallen into the enemy's hands. It was not until then that some change took place in the proportion of enemy forces engaged on the two fronts. Even so, at the moment of making this report, of the 40 divisions comprising 580,000 Japanese soldiers in China (not counting those in the three northeastern provinces), $22^{1}/_{2}$ divisions, comprising 320,000 men or 56 per cent of the total forces, are engaged on the front of the Liberated Areas, and no more than $17^{1}/_{2}$ divisions, comprising 260,000 men or 44 per cent, are engaged on the Kuomintang front. As for the puppet troops engaged on the two fronts, the ratio has not changed at all.

It should also be pointed out that the puppet troops, numbering more than 800,000 men (in both the regular and the local forces), are chiefly composed either of units that surrendered under their Kuomintang commanders or of units organized by the Kuomintang officers after their surrender. The Kuomintang reactionaries have furnished these puppet troops in advance with a false and traitorous theory, namely, "saving the nation by a devious path", and have given them moral and organizational support since their surrender, directing them to attack the Chinese people's Liberated Areas in co-ordination with the Japanese aggressors. These reactionaries have also mustered large forces, totalling no less than 797,000 men, to blockade and attack the Shensi-Kansu-Ningsia Border Region and other Liberated Areas. This grave situation is being kept from the knowledge of many Chinese and foreigners by the Kuomintang government's policy of suppressing news.

CHINA'S LIBERATED AREAS

China's Liberated Areas, led by the Communist Party, now have a population of 95,500,000. They exist from Inner Mongolia in the north to Hainan Island in the south; almost everywhere the enemy goes, he finds the Eighth Route Army, the New Fourth Army or some other people's forces in operation. This vast liberated territory consists of nineteen major Liberated Areas, covering greater or lesser parts of the provinces of Liaoning, Jehol, Chahar, Suiyuan, Shensi, Kansu, Ningsia, Shansi, Hopei, Honan, Shantung, Kiangsu, Chekiang, Anhwei, Kiangsi, Hupeh, Hunan, Kwangtung and Fukien. Yenan is the centre from which guidance is given to all these Liberated Areas. The Shensi-Kansu-Ningsia Border Region west of the Yellow River, with a population of only 1,500,000, is but one of the nineteen areas forming this vast liberated part of China and, indeed, the smallest in population except for one in eastern Chekiang Province and another on Hainan Island. Unaware of this, some people think China's liberated territory consists chiefly of the Shensi-Kansu-Ningsia Border Region. This misconception arises from the Kuomintang government's blockade. In every one of the Liberated Areas, all the requisite policies of the Anti-Japanese National United Front have been put into practice, and popularly elected governments, that is, local coalition governments, have been or are being set up, in which Communists and representative personalities of other anti-Japanese parties or without any party affiliation are co-operating. The entire strength of the people has been mobilized in the Liberated Areas. As a result, despite the formidable pressure of the enemy, the Kuomintang's military blockade and attacks and the complete absence of outside help, China's Liberated Areas have stood firm and have grown steadily, reducing the territory occupied by the enemy and extending their own; they have become the model for a democratic China and the main force driving out the Japanese aggressors and liberating the Chinese people in military co-operation with the allied countries. The armed forces of China's Liberated Areas, the Eighth Route Army, the New Fourth Army and the other armed forces of the people, have not only set a heroic example in fighting Japan, but have also set an example in carrying out the democratic policies of the Anti-Japanese National United Front. The declaration issued by the Central Committee of the Communist Party of China on September 22, 1937 affirming that "Dr. Sun Yat-sen's Three People's Principles being what China needs today, our Party is ready to fight for their complete realization", has been completely carried into effect in China's Liberated Areas.

THE KUOMINTANG AREAS

Persisting in its dictatorial rule, the chief ruling clique of the Kuo-mintang has followed a policy of passive resistance to Japan and a domestic policy directed against the people. In consequence, its armed forces have shrunk to less than half their original size and most of them have virtually lost their combat effectiveness; there is a profound rift between this clique and the broad masses and a grave crisis of mass impoverishment, seething discontent and widespread revolt; not only has its role in the war been sharply reduced, but it has also become an obstacle to the mobilization and unity of all the anti-Japanese forces of the Chinese people.

Why has such a grave situation arisen under the leadership of the Kuomintang's chief ruling clique? It has arisen because that clique represents the interests of China's big landlords, big bankers and big compradors. The handful of people forming this reactionary stratum monopolize all the important military, political, economic and cultural organizations under the Kuomintang government. They place the safe-guarding of their own interests above resistance to Japan. They too say "the nation above all", but their actions do not accord with the demands of the great majority of the nation. They too say "the state above all", but what they mean is the feudal-fascist dictatorship of the big landlords, big bankers and big compradors, and not a democratic state of the people. Therefore they are afraid of the rise of the people, afraid of the democratic movement and afraid of full mass mobilization for war against Japan. Herein lies the root cause of their policy of passive resistance to Japan and their reactionary domestic policy against the people, democracy and the Communist Party. They have a double-faced policy in everything. For instance, on the one hand they are resisting Japan but on the other they are pursuing a passive war policy, and moreover they are the constant target of Japanese inducements to surrender. They talk about developing China's economy, but in fact they build up their own bureaucrat-capital, *i.e.*, the capital of the big landlords, bankers and compradors, and monopolize the lifelines of China's economy, ruthlessly oppressing the peasants, the workers, the petty bourgeoisie and the non-monopoly bourgeoisie. They talk about putting "democracy" into practice and "handing state power back to the people", yet they ruthlessly suppress the people's movement for democracy and refuse to introduce the mildest democratic reform. They say that "the Communist problem is a political one and should be solved politically", yet they ruthlessly suppress the Chinese Communist Party militarily, politically and economically, regarding it as "enemy No. 1" and the Japanese aggressors as only "enemy No. 2", and day in and day out they busy themselves with preparations for a civil war and plots to annihilate the Communist Party. They say they will establish a "modern state", yet they work desperately to maintain the feudal-fascist dictatorship of the big landlords, bankers and compradors. While maintaining formal diplomatic relations with the Soviet Union, they are in fact hostile to it. They chant "Asia before Europe" in chorus with the U.S. isolationists in order to prolong the life of fascist Germany, which amounts to prolonging the life of fascists everywhere, including their own fascist rule over the Chinese people, yet at the same time they indulge in diplomatic manoeuvres, masquerading as anti-fascist heroes. If you look for the root of these contradictory double-faced policies, you will find they all stem from the social stratum of the big landlords, bankers and compradors.

Nevertheless, the Kuomintang is not a homogeneous political party. Though it is controlled and led by the reactionary clique representing the stratum of the big landlords, bankers and compradors, it must not be entirely identified with this clique. Some Kuomintang leaders do not belong to this clique by which they are even slighted, pushed aside or attacked. Many of its cadres and rank and file and many members of the Three People's Principles Youth League are dissatisfied with the leadership of this clique, and some even oppose it. The same is true of all the Kuomintang armies, government organs and economic and cultural institutions which this reactionary clique controls. There are quite a number of democratic elements in all of them. Moreover, the reactionary clique itself, divided as it is into several contending factions, is not a close-knit body. Undoubtedly it is wrong to regard the Kuomintang as a homogeneous body of reactionaries.

A CONTRAST

The Chinese people have come to see the sharp contrast between the Liberated Areas and the Kuomintang areas.

Are not the facts clear enough? Here are two lines, the line of a people's war and the line of passive resistance, which is against a people's war; one leads to victory even in the difficult conditions in China's Liberated Areas with their total lack of outside aid, and the other leads to defeat even in the extremely favourable conditions in the Kuomintang areas with foreign aid available.

The Kuomintang government attributes its failures to lack of arms. Yet one may ask, which of the two are short of arms, the Kuomintang troops or the troops of the Liberated Areas? Of all China's forces, those of the Liberated Areas lack arms most acutely, their only weapons being those they capture from the enemy or manufacture under the most adverse conditions.

Is it not true that the forces directly under the Kuomintang central government are far better armed than the provincial troops? Yet in combat effectiveness most of the central forces are inferior to the provincial troops.

The Kuomintang commands vast reserves of manpower, yet its wrong recruiting policy makes manpower replenishment very difficult. Though cut off from each other by the enemy and engaged in constant fighting, China's Liberated Areas are able to mobilize inexhaustible manpower because the militia and self-defence corps system, which is well-adapted to the needs of the people, is applied everywhere, and because misuse and waste of manpower are avoided.

Although the Kuomintang controls vast areas abounding in grain and the people supply it with 70-100 million *tan* annually, its army is always short of food and its soldiers are emaciated because the greater part of the grain is embezzled by those through whose hands it passes. But although most of China's Liberated Areas, which are located in the enemy rear, have been devastated by the enemy's policy of "burn all, kill all, loot all", and although some regions like northern Shensi are very arid, we have successfully solved the grain problem through our own efforts by increasing agricultural production.

The Kuomintang areas are facing a very grave economic crisis; most industries are bankrupt, and even such necessities as cloth have to be imported from the United States. But China's Liberated Areas are able to meet their own needs in cloth and other necessities through the development of industry.

In the Kuomintang areas, the workers, peasants, shop assistants, government employees, intellectuals and cultural workers live in extreme misery. In the Liberated Areas all the people have food, clothing and work.

It is characteristic of the Kuomintang areas that, exploiting the national crisis for profiteering purposes, officials have concurrently become traders and habitual grafters without any sense of shame or decency. It is characteristic of China's Liberated Areas that, setting an example of plain living and hard work, the cadres take part in production in addition to their regular duties; honesty is held in high esteem while graft is strictly prohibited.

In the Kuomintang areas the people have no freedom at all. In China's Liberated Areas the people have full freedom.

Who is to blame for all the anomalies which confront the Kuomintang rulers? Are others to blame, or they themselves? Are foreign countries to blame for not giving them enough aid, or are the Kuomintang government's dictatorial rule, corruption and incompetence to blame? Isn't the answer obvious?

WHO IS "SABOTAGING THE WAR OF RESISTANCE AND ENDANGERING THE STATE"?

In the light of the indisputable evidence, is it not the Kuomintang government itself that has been sabotaging the Chinese people's War of Resistance and endangering our country? For fully ten years that government devoted itself wholly to civil war, turning the edge of its sword against the people while utterly neglecting national defence, and by its policy of non-resistance it gave away the four northeastern provinces. When the Japanese aggressors drove south of the Great

Wall, it put up a flurry of resistance and then retreated from Lukouchiao all the way to the province of Kweichow. Yet the Kuomintang
alleges that "the Communist Party is sabotaging the War of Resistance
and endangering the state" (see resolutions of the Eleventh Plenary
Session of the Central Executive Committee of the Kuomintang, held
in September 1943). Its only evidence is that the Communist Party has
united with all sections of the people to create the Liberated Areas
which are heroically resisting Japan. The logic of the Kuomintang is
so different from that of the Chinese people that the failure to arrive
at a common language on many problems is not to be wondered at.

Here are two questions.

First, what exactly has made the Kuomintang government abandon
so vast and so well populated a territory, stretching from Heilungkiang
Province to Lukouchiao and from Lukouchiao to Kweichow? Can
it be anything other than its policy first of non-resistance and then
of passive resistance to Japan, and its domestic policy of opposing
the people?

Second, what exactly has enabled China's Liberated Areas to
smash the ruthless and prolonged attacks of the Japanese and puppet
forces, to recover such vast territories and liberate such an immense
population from the grip of the national enemy? Can it be anything
other than our correct line, the line of a people's war?

"DISOBEDIENCE TO GOVERNMENTAL AND MILITARY ORDERS"

The Kuomintang government also constantly accuses the Chinese
Communist Party of "disobedience to governmental and military
orders". All we need say is that fortunately the Chinese Communists,
sharing the common sense of the Chinese people, have not obeyed
such "governmental and military orders" as in fact would have meant
handing over to the Japanese aggressors the Liberated Areas which
the Chinese people had recaptured from them amid great difficulties
and hardships. Some examples are the "Measures for Restricting the
Activities of Alien Parties" in 1939, the orders for the "disbandment
of the New Fourth Army" and for its "withdrawal north of the old
course of the Yellow River" in 1941, the order for the "dissolution of
the Communist Party of China" in 1943, the order for us to "disband
all the troops except for ten divisions within a definite time limit"
in 1944, and the proposal which the Kuomintang government called
"a concession" in the recent talks with us and which would require us

to hand over our armed forces and local governments in exchange for a few posts in its dictatorial government, but without the formation of a coalition government. Fortunately we have not submitted to this sort of thing and have thus preserved an undefiled stretch of soil and a heroic anti-Japanese army for the Chinese people. Should not the Chinese people congratulate themselves on such "disobedience"? Does not the Kuomintang government feel it has done enough after presenting the Japanese aggressors with the vast populated area from Heilungkiang to Kweichow through its own fascist government decrees and defeatist military orders? The Japanese aggressors and the reactionaries welcome these "governmental and military orders", but can such things be welcomed by any upright Chinese patriot? Unless there is a coalition government, not in form but in fact, not a fascist dictatorship but a democratic government, is it conceivable that the Chinese people would permit the Chinese Communists to hand over the Liberated Areas where the people have won freedom as well as the people's armies that have performed signal service in the War of Resistance to the present Kuomintang government, which is defeatist, fascist and dictatorial? Without the Liberated Areas and the people's army, could the anti-Japanese cause of the Chinese people be what it is today? And can one possibly conceive what the future of the Chinese nation would be?

THE DANGER OF CIVIL WAR

To this day the chief ruling clique in the Kuomintang is persisting in its reactionary policy of dictatorship and civil war. There are many signs that it has long been making, and is now stepping up, preparations to unleash civil war as soon as the forces of a certain allied country have cleared a considerable part of the Chinese mainland of the Japanese aggressors. It also hopes that the generals of certain allied countries will do the same job in China as the British General Scobie[5] has been doing in Greece. It applauds the butchery perpetrated by Scobie and the reactionary Greek government. It is planning to plunge China once again into the maelstrom of civil war, as in 1927-37. Behind the smokescreen of "convening the national assembly" and "political settlement", it is secretly preparing civil war. If our fellow-countrymen fail to take note, fail to expose its schemes and put a stop to these preparations, then one fine morning they will hear the cannonade of civil war.

NEGOTIATIONS

After obtaining the consent of other democratic parties, the Communist Party of China put forward the demand at the People's Political Council in September 1944 that the Kuomintang one-party dictatorship be abolished immediately and a democratic coalition government be formed for the purpose of defeating the Japanese aggressors, building a new China and preventing civil war. This was undoubtedly a timely demand, and in the space of a few months it has won the warm response of the broad masses.

We have had many rounds of negotiations with the Kuomintang government on the question of abolishing the one-party dictatorship, forming a coalition government and instituting essential democratic reforms, but it has rejected all our proposals. Not only is the Kuomintang unwilling to abolish the one-party dictatorship and form a coalition government, it is unwilling to introduce a single one of the urgently needed democratic reforms, such as the abolition of the secret police, the annulment of the reactionary laws and decrees that suppress the people's freedom, the release of political prisoners, recognition of the legal status of the political parties, recognition of the Liberated Areas and the withdrawal of the armies blockading and attacking them. Consequently political relations in China have become very strained.

TWO PROSPECTS

In the light of the situation as a whole and of the above analysis of the actual international and domestic state of affairs, I would ask everyone here to be on the alert and not to expect that our cause will proceed smoothly and easily. No, it will not. Actually there are two possibilities, two prospects, one good and one bad. One possibility or prospect is that the fascist dictatorship will continue and democratic reforms will not be allowed, that the stress will be on opposing the people instead of the Japanese aggressors, and even that civil war may break out after the Japanese aggressors are defeated, dragging China back into her old miserable state, without independence, freedom, democracy, unity, prosperity or strength. This possibility or prospect is still there, and it has not ceased to exist or has not automatically vanished simply because of the favourable international situation and the increased political consciousness and organized strength of our people. Those who hope that this possibility or prospect will become a reality in China are the reactionary clique within the

Kuomintang at home and the imperialist-minded reactionaries abroad. This is one aspect which must be taken into account.

But there is another aspect and, again in the light of the situation as a whole and the foregoing analysis of the international and domestic state of affairs, we can gain added confidence and courage in striving for the second possibility or prospect. It is that of overcoming all difficulties, uniting the whole people, abolishing the Kuomintang's fascist dictatorship, carrying out democratic reforms, consolidating and expanding the anti-Japanese forces, thoroughly defeating the Japanese aggressors and building an independent, free, democratic, united, prosperous and powerful new China. Those who hope that this possibility or prospect will become a reality in China are the masses, the Communist Party and the other democratic parties at home, and all the nations that treat us as equals and the progressives and the masses abroad.

We know full well that we Communists together with the whole Chinese people still face great difficulties and many obstacles and have a long and tortuous road to travel. But we know equally well that, together with the whole Chinese people, we shall overcome all the difficulties and obstacles and accomplish the task which history has entrusted China. The great task for us and for the whole people is to avert the first possibility or prospect and work for the second with every ounce of our energy. Essentially the international and domestic situation favours us Communists together with the Chinese people as a whole. This I have already made quite clear. We hope that the Kuomintang authorities will have the courage to change their present wrong policies in view of the general world trend and the popular feeling in China, so that the war can be won, the sufferings of the Chinese people can be reduced and a new China can soon be brought into being. It must be understood that, however tortuous the road, the Chinese people will certainly accomplish the task of achieving independence and liberation, and that the time has come for them to do so. It falls to our generation to fulfil the great aspirations cherished by countless martyrs in the past century, and any attempt to stop us will undoubtedly end in failure.

IV. THE POLICY OF THE CHINESE COMMUNIST PARTY

I have analysed the two lines in China's War of Resistance. Such an analysis is absolutely necessary. For up to this very moment many

Chinese people still do not know what is really going on in this war. Many people in the Kuomintang areas and in foreign countries are being kept in the dark by the Kuomintang government's policy of blockade. They knew practically nothing about China's Liberated Areas until a group of Chinese and foreign correspondents came here in 1944 on a tour of observation. As soon as this group returned, the Kuomintang government, which was very much afraid of the true situation in the Liberated Areas becoming known outside, bolted the door and refused to let any other correspondent come here. Similarly it has suppressed the truth about the Kuomintang areas. Therefore I feel that we have the duty to give the public as much of the true picture of "the two areas" as possible. Only when people see the whole situation in China clearly will they understand why there is such a difference in policy between the Communist Party and the Kuomintang, the two biggest political parties in China, and why there is such a struggle between the two lines. Only then will people understand that the dispute between the two parties is not an unnecessary or unimportant or merely captious dispute, as some have alleged, but is one of principle on which the lives of hundreds of millions of people depend.

In China's present grave situation, the people, the democrats and democratic parties at home and the people in other countries who are concerned about the Chinese situation all hope that unity will replace disunity and that democratic reforms will be introduced, and they all want to know what the policy of the Chinese Communist Party is for solving the many vital problems of today. The members of our Party, of course, have a still deeper interest in these matters.

Our policies of the Anti-Japanese National United Front in the war have always been clear and definite, and they have been tested in the eight years of war. Our congress should draw conclusions from them as a guide for our future struggles.

Here I shall explain a number of the definite conclusions arrived at by our Party concerning the major policies for solving China's problems.

OUR GENERAL PROGRAMME

An agreed common programme is urgently needed by the Chinese people, the Chinese Communist Party and all the anti-Japanese democratic parties for the purpose of mobilizing and uniting all the anti-Japanese forces of the Chinese people, completely wiping out the

Japanese aggressors and building a new China that is independent, free, democratic, united, prosperous and powerful.

Such a common programme may be divided into two parts, the general and the specific. Let us consider first the general and then the specific programme.

On the major premise that the Japanese aggressors must be completely destroyed and a new China must be built, we Communists and the overwhelming majority of the population are agreed on the following fundamental propositions at the present stage of China's development. First, China should not have a feudal, fascist and anti-popular state system under the dictatorship of the big landlords and big bourgeoisie, because eighteen years of government by the chief ruling clique of the Kuomintang have already proved its complete bankruptcy. Second, China cannot possibly establish the old type of democratic dictatorship — a purely national-bourgeois state — and therefore should not attempt to do so, because on the one hand the Chinese national bourgeoisie has proved itself very flabby economically and politically, and on the other, for a long time now a new factor has been present, namely, the awakened Chinese proletariat with its leader, the Chinese Communist Party, which has demonstrated great capacity in the political arena and assumed leadership of the peasant masses, the urban petty bourgeoisie, the intelligentsia and other democratic forces. Third, it is likewise impossible for the Chinese people to institute a socialist state system at the present stage when it is still their task to fight foreign and feudal oppression and the necessary social and economic conditions for a socialist state are still lacking.

What then do we propose? We propose the establishment, after the thorough defeat of the Japanese aggressors, of a state system which we call New Democracy, namely, a united-front democratic alliance based on the overwhelming majority of the people, under the leadership of the working class.

It is this kind of state system that truly meets the demands of the overwhelming majority of the Chinese population, because it can win and indeed has been winning the approval, first, of millions of industrial workers and tens of millions of handicraftsmen and farm labourers, second, of the peasantry, which constitutes 80 per cent of China's population, i.e., 360 million out of a population of 450 million, and third, of the large numbers of the urban petty bourgeoisie as well as the national bourgeoisie, the enlightened gentry and other patriots.

Of course, there are still contradictions among these classes, notably the contradiction between labour and capital, and consequently each has its own particular demands. It would be hypocritical and wrong to deny the existence of these contradictions and differing demands. But throughout the stage of New Democracy, these contradictions, these differing demands, will not grow and transcend the demands which all have in common and should not be allowed to do so; they can be adjusted. Given such adjustment, these classes can together accomplish the political, economic and cultural tasks of the new-democratic state.

The politics of New Democracy which we advocate consists in the overthrow of external oppression and of internal feudal and fascist oppression, and then the setting up not of the old type of democracy but of a political system which is a united front of all the democratic classes. These views of ours are completely in accord with the revolutionary views of Dr. Sun Yat-sen. In the Manifesto of the First National Congress of the Kuomintang, Dr. Sun wrote:

> The so-called democratic system in modern states is usually monopolized by the bourgeoisie and has become simply an instrument for oppressing the common people. On the other hand, the Kuomintang's Principle of Democracy means a democratic system shared by all the common people and not privately owned by the few.

This is a great political injunction of Dr. Sun's. The Chinese people, the Chinese Communist Party and all other democrats must respect it, firmly put it into practice and wage a determined fight against all individuals and groups that violate or oppose it, and so defend and develop this perfectly correct political principle of New Democracy.

The organizational principle of the new-democratic state should be democratic centralism, with the people's congresses determining the major policies and electing the governments at the various levels. It is at once democratic and centralized, that is, centralized on the basis of democracy and democratic under centralized guidance. This is the only system that can give full expression to democracy with full powers vested in the people's congresses at all levels and, at the same time, guarantee centralized administration with the governments at each level exercising centralized management of all the affairs entrusted to them by the people's congresses at the corresponding level and safeguarding whatever is essential to the democratic life of the people.

The army and the other armed forces constitute an important part of the apparatus of the new-democratic state power, without which the state cannot be defended. As with all other organs of power, the armed forces of the new-democratic state belong to the people and protect the people; they have nothing in common with the army, police, etc. of the old type which belong to the few and oppress the people.

The economy of New Democracy which we advocate is likewise in accord with Dr. Sun's principles. On the land question, Dr. Sun championed "land to the tiller". On the question of industry and commerce, Dr. Sun stated in the Manifesto quoted above:

> Enterprises, such as banks, railways and airlines, whether Chinese-owned or foreign-owned, which are either monopolistic in character or too big for private management, shall be operated and administered by the state, so that private capital cannot dominate the livelihood of the people: this is the main principle of the regulation of capital.

In the present stage, we fully agree with these views of Dr. Sun's on economic questions.

Some people suspect that the Chinese Communists are opposed to the development of individual initiative, the growth of private capital and the protection of private property, but they are mistaken. It is foreign oppression and feudal oppression that cruelly fetter the development of the individual initiative of the Chinese people, hamper the growth of private capital and destroy the property of the people. It is the very task of the New Democracy we advocate to remove these fetters and stop this destruction, to guarantee that the people can freely develop their individuality within the framework of society and freely develop such private capitalist economy as will benefit and not "dominate the livelihood of the people", and to protect all appropriate forms of private property.

In accordance with Dr. Sun's principles and the experience of the Chinese revolution, China's national economy at the present stage should be composed of the state sector, the private sector and the co-operative sector. But the state here must certainly not be one "privately owned by the few", but a new-democratic state "shared by all the common people" under the leadership of the proletariat.

The culture of New Democracy should likewise be "shared by all the common people", that is, it should be a national, scientific and mass culture, and must under no circumstances be a culture "privately owned by the few".

Such is the general or fundamental programme which we Communists advocate for the present stage, the entire stage of the bourgeois-democratic revolution. This is our minimum programme as against our future or maximum programme of socialism and communism. Its realization will carry the Chinese state and Chinese society a step forward, from a colonial, semi-colonial and semi-feudal to a new-democratic state and society.

The political leadership of the proletariat and the proletarian-led state and co-operative sectors of the economy required by our programme are socialist factors. Yet the fulfilment of this programme will not turn China into a socialist society.

We Communists do not conceal our political views. Definitely and beyond all doubt, our future or maximum programme is to carry China forward to socialism and communism. Both the name of our Party and our Marxist world outlook unequivocally point to this supreme ideal of the future, a future of incomparable brightness and splendour. On joining the Party, every Communist has two clearly-defined objectives at heart, the new-democratic revolution now and socialism and communism in the future, and for these he will fight despite the animosity of the enemies of communism and their vulgar and ignorant calumny, abuse and ridicule, which we must firmly combat. As for the well-meaning sceptics, we should explain things to them with goodwill and patience and not attack them. All this is very clear, definite and unequivocal.

But all Communists and sympathizers with communism in China must struggle to achieve the objective of the present stage; they must struggle against foreign and feudal oppression to deliver the Chinese people from their miserable colonial, semi-colonial and semi-feudal plight and establish a proletarian-led new-democratic China whose main task is the liberation of the peasantry, a China of the revolutionary Three People's Principles of Dr. Sun Yat-sen, a China which is independent, free, democratic, united, prosperous and powerful. This is what we have actually been doing. Together with the masses of the Chinese people, we Communists have been fighting heroically for this objective for the past twenty-four years.

If any Communist or Communist sympathizer talks about socialism and communism but fails to fight for this objective, if he belittles this bourgeois-democratic revolution, relaxes or slows down ever so slightly and shows the least disloyalty and coolness or is reluctant to shed his blood or give his life for it, then wittingly or unwittingly, such a person is betraying socialism and communism to a greater or lesser extent and is certainly not a politically conscious and staunch fighter for communism. It is a law of Marxism that socialism can be attained only via the stage of democracy. And in China the fight for democracy is a protracted one. It would be a sheer illusion to try to build a socialist society on the ruins of the colonial, semi-colonial and semi-feudal order without a united new-democratic state, without the development of the state sector of the new-democratic economy, of the private capitalist and the co-operative sectors, and of a national, scientific and mass culture, *i.e.*, a new-democratic culture, and without the liberation and the development of the individuality of hundreds of millions of people — in short, without a thoroughgoing bourgeois-democratic revolution of a new type led by the Communist Party.

Some people fail to understand why, so far from fearing capitalism, Communists should advocate its development in certain given conditions. Our answer is simple. The substitution of a certain degree of capitalist development for the oppression of foreign imperialism and domestic feudalism is not only an advance but an unavoidable process. It benefits the proletariat as well as the bourgeoisie, and the former perhaps more. It is not domestic capitalism but foreign imperialism and domestic feudalism which are superfluous in China today; indeed, we have too little of capitalism. Strangely enough, some spokesmen of the Chinese bourgeoisie fight shy of openly advocating the development of capitalism, but refer to it obliquely. There are other people who flatly deny that China should permit a necessary degree of capitalist development and who talk about reaching socialism in one stride and "accomplishing at one stroke" the tasks of the Three People's Principles and socialism. Obviously, these opinions either reflect the weakness of the Chinese national bourgeoisie or are a demagogic trick on the part of the big landlords and the big bourgeoisie. From our knowledge of the Marxist laws of social development, we Communists clearly understand that under the state system of New Democracy in China it will be necessary in the interests of social progress to facilitate the development of the private capitalist sector of the economy (provided it does not dominate the livelihood of the people) besides the development of the state sector and of the individual and co-operative sectors run by the labouring people. We Communists will not let empty talk or deceitful tricks befuddle us.

There are some people who doubt whether we Communists are sincere when we declare that "the Three People's Principles being what

China needs today, our Party is ready to fight for their complete realization". This is the result of their failure to understand that the basic tenets of the Three People's Principles, which Dr. Sun Yat-sen enunciated in the Manifesto of the First National Congress of the Kuomintang in 1924 and which we have accepted, coincide with certain basic tenets of our Party's programme for the present stage, that is, of our minimum programme. It should be pointed out that these Three People's Principles of Dr. Sun Yat-sen coincide with our Party's programme for the present stage only in certain basic tenets and not in everything. Our Party's programme of New Democracy is of course much more comprehensive than Dr. Sun's principles, particularly as our Party's theory, programme and practice of New Democracy have greatly developed with the development of the Chinese revolution in the twenty years since Dr. Sun's death, and will develop still further. In essence, however, these Three People's Principles are a programme of New Democracy, as distinguished from the previous, old Three People's Principles; naturally they are "what China needs today" and naturally "our Party is ready to fight for their complete realization". To us Chinese Communists, the struggle for our Party's minimum programme and the struggle for Dr. Sun's revolutionary, or new, Three People's Principles are basically (though not in every respect) one and the same thing. Therefore, as in the past and the present, the Chinese Communists will prove to be the most sincere and thoroughgoing executors of the revolutionary Three People's Principles in the future as well.

Some people are suspicious and think that once in power, the Communist Party will follow Russia's example and establish the dictatorship of the proletariat and a one-party system. Our answer is that a new-democratic state based on an alliance of the democratic classes is different in principle from a socialist state under the dictatorship of the proletariat. Beyond all doubt, our system of New Democracy will be built under the leadership of the proletariat and of the Communist Party, but throughout the stage of New Democracy China cannot possibly have a one-class dictatorship and one-party government and therefore should not attempt it. We have no reason for refusing to co-operate with all political parties, social groups and individuals, provided their attitude to the Communist Party is co-operative and not hostile. The Russian system has been shaped by Russian history; in Russia the exploitation of man by man has been abolished as a social system, the political, economic and cultural system of the newest type of democracy, *i.e.*, socialism, has been put into effect, and the people support the Bolshevik Party alone, having discarded all the anti-socialist parties. All this has shaped the Russian system, which is perfectly necessary and reasonable there. But even in Russia, where the Bolshevik Party is the sole political party, the system practised in the organs of state power is still one of an alliance of workers, peasants and intellectuals and an alliance of Party members and non-Party people, and not a system in which the working class and the Bolsheviks alone may work in the organs of government. The Chinese system for the present stage is being shaped by the present stage of Chinese history, and for a long time to come there will exist a special form of state and political power, a form that is distinguished from the Russian system but is perfectly necessary and reasonable for us, namely, the new-democratic form of state and political power based on the alliance of the democratic classes.

OUR SPECIFIC PROGRAMME

Our Party must also have a specific programme for each period based on this general programme. Our general programme of New Democracy will remain unchanged throughout the stage of the bourgeois-democratic revolution, that is, for several decades. But from phase to phase during this stage, conditions have changed or are changing and it is only natural that we have to change our specific programme accordingly. For example, our general programme of New Democracy has remained the same throughout the periods of the Northern Expedition, the Agrarian Revolutionary War and the War of Resistance Against Japan, but there have been changes in our specific programme, because our friends and enemies have not remained the same in the three periods.

The Chinese people now find themselves in the following situation:

(1) the Japanese aggressors have not yet been defeated;

(2) the Chinese people urgently need to work together for a democratic change in order to achieve national unity, rapidly mobilize and unite all anti-Japanese forces, and defeat the Japanese aggressors in co-operation with the allies; and

(3) the Kuomintang government is disrupting national unity and obstructing such a democratic change.

What is our specific programme in the circumstances or, in other words, what are the immediate demands of the people?

We consider the following to be appropriate and minimum demands:

Mobilize all available forces for the thorough defeat of the Japanese aggressors and the establishment of international peace in co-operation with the allies;

Abolish the Kuomintang one-party dictatorship and establish a democratic coalition government and a joint supreme command;

Punish the pro-Japanese elements, fascists and defeatists who are opposing the people and disrupting national unity, and so help to build national unity;

Punish the reactionaries who are creating the danger of civil war, and so help to ensure internal peace;

Punish the traitors, take punitive action against officers who surrender to the enemy, and punish the agents of the Japanese;

Liquidate the reactionary secret service and all its repressive activities and abolish the concentration camps;

Revoke all reactionary laws and decrees aimed at suppressing the people's freedom of speech, press, assembly, association, political conviction and religious belief and freedom of the person, and guarantee full civil rights to the people;

Recognize the legal status of all democratic parties and groups;

Release all patriotic political prisoners;

Withdraw all troops encircling and attacking China's Liberated Areas and dispatch them to the anti-Japanese front;

Recognize the anti-Japanese armed forces and popularly elected governments of China's Liberated Areas;

Consolidate and expand the Liberated Areas and their armed forces, and recover all lost territory;

Help the people in the Japanese-occupied areas to organize underground armed forces for armed uprisings;

Allow the Chinese people to arm themselves and defend their homes and their country;

Bring about the political and military transformation of those armies directly under the Kuomintang supreme command, which constantly lose battles, oppress the people and discriminate against armies not directly under it, and punish the commanders who are responsible for disastrous defeats;

Improve the recruiting system and the living conditions of the officers and men;

Give preferential treatment to the families of the soldiers fighting in the anti-Japanese war, so that the officers and men at the front are free from domestic worries;

Provide preferential treatment for disabled soldiers and for the families of the soldiers who give their lives for the country, and help demobilized soldiers to settle down and earn a living;

Develop war industries to facilitate the prosecution of the war;

Distribute the military and financial aid received from the allies impartially to all the armies fighting in the War of Resistance;

Punish corrupt officials and institute clean government;

Improve the pay of the middle and lower grade government employees;

Give the Chinese people democratic rights;

Abolish the oppressive *pao-chia* system;[6]

Provide the war refugees and the victims of natural disasters with relief;

Appropriate substantial funds after the recovery of China's lost territory for the extensive relief of people who have suffered under enemy occupation;

Abolish exorbitant taxes and miscellaneous levies and establish a consolidated progressive tax;

Introduce rural reforms, reduce rent and interest, provide suitable safeguards for the rights of tenants, grant low-interest loans to impoverished peasants and help the peasants to organize, in order to facilitate the expansion of agricultural production;

Outlaw bureaucrat-capital;

Abolish the present policy of economic controls;

Check the unbridled inflation and rocketing prices;

Assist private industry and provide it with facilities for obtaining loans, purchasing raw materials and marketing its products;

Improve the livelihood of the workers, provide relief for the unemployed and help the workers to organize, in order to facilitate the expansion of industrial production;

Abolish Kuomintang indoctrination in education and promote a national, scientific and mass culture and education;

Guarantee the livelihood of the teachers and other staff members of educational institutions and guarantee academic freedom;

Protect the interests of the youth, women and children — provide assistance to young student refugees, help the youth and women to organize in order to participate on an equal footing in all work useful to the war effort and to social progress, ensure freedom of marriage and equality as between men and women, and give young people and children a useful education;

Give the minority nationalities in China better treatment and grant them autonomous rights;

Protect the interests of the overseas Chinese and assist those who have returned to the motherland;

Protect foreign nationals who have fled to China from the Japanese oppression and support their struggle against the Japanese aggressors;

Improve Sino-Soviet relations.

To achieve these demands, the most important thing is the immediate abolition of the Kuomintang one-party dictatorship and the establishment of a democratic provisional central government, a coalition government enjoying nation-wide support and including representatives of all the anti-Japanese parties and people without party affiliation. Without this prerequisite it is impossible to make any genuine change in the Kuomintang areas, and therefore in the country as a whole.

These demands voice the desires of the Chinese masses and also of broad sections of democratic public opinion in the allied countries.

A minimum specific programme which is agreed upon by all the anti-Japanese democratic parties is absolutely indispensable, and we are prepared to consult with them on the basis of the programme outlined above. Different parties may have different demands, but all should reach agreement on a common programme.

As far as the Kuomintang areas are concerned, such a programme is still at the stage of being a demand of the people; as far as the Japanese-occupied areas are concerned, it is a programme whose fulfilment must await their recovery, except for the item on the organization of underground forces for armed uprisings; as far as the Liberated Areas are concerned, it is a programme which has already been, is being and should continue to be, put into practice.

The immediate demands or specific programme of the Chinese people outlined above involve many vital war-time and post-war problems which require further elucidation. In explaining these problems below we shall criticize some of the wrong viewpoints held by the chief ruling clique of the Kuomintang and at the same time answer some questions raised by other people.

1. Destroy the Japanese Aggressors Completely, Allow No Compromise Halfway

The Cairo conference[7] rightly decided that the Japanese aggressors must be made to surrender unconditionally. But the Japanese aggressors are now working behind the scenes for a compromise peace, while the pro-Japanese elements in the Kuomintang government are hitching up with Japan's secret emissaries through the Nanking puppet government, and no stop has been put to this. Hence the danger of a halfway compromise is not yet entirely over. The Cairo conference made another good decision, namely, that the four northeastern provinces, Taiwan and the Penghu Islands should be returned to China. But, given its present policies, the Kuomintang government cannot possibly be relied upon to fight all the way to the Yalu River and recover all our lost territory. What should the Chinese people do in these circumstances? They should demand that the Kuomintang government should destroy the Japanese aggressors completely and allow no compromise halfway. All intrigues for a compromise must immediately be stopped. The Chinese people should demand that the Kuomintang government should change its present policy of passive resistance and employ all its military strength in active warfare against Japan. They should expand their own armed forces — the Eighth Route Army, the New Fourth Army and the other armed units of the people — and on their own initiative develop anti-Japanese armed forces on an extensive scale wherever the enemy has reached, and they should prepare to recover all the lost territory by fighting in direct co-operation with the allies; under no circumstances must they place their reliance solely on the Kuomintang. It is the sacred right of the Chinese people to defeat the Japanese aggressors. If the reactionaries try to deprive them of this right, suppress their anti-Japanese activities or undermine their strength, then the Chinese people should firmly strike back in self-defence if persuasion proves unavailing. For such acts of national treachery on the part of the Chinese reactionaries only aid and abet the Japanese aggressors.

2. Abolish the Kuomintang One-Party Dictatorship, Establish a Democratic Coalition Government

To wipe out the Japanese aggressors it is necessary to effect democratic reforms throughout the country. Yet this will be impossible unless the one-party dictatorship of the Kuomintang is abolished and a democratic coalition government is established.

The one-party dictatorship of the Kuomintang is in reality the dictatorship of the anti-popular clique within the Kuomintang, and this dictatorship is the disruptor of China's national unity, the author of the defeats on the Kuomintang front in the war, and the basic obstacle to the mobilization and unification of the anti-Japanese forces of the Chinese people. The Chinese people have become fully aware of the evils of this dictatorship through eight years of bitter experience in the War of Resistance, and they naturally demand its immediate abolition. This reactionary dictatorship is also the breeder of civil war and, unless it is immediately abolished, it will again bring the calamity of civil war upon them.

So widespread and resounding is the outcry of the Chinese people for the abolition of the anti-popular dictatorship that the Kuomintang authorities themselves have been forced to agree publicly to the "earlier termination of political tutelage", which shows how far this "political tutelage" or one-party dictatorship has forfeited popular support and prestige. There is not a single person in China who still dares to assert that "political tutelage" or one-party dictatorship is any good or that it should not be abolished or "terminated", and that marks a great change in the situation.

It is definite and beyond all doubt that it should be "terminated". But opinions differ as to how to do it. Some say, terminate it at once and establish a provisional democratic coalition government. Others say, wait a bit, convene the "national assembly", and "hand state power back to the people" and not to a coalition government.

What does this mean?

It means there are two ways of doing things, the honest way and the dishonest way.

First, the honest way. The honest way is immediately to proclaim the abolition of the Kuomintang one-party dictatorship, to establish a provisional central government composed of representatives of the Kuomintang, the Communist Party, the Democratic League and people with no party affiliation, and to promulgate a democratic

programme of political action such as the immediate demands of the
Chinese people which we have set forth above, with the aim of re-
storing national unity and defeating the Japanese aggressors. A round-
table conference of the representatives of the various parties and
people with no party affiliation should be convened to discuss and
reach agreement on these matters, and action should then be taken
accordingly. This is the road of unity, which the Chinese people will
firmly support.

Second, the dishonest way. The dishonest way is to disregard the
demands of the masses and of all the democratic parties and to insist
on convening a so-called national assembly stage-managed by the anti-
popular clique in the Kuomintang and have it adopt a "constitution"
which in practice will be anti-democratic and will buttress the dictatorship of this clique, for the purpose of providing a cloak of legality for
an illegal "National Government" — a government formed privately
through the appointment of a few dozen Kuomintang members, imposed
on the people and utterly devoid of any foundation in the popular
will — thus making a pretence of "handing state power back to the
people" while actually "handing it back" to the selfsame reactionary
clique within the Kuomintang. Whoever disapproves will be accused
of sabotaging "democracy" and "unity", which will then be a "reason"
for ordering punitive action against him. This is the road of disruption,
which the Chinese people will firmly oppose.

The steps our reactionary heroes are preparing to take in line with
this splitting policy will probably lead them to destruction. They are
putting a noose round their own necks and fastening it there, and this
noose is the "national assembly". Their intention is to use the "national
assembly" as a magic weapon, first, to prevent the formation of a
coalition government, second, to maintain their dictatorship, and third,
to prepare a justification of civil war. However, the logic of history
runs counter to their wishes, and they will be "lifting a rock only to
drop it on their own toes". For it is now obvious to all that the people
in the Kuomintang areas have no freedom and the people in the
Japanese-occupied areas cannot take part in elections, while the
Liberated Areas which have freedom are not recognized by the Kuomintang government. Such being the case, how can there be national
delegates? How can there be a "national assembly"? The national
assembly they are clamouring for is the one the Kuomintang dictatorship rigged up in every detail eight years ago during the civil war
period. If such an assembly is convened, the whole nation will inevitably

rise up against it, and how, it may be asked, will our reactionary heroes get out of that predicament? All in all, the convening of the bogus national assembly will only lead them to destruction.

We Communists propose two steps for the termination of the Kuomintang one-party dictatorship. First, at the present stage, to establish a provisional coalition government through common agreement among representatives of all parties and people with no party affiliation. Second, in the next stage, to convene a national assembly after free and unrestricted elections and form a regular coalition government. In both cases there will be a coalition government in which the representatives of all classes and political parties willing to take part are united on a democratic common programme in the fight against Japan today and for national construction tomorrow.

This is the only course China can take, whatever the intentions of the Kuomintang or other parties, groups or individuals, whether they like it or not, and whether or not they are conscious of it. This is a historical law, an inexorable trend which no force can reverse.

On this and all other problems of democratic reform, we Communists declare that although the Kuomintang authorities are still stubbornly persisting in their wrong policies and using negotiations to play for time and allay public opinion, we are ready to resume negotiations with them the moment they show willingness to renounce their present wrong policies and agree to democratic reforms. But the negotiations must be based on the general principle of resistance, unity and democracy, and we will not agree to any so-called measures, plans or empty pronouncements that depart from this general principle, however pleasing they may sound.

3. Freedom for the People

At present the Chinese people's struggle for freedom is primarily directed against the Japanese aggressors. But the Kuomintang government is preventing them from fighting the Japanese aggressors by depriving them of their freedom and binding them hand and foot. Unless this problem is solved, it will be impossible to mobilize and unify all the anti-Japanese forces of the nation. It is precisely to untie the people's bonds so that they can have the freedom to resist Japan, to unite and to win democracy that our programme puts forward such demands as the abolition of the one-party dictatorship; the establishment of a coalition government; the liquidation of the secret police; the revocation of repressive laws and decrees; the punishment of traitors, spies, pro-Japanese elements, fascists and corrupt officials; the release of political prisoners; the recognition of the legal status of all the democratic parties; the withdrawal of troops encircling or attacking the Liberated Areas; the recognition of the Liberated Areas; the abolition of the *pao-chia* system; and the many other demands relating to the economy, culture and the mass movement.

Freedom is won by the people through struggle, it is not bestowed by anyone as a favour. The people in China's Liberated Areas have already won freedom, and the people can and must win freedom in the other areas too. The greater the freedom of the Chinese people and the stronger their organized democratic forces, the greater the possibility of forming a provisional and unified coalition government. Once formed, this coalition government will in its turn provide full freedom for the people and so consolidate its own foundations. Only then will it be possible to hold free and unrestricted elections throughout the land after the overthrow of the Japanese aggressors, to create a democratic national assembly and to establish a regular and unified coalition government. Unless the people have freedom, there can be no national assembly or government genuinely elected by the people. Is this not clear enough?

Freedom of speech, press, assembly, association, political conviction and religious belief and freedom of the person are the people's most important freedoms. In China only the Liberated Areas have given full effect to these freedoms.

In 1925 Dr. Sun Yat-sen declared in his deathbed Testament:

> For forty years I have devoted myself to the cause of the national revolution with the aim of winning freedom and equality for China. My experience during these forty years has firmly convinced me that to achieve this aim we must arouse the masses of the people and unite in a common fight with those nations of the world who treat us as equals.

The unworthy successors of Dr. Sun, who have betrayed him, oppress the masses of the people instead of arousing them, and deprive them of all their freedom of speech, press, assembly, association, political conviction and religious belief and freedom of the person. They attach the labels "traitor party", "traitor army", and "traitor areas" to the Communist Party, the Eighth Route and New Fourth Armies and the Liberated Areas, which are all genuinely arousing the masses of the people and protecting their freedoms and rights. We hope that there will soon be an end to this reversal of right and wrong. If it lasts much longer, the Chinese people will lose all patience.

4. Unity of the People

It is imperative to turn a divided China into a united China in order to destroy the Japanese aggressors, prevent civil war and build a new China; such is the historical task of the Chinese people.

But how is China to be united? Through autocratic unification by a dictator or democratic unification by the people? From the time of Yuan Shih-kai[8] the Northern warlords concentrated on autocratic unification. But what was the result? Contrary to their desires, what they obtained was not unification but division, and finally they tumbled from power. Following in Yuan Shih-kai's footsteps, the anti-popular clique of the Kuomintang sought autocratic unification and waged civil war for fully ten years, only to let in the Japanese aggressors while they themselves withdrew to Mount Omei.[9] And now from their mountain top they are again shouting about their theory of autocratic unification. To whom are they shouting? Will any upright patriotic Chinese listen to them? Having lived through sixteen years of Northern warlord rule and eighteen years of dictatorial Kuomintang rule, the people have acquired ample experience and discerning eyes. They want democratic unification by the masses and not autocratic unification by a dictator. As early as 1935, we Communists put forward the policy of the Anti-Japanese National United Front, and we have fought for it ever since. In 1939, when the Kuomintang was enforcing its reactionary "Measures for Restricting the Activities of Alien Parties", thus creating the imminent danger of capitulation, split and retrogression, and when it was shouting about its theory of autocratic unification, we again declared: There must be unification based on resistance and not on capitulation, on unity and not on splitting, on progress and not on retrogression. Only unification based on resistance, unity and progress is genuine and any other kind would be a sham. Six years have passed, but the issue remains the same.

Can there be unity if the people have no freedom or democracy? There will be unity as soon as they have both. The Chinese people's movement for freedom, democracy and a coalition government is at the same time a movement for unity. When we put forward many demands for freedom, democracy and a coalition government in our specific programme, we are at the same time aiming at unity. It is plain common sense that unless the dictatorship of the anti-popular

Kuomintang clique is abolished and a democratic coalition government is formed, not only will it be impossible to carry out any democratic reform in the Kuomintang areas or to mobilize the armies and the people there for the defeat of the Japanese aggressors, but the calamity of civil war will ensue. Why do so many democrats, with and without party affiliation, including many in the Kuomintang, unanimously demand a coalition government? Because they are clearly aware of the present crisis and realize that there is no other way to overcome it and achieve both unity against the enemy and unity for national construction.

5. The People's Army

Without an army standing on the people's side, it is impossible for the Chinese people to win freedom and unification, establish a coalition government, thoroughly defeat the Japanese aggressors and build a new China. At present the only armed forces that stand wholly on the people's side are the Liberated Areas' Eighth Route and New Fourth Armies, which are not very large; they are far from sufficient. Yet the Kuomintang group which opposes the people is ceaselessly intriguing to undermine and destroy the armies of the Liberated Areas. In 1944 the Kuomintang government presented a so-called memorandum demanding that the Communist Party should "disband, within a definite time limit", four-fifths of the armed forces of the Liberated Areas. In 1945, during the most recent negotiations, it has further demanded the handing over of all the armed forces of the Liberated Areas by the Communist Party, after which it would grant the Communist Party "legal status".

These people tell the Communists, "Hand over your troops and we will grant you freedom." According to their theory, a political party that does not have any army should enjoy freedom. Yet whatever freedom the Chinese Communist Party enjoyed during 1924-27, when it had only a small armed force, vanished with the Kuomintang government's policies of "party purge" and massacre. And today, the China Democratic League and the democrats within the Kuomintang, who have no armed forces, have no freedom either. Let us take the workers, peasants and students and the progressively inclined people in cultural, educational and industrial circles under the Kuomintang regime — for the last eighteen years none of them have had any armed forces, and none of them have had any freedom. Can it be that all these democratic parties and people have been denied freedom because they organized armies, perpetrated "feudal separatism", created "traitor areas" and violated "governmental and military orders"? Not in the least. On the contrary, they have been denied freedom precisely because they have done none of these things.

"The army belongs to the state" — that is perfectly true, and there is not an army in the world that does not belong to a state. But what kind of state? A state under the feudal and fascist dictatorship of the big landlords, big bankers and big compradors, or a new-democratic state of the broad masses of the people? The only kind of state for China to establish is a new-democratic state and, on this basis, she should establish a new-democratic coalition government; all the armed forces of China must belong to such a government of such a state so that they may safeguard the people's freedom and effectively fight foreign aggressors. The moment a new-democratic coalition government comes into being in China, the Liberated Areas of China will hand their armed forces over to it. But all the Kuomintang armed forces will have to be handed over to it at the same time.

In 1924 Dr. Sun Yat-sen said, "Today should mark the beginning of a new epoch in the national revolution. . . . The first step is to unite the armed forces with the people, and the next step is to turn them into the armed forces of the people."[10] It is because they have applied this policy that the Eighth Route and New Fourth Armies have become "the armed forces of the people", that is, the people's army, and have been able to win victories. During the earlier period of the Northern Expedition, the Kuomintang armies took Dr. Sun's "first step", and hence won victories. In the latter period of the Northern Expedition they abandoned even the "first step", took a stand against the people, and hence from that time right down to the present they have become more and more corrupt and degenerate; in their element when fighting internal war, they cannot but be out of their element when it comes to fighting external war. Every patriotic officer in the Kuomintang army who has a conscience should set about reviving the Sun Yat-sen spirit and transforming his troops.

In the work of transforming the old armies, a suitable education should be given to all officers who are capable of being re-educated to help them to get rid of their obsolete outlook and acquire a correct outlook, so that they can remain and serve in the people's army.

It is the duty of the whole nation to struggle for the creation of the army of the Chinese people. Without a people's army the people have nothing. On this question there must be no empty theorizing whatsoever.

We Communists are ready to give our support to the task of transforming the Chinese army. All those military forces which are willing to unite with the people and to oppose the Japanese aggressors instead of opposing the armed forces of the Chinese Liberated Areas should be regarded as friendly troops and be given proper assistance by the Eighth Route and New Fourth Armies.

6. The Land Problem

To wipe out the Japanese aggressors and build a new China, it is imperative to reform the land system and emancipate the peasants. Dr. Sun Yat-sen's thesis of "land to the tiller" is correct for the present period of our revolution, which is bourgeois-democratic in nature.

Why do we say our revolution in the present period is bourgeois-democratic in nature? We mean that the target of this revolution is not the bourgeoisie in general but national and feudal oppression, that the measures taken in this revolution are in general directed not at abolishing but at protecting private property, and that as a result of this revolution the working class will be able to build up the strength to lead China in the direction of socialism, though capitalism will still be enabled to grow to an appropriate extent for a fairly long period. "Land to the tiller" means transferring the land from the feudal exploiters to the peasants, turning the private property of the feudal landlords into the private property of the peasants and emancipating them from feudal agrarian relations, thereby making possible the transformation of an agricultural country into an industrial country. Thus, "land to the tiller" is in the nature of a bourgeois-democratic and not a proletarian-socialist demand; it is the demand of all revolutionary democrats and not the demand of us Communists alone. The difference is that, in China's circumstances, we Communists alone treat this demand with special seriousness, and do not just talk about it but put it into practice. Who are the revolutionary democrats? Apart from the proletariat who are the most thoroughgoing of the revolutionary democrats, the peasants form by far the largest group. The overwhelming majority of the peasants, that is, all except the rich peasants who have a feudal tail, actively demand "land to the tiller". The urban petty bourgeoisie are also revolutionary democrats and "land to the tiller" will prove to be to their advantage as well, for it will help to develop the productive forces in agriculture. The national bourgeoisie are a vacillating class — they also approve of "land to the tiller" because they need markets, but many of them are afraid of it because for the most part they have ties with landed property. Dr. Sun Yat-sen was the earliest revolutionary democrat in China. Representing the revolutionary section of the national bourgeoisie as well as the urban petty bourgeoisie and the peasants, he carried out an armed revolution and put forward his thesis of "equalization of landownership" and "land to the tiller". But unfortunately he did not take the initiative and reform the land system when he was in power. And when the anti-popular clique of the Kuomintang took power, it completely betrayed what he stood for. It is this clique that is now stubbornly opposing "land to the tiller" because it represents the stratum of big landlords, bankers and compradors. As China has no political party exclusively representing the peasants and the political parties of the national bourgeoisie have no thoroughgoing land programme, the Chinese Communist Party has become the leader of the peasants and all the other revolutionary democrats, being the only party that has formulated and carried out a thoroughgoing land programme, fought earnestly for the peasants' interests and therefore won the overwhelming majority of the peasants as its great ally.

From 1927 to 1936, the Chinese Communist Party adopted various measures for the thorough reform of the land system and put Dr. Sun's "land to the tiller" into effect. It was precisely the reactionary clique of the Kuomintang, that gang of unworthy followers of Dr. Sun Yat-sen, who bared their teeth, showed their claws and fought against "land to the tiller" in ten years of war against the people.

The Communist Party has made a major concession in the anti-Japanese war period by changing the policy of "land to the tiller" to one of reducing rent and interest. This concession is a correct one, for it helped to bring the Kuomintang into the war against Japan and lessened the resistance of the landlords in the Liberated Areas to our mobilization of the peasants for the war. If no special obstacle arises, we are prepared to continue this policy after the war, first extending rent and interest reduction to the whole country and then taking proper measures for the gradual achievement of "land to the tiller".

However, those who have betrayed Dr. Sun oppose the reduction of rent and interest, let alone "land to the tiller". The Kuomintang government has not carried out the decree for a "25 per cent reduction in rent" and similar decrees which it has promulgated itself; only we in the Liberated Areas have enforced them, and for this crime the Liberated Areas have been labelled "traitor areas".

In the course of the anti-Japanese war a so-called theory of two stages, a stage of "national revolution" and a stage of "revolution for democracy and the people's livelihood", has made its appearance. This theory is wrong.

"Faced with a formidable enemy, we should not raise the question of democratic reforms or the people's livelihood; better wait until the Japanese are gone" — such is the absurd theory put forward by the reactionary clique of the Kuomintang for the purpose of preventing complete victory in the war. Yet there are people who have been echoing this theory and have become its servile adherents.

"Faced with a formidable enemy, it is impossible for us to build up bases against the Japanese and resist their attacks unless we settle the question of democracy and the people's livelihood" — this is what the Chinese Communist Party has been advocating and, moreover, has already put into practice with excellent results.

In the period of the anti-Japanese war, reduction of rent and interest and the other democratic reforms all serve the war. In order to lessen the landlords' resistance to the war effort we have abstained from abolishing their ownership of land and have only reduced rent and interest; at the same time, we have encouraged them to transfer their assets to industry and given the enlightened gentry the opportunity to take part in public activities for the war and in the work of government alongside other representatives of the people. As for the rich peasants, we have encouraged them to develop production. All this is part of the resolute line of democratic reforms in the rural areas and is absolutely necessary.

There are two lines. Either stubbornly oppose the Chinese peasants' endeavour to settle the problem of democracy and the people's livelihood, and become corrupt, ineffectual and utterly incapable of fighting Japan; or firmly support the Chinese peasants in their endeavour, and gain the greatest of allies, constituting 80 per cent of the population, thereby forging tremendous fighting strength. The former is the line of the Kuomintang government, the latter is the line of China's Liberated Areas.

The line of the opportunists is to vacillate between the two, to profess support for the peasants and yet lack the resolve to reduce rent and interest, arm the peasants or establish democratic political power in the rural areas.

Using all the forces at its command, the anti-popular clique of the Kuomintang has directed every kind of vicious attack, open and secret, military and political, both with bloodshed and without, against the Chinese Communist Party. Taken in its social setting, the dispute between the two parties is essentially over this issue of agrarian relations. Where exactly did we give offence to the Kuomintang reactionary clique? Is it not on this score? Has it not been precisely by rendering the Japanese aggressors great help on this score that this clique has won favour and encouragement from them? Have not all the charges against the Chinese Communist Party — "sabotaging the War of Resistance and endangering the state", "traitor party", "traitor army", "traitor areas", and "disobedience to governmental and military orders" — been levelled precisely because it has done conscientious work in the true interests of the nation in this sphere?

It is the peasants who are the source of China's industrial workers. In the future, additional tens of millions of peasants will go to the cities and enter factories. If China is to build up powerful national industries and many large modern cities, there will have to be a long process of transformation of rural into urban inhabitants.

It is the peasants who constitute the main market for China's industry. Only they can supply foodstuffs and raw materials in great abundance and absorb manufactured goods in great quantities.

It is the peasants who are the source of the Chinese army. The soldiers are peasants in military uniform, the mortal enemies of the Japanese aggressors.

It is the peasants who are the main political force for democracy in China at the present stage. Chinese democrats will achieve nothing unless they rely on the support of the 360 million peasants.

It is the peasants who are the chief concern of China's cultural movement at the present stage. If the 360 million peasants are left out, do not the "elimination of illiteracy", "popularization of education", "literature and art for the masses" and "public health" become largely empty talk?

In saying this, I am of course not ignoring the political, economic and cultural importance of the rest of the people numbering about 90 million, and in particular am not ignoring the working class, which is politically the most conscious and therefore qualified to lead the whole revolutionary movement. Let there be no misunderstanding.

It is absolutely necessary not only for Communists but for every democrat in China to grasp these points.

When there is reform of the land system — even such an elementary reform as reduction of rent and interest — the peasants become more interested in production. Then as the peasants are helped to organize farming and other co-operatives step by step on a voluntary basis, the productive forces will grow. The farming co-operatives at present can only be collective, mutual-aid labour organizations based on an individual peasant economy (*i.e.*, on private ownership by the peasants), such as labour-exchange teams, mutual-aid teams and work-exchange groups; even so the increase in labour productivity and output is already astonishing. Such organizations have been widely developed in China's Liberated Areas and from now on should be spread as much as possible.

It might be mentioned that co-operative organization of the labour-exchange team type has existed among the peasants for a long time, but in the past it was only a means by which they tried to alleviate their wretchedness. Today the labour-exchange teams in China's Liberated Areas are different both in form and in content; they have become a means by which the peasant masses increase production and strive for a better life.

In the last analysis, the impact, good or bad, great or small, of the policy and the practice of any Chinese political party upon the people depends on whether and how much it helps to develop their productive forces, and on whether it fetters or liberates these forces. The social productive forces of China can be liberated only by destroying the Japanese aggressors, carrying out land reform, emancipating the peasants, developing modern industry and establishing an independent, free, democratic, united, prosperous and powerful new China — and this will win the approbation of the Chinese people.

It should be pointed out further that it is not easy for city intellectuals who come to work in the countryside to understand the characteristics of the rural areas, *i.e.*, that they are still based on a scattered and backward, individual economy, and that, moreover, the Liberated Areas are temporarily cut off from one another by the enemy and involved in a guerrilla war. Failing to understand these characteristics, they often inappropriately approach and handle rural problems and rural work from the viewpoint of life and work in the cities, and so divorce themselves from the realities of the countryside and fail to identify themselves with the peasants. It is necessary to overcome this by education.

China's numerous revolutionary intellectuals must awaken to the necessity of becoming one with the peasants. The peasants need them and await their help. They should go to the countryside enthusiastically, doff their student garb and put on rough clothing, and willingly start with any work however trivial; they should learn what the peasants want and help to arouse and organize them in the struggle to accomplish the democratic revolution in the countryside, which is one of the most important tasks in China's democratic revolution.

After the Japanese aggressors are wiped out, we should confiscate the land usurped by them and the chief traitors and distribute it among those peasants who have little or no land.

7.   The Problem of Industry

In order to defeat the Japanese aggressors and build a new China it is necessary to develop industry. But under the Kuomintang government there is dependence on foreign countries for everything, and its financial and economic policy is ruining the entire economic life of the people. A few small industrial enterprises are all that is to be found in the Kuomintang areas, and in most cases they have been unable to avoid bankruptcy. In the absence of political reforms all the productive forces are being ruined, and this is true both of agriculture and of industry.

By and large, it will be impossible to develop industry unless China is independent, free, democratic and united. To wipe out the Japanese aggressors is to seek independence. To abolish the Kuomintang's one-party dictatorship, establish a democratic and united coalition government, transform all China's troops into a people's armed force, carry out land reform and emancipate the peasants is to seek freedom, democracy and unity. Without independence, freedom, democracy and unity it is impossible to build industry on a really large scale. Without industry there can be no solid national defence, no well-being for the people, no prosperity or strength for the nation. The history of the 105 years since the Opium War of 1840,[11] and especially of the eighteen years since the Kuomintang came to power, has brought this important point home to the Chinese people. A China that is not poor and weak but prosperous and strong implies a China that is not colonial or semi-colonial but independent, not semi-feudal but free and democratic, not divided but united. In semi-colonial, semi-feudal and divided China, many people have for years dreamed of developing industry, building up national defence, and bringing well-being to the people and prosperity and power to the nation, but all their dreams have been shattered. Many well-intentioned educators, scientists and students have buried themselves in their own work or studies and paid no attention to politics in the belief that they could serve the country with their knowledge, but this too has turned out to be a dream, a dream that has been shattered. This indeed is a good sign, for the shattering of these childish dreams marks a starting-point on China's road towards prosperity and strength. The Chinese people have learned many things in the war; they know that after the defeat of the Japanese aggressors they must build a new-democratic China enjoying independence, freedom, democracy, unity, prosperity and strength, all of which are interrelated and indispensable. If they do so, then a bright future lies before China. The productive forces of the Chinese people will be released and given every possibility to develop only when the political system of New Democracy obtains in all parts of China. More and more people are coming to understand this point every day.

When the political system of New Democracy is won, the Chinese people and their government will have to adopt practical measures in order to build heavy and light industry step by step over a number of years and transform China from an agricultural into an industrial country. The new-democratic state cannot be consolidated unless it has a solid economy as its base, a much more advanced agriculture than at present, and a large-scale industry occupying a predominant position in the national economy, with communications, trade and finance to match.

We Communists are ready to fight for this objective in co-operation with all the democratic parties and industrial circles throughout the country. The Chinese working class will play a great role in this undertaking.

Ever since World War I, the Chinese working class has consciously fought for the independence and liberation of China. The year 1921 witnessed the birth of the Communist Party of China, the vanguard of the working class, and China's struggle for liberation then entered a new stage. During the ensuing three periods, the Northern Expedition, the Agrarian Revolutionary War and the War of Resistance Against Japan, the working class and Communist Party of China have worked extremely hard and made an invaluable contribution to the cause of the liberation of the Chinese people. In the struggle for the final defeat of the Japanese aggressors, and especially for the recovery of the big cities and important lines of communications, the Chinese working class will play a very great role. And it can be predicted that after the anti-Japanese war, the effort and contribution of the Chinese working class will be even greater. The task of the Chinese working class is to struggle not only for the establishment of a new-democratic state but also for China's industrialization and the modernization of her agriculture.

The policy of adjusting the interests of labour and capital will be adopted under the new-democratic state system. On the one hand, it will protect the interests of the workers, institute an eight- to ten-hour working day according to circumstances, provide suitable unemployment relief and social insurance and safeguard trade union rights; on the other hand, it will guarantee legitimate profits to properly managed state, private and co-operative enterprises — so that both the public and the private sectors and both labour and capital will work together to develop industrial production.

The enterprises and property in China of the Japanese aggressors and of the chief traitors will be confiscated and placed at the disposal of the government when Japan is defeated.

8.   The Problem of Culture, Education and the Intellectuals

The calamities brought upon the Chinese people by foreign and feudal oppression also affect our national culture. The progressive cultural and educational institutions and progressive cultural workers and educators have particularly suffered. To sweep away foreign and feudal oppression and build a new-democratic China, we need large numbers of educators and teachers for the people, and also people's scientists, engineers, technicians, doctors, journalists, writers, men of letters, artists and rank-and-file cultural workers. They must be imbued with the spirit of serving the people and must work hard. Provided they serve the people creditably, all intellectuals should be esteemed and regarded as valuable national and social assets. The problem of the intellectuals becomes particularly important in China because the country is culturally backward as a result of foreign and feudal oppression and because intellectuals are urgently needed in the people's struggle for liberation. The numerous revolutionary intellectuals have played a very great role in the people's struggle for liberation in the past half-century, and especially since the May 4th Movement of 1919 and in the eight years of the anti-Japanese war. They will play an even greater role in the struggles to come. Therefore, the task of a people's government is systematically to develop all kinds of intellectually equipped cadres from among the ranks of the people and at the same time take care to unite with and re-educate all the useful intellectuals already available.

The elimination of illiteracy among 80 per cent of the population is a vital task for the new China.

Proper and firm steps should be taken to eliminate all enslaving feudal and fascist culture and education.

Vigorous action should be taken to prevent and cure endemic and other diseases among the people and to expand the people's medical and health services.

The old type of cultural and educational workers and doctors should be given suitable re-education so that they can acquire a new outlook and new methods to serve the people.

The Chinese people's culture and education should be new-democratic, that is to say, China should establish her own new national, scientific and mass culture and education.

As for foreign culture, it would be a wrong policy to shut it out, rather we should as far as possible draw on what is progressive in it for use in the development of China's new culture; it would also be wrong to copy it blindly, rather we should draw on it critically to meet the actual needs of the Chinese people. The new culture created in the Soviet Union should be a model for us in building our people's culture. Similarly, ancient Chinese culture should neither be totally rejected nor blindly copied, but should be accepted discriminatingly so as to help the progress of China's new culture.

9. The Problem of the Minority Nationalities

The anti-popular clique of the Kuomintang denies that many nationalities exist in China, and labels all excepting the Han nationality as "tribes". It has taken over the reactionary policy of the governments of the Ching Dynasty and of the Northern warlords in relation to the minority nationalities, oppressing and exploiting them in every possible way. Clear cases in point are the massacre of Mongolians of the Ikhchao League in 1943, the armed suppression of the minority nationalities in Sinkiang since 1944 and the massacres of the Hui people in Kansu Province in recent years. These are manifestations of a wrong Han-chauvinistic ideology and policy.

In 1924 Dr. Sun Yat-sen wrote in the Manifesto of the First National Congress of the Kuomintang that "the Kuomintang's Principle of

Nationalism has a twofold meaning, first, the liberation of the Chinese nation, and second, the equality of all the nationalities in China" and that "the Kuomintang solemnly declares that it recognizes the right to self-determination of all the nationalities in China and that a free and united republic of China (a free union of all the nationalities) will be established when the anti-imperialist and anti-warlord revolution is victorious".

The Communist Party of China is in full agreement with Dr. Sun's policy on nationalities as stated here. Communists must actively help the people of all the minority nationalities to fight for it, and help them, including all their leaders who have ties with the masses, to fight for their political, economic and cultural emancipation and development and to establish their own armies which will safeguard the people's interests. Their spoken and written languages, their manners and customs and their religious beliefs must be respected.

The attitude which the Shensi-Kansu-Ningsia Border Region and the Liberated Areas in northern China have for years adopted towards the Mongolian and Hui nationalities is correct, and the work they have done has been fruitful.

10. The Problem of Foreign Policy

The Communist Party of China agrees with the Atlantic Charter and with the decisions of the international conferences of Moscow, Cairo, Teheran and the Crimea,[12] because these decisions all contribute to the defeat of the fascist aggressors and the maintenance of world peace.

The fundamental principle of the foreign policy advocated by the Chinese Communist Party is as follows: China shall establish and strengthen diplomatic relations with all countries and settle all questions of common concern, such as co-ordination of military operations in the war, peace conferences, trade and investment, on the basic conditions that the Japanese aggressors must be completely defeated and world peace maintained, that there must be mutual respect for national independence and equality, and that there must be promotion of mutual interests and friendship between states and between peoples.

The Chinese Communist Party fully agrees with the proposals of the Dumbarton Oaks conference and the decisions of the Crimea conference on the establishment of an organization to safeguard international peace and security after the war. It welcomes the United Nations Conference on International Organization in San Francisco.

It has appointed its own representative on China's delegation to this conference in order to express the will of the Chinese people.[13]

We hold that the Kuomintang government must cease its hostility towards the Soviet Union and speedily improve Sino-Soviet relations. The Soviet Union was the first country to renounce the unequal treaties and sign new, equal treaties with China. At the time of the Kuomintang's First National Congress called by Dr. Sun Yat-sen in 1924 and the subsequent Northern Expedition, the Soviet Union was the only country to help China's war of liberation. When the anti-Japanese war broke out in 1937, the Soviet Union was again the first country to help China against the Japanese aggressors. The Chinese people are grateful to the Soviet government and people for this help. We believe that no final and thorough settlement of the problems of the Pacific is possible without the participation of the Soviet Union.

We ask the governments of all the allied countries, and of the United States and Britain in the first place, to pay serious attention to the voice of the Chinese people and not to impair friendship with them by pursuing foreign policies that run counter to their will. We maintain that if any foreign government helps the Chinese reactionaries and opposes the Chinese people's democratic cause, it will be committing a gross mistake.

The Chinese people welcome the steps taken by many foreign governments in renouncing their unequal treaties and concluding new, equal treaties with China. However, we maintain that the conclusion of equal treaties does not in itself mean that China has actually won genuine equality. Genuine and actual equality is never the gift of foreign governments, but must be won mainly by the Chinese people through their own efforts, and the way to win it is to build a new-democratic China politically, economically and culturally; otherwise there will be only nominal and not actual independence and equality. That is to say, China can never win genuine independence and equality by following the present policy of the Kuomintang government.

We consider that, after the defeat and unconditional surrender of the Japanese aggressors, it will be necessary to help all the democratic forces of the Japanese people to establish their own democratic system so that Japanese fascism and militarism may be thoroughly wiped out, together with their political, economic and social roots. Unless the Japanese people have a democratic system, it will be impossible thoroughly to wipe out Japanese fascism and militarism and impossible to ensure peace in the Pacific.

We consider the decision of the Cairo conference regarding the independence of Korea to be correct. The Chinese people should help the Korean people to win liberation.

We hope that India will attain independence. For an independent and democratic India is not only needed by the Indian people but is essential for world peace.

As regards the Southeast Asian countries — Burma, Malaya, Indonesia, Viet Nam and the Philippines — we hope that after the defeat of the Japanese aggressors their people will exercise their right to establish independent and democratic states of their own. As for Thailand, she should be treated like the fascist satellite states in Europe.

*   *   *

So much for the major points of our specific programme.

To repeat, none of the points in this specific programme can be successfully carried out on a nation-wide scale without a democratic coalition government enjoying the support of the entire nation.

By its twenty-four years of struggle for the cause of the liberation of the Chinese people, the Communist Party of China has attained a position such that any political party or social group or any Chinese or foreigner ignoring its opinion on questions concerning China will be making a serious mistake and courting certain failure. There were, and still are, people who try to ignore our opinions and to follow their own bigoted course, but they have all ended in a blind alley. Why? Simply because our opinions conform to the interests of the Chinese masses. The Chinese Communist Party is the most faithful spokesman of the Chinese people, and whoever fails to respect it in fact fails to respect the Chinese masses and is doomed to defeat.

THE TASKS IN THE KUOMINTANG AREAS

I have now given a detailed explanation of our Party's general and specific programmes. There is no doubt that these programmes will eventually be put into effect throughout China; this is the vista that the international and domestic situation as a whole has opened up for the Chinese people. However, at the moment conditions in the Kuomintang areas, the enemy-occupied areas and the Liberated Areas differ from each other, making it necessary for us to distinguish between them in implementing our programme. Different conditions give rise to different tasks. Some of these tasks I have already explained above, while others still need elaboration.

In the Kuomintang areas, the people are not free to engage in patriotic activity, and democratic movements are considered illegal, and yet various social strata, democratic parties and individuals are becoming increasingly active. The China Democratic League issued a manifesto in January this year demanding the termination of the Kuomintang's one-party dictatorship and the establishment of a coalition government. Many sections of the people have made similar declarations. Within the Kuomintang, too, many people are showing increasing doubt and discontent over the policies of the leading bodies of their own party, are becoming increasingly aware of the danger of their party's isolation from the people, and are therefore demanding democratic reforms suited to the times. In Chungking and other places democratic movements are growing among the workers, the peasants, cultural circles, the students, educational circles, women, industrial and commercial circles, government employees and even among some of the soldiers and officers. These facts indicate that the democratic movements of all the oppressed strata are gradually converging on a common objective. One weakness of the present movements is that the basic sections of society have not yet joined it on a wide scale and that the most important forces, namely, the peasants, workers, soldiers and the lower-ranking government employees and teachers, who are all suffering so bitterly, are not yet organized. Another weakness is that many of the democratic personalities in the movement are still unclear and hesitant about the fundamental policy, namely, that a change in the situation must be sought through the waging of struggle on a democratic mass basis. However, the objective situation is compelling all the oppressed strata, political parties and social groups gradually to awaken and unite. No suppression by the Kuomintang government can stop the advance of this movement.

All the oppressed strata, political parties and social groups in the Kuomintang areas must extend their democratic movement on a broad scale and gradually weld their scattered forces together in order to fight for national unity, the establishment of a coalition government, the defeat of the Japanese aggressors and the building of a new China. The Communist Party of China and the people of the Liberated Areas should give them every possible help.

In the Kuomintang areas the Communists should continue to pursue the policy of a broad National United Front Against Japan. In the fight for common objectives, we should co-operate with anyone who does not oppose us today, even though he might have done so yesterday.

THE TASKS IN THE JAPANESE-OCCUPIED AREAS

In the occupied areas, Communists should call on all who oppose Japan to follow the French and Italian examples and form organizations and underground forces to prepare armed uprisings, so that when the time comes they can act from the inside in co-ordination with the armies attacking from the outside and so wipe out the Japanese aggressors. The atrocities, plunder, rape and humiliation suffered by our brothers and sisters in the occupied areas at the hands of the Japanese aggressors and their servile lackeys have aroused the burning wrath of all Chinese, and the hour of revenge is fast approaching. The victories in the European theatre of war and the victories of our Eighth Route and New Fourth Armies have stimulated and heightened the anti-Japanese spirit of the people in the occupied areas. They urgently want to become organized so as to achieve liberation as quickly as possible. Therefore, we must raise our work in the occupied areas to the same level of importance as that in the Liberated Areas. Large numbers of our working personnel must be sent to work there. Large numbers of activists among the people there must be trained and promoted and must take part in local work. We must intensify our underground work in the four northeastern provinces which have been occupied longer than any other region and which form a key industrial and troop concentration area for the Japanese aggressors. With a view to the recovery of these lost territories, we should strengthen our solidarity with the people who have fled south from the Northeast.

Communists should pursue the broadest united front policy in all the occupied areas. For the overthrow of the common enemy they must unite with anyone who is opposed to the Japanese aggressors and their servile lackeys.

We should warn all the puppet armies, the puppet police and others who are helping the enemy and opposing their countrymen that they must quickly recognize the criminal nature of their actions, repent in time and atone for their crimes by helping their countrymen against the enemy. Otherwise the nation will certainly call them to account the day the enemy collapses.

Communists should direct persuasive propaganda at all puppet organizations with a mass following so as to win the masses who have been misled over to our side against the national enemy. At the same time, evidence should be collected about those impenitent collaborators who have committed the most heinous crimes, so that they can be brought to justice when the lost territories are recovered.

Those Kuomintang reactionaries who have betrayed the nation by organizing open collaborators to fight the Chinese people, the Communist Party, the Eighth Route Army, the New Fourth Army and other armed forces of the people must be warned to repent in time. Otherwise, when the lost territories are recovered, they will certainly be punished for their crimes along with the collaborators with Japan and will be shown no mercy.

THE TASKS IN THE LIBERATED AREAS

Our Party has put its whole new-democratic programme into practice in the Liberated Areas with striking results, and so built up tremendous anti-Japanese strength, and from now on this strength should be developed and consolidated in every way.

In the prevailing circumstances, the troops of the Liberated Areas should launch extensive attacks on all places that can be captured from the Japanese and puppets in order to expand the Liberated Areas and reduce the occupied areas.

But at the same time it should be borne in mind that the enemy is still strong and may launch further attacks on the Liberated Areas. The army and the people of our areas must be ready at all times to smash his attacks and must work in every way to consolidate these areas.

We must expand the armies, the guerrilla units, the people's militia and the self-defence corps of the Liberated Areas, and increase their combat effectiveness by speeding up their training and consolidation in order to build up adequate strength for the final defeat of the aggressors.

The army in the Liberated Areas must support the government and cherish the people, while the democratic governments must lead the people in the work of supporting the army and taking good care of the families of soldiers fighting Japan. In this way relations between the army and the people will become still better.

In the work of the local coalition governments and mass organizations, Communists should continue to co-operate closely with all anti-Japanese democrats on the basis of the new-democratic programme.

Similarly in military work, Communists should co-operate closely with all anti-Japanese democrats who are willing to co-operate with us, whether or not they are members of the armies of the Liberated Areas.

To increase the enthusiasm of the masses of the workers, peasants and other working people for the war and for production, we must thoroughly apply the policy of reducing rent and interest and of increasing the pay of workers and office staff. The cadres of the Liberated Areas must diligently learn to do economic work. All available forces must be mobilized for the extensive development of agriculture, industry and trade and the improvement of the livelihood of the soldiers and the people. For this purpose there must be labour emulation campaigns, and rewards should be given to labour heroes and model workers. When the Japanese aggressors are driven out of the cities, our personnel must rapidly learn how to do urban economic work.

Our cultural and educational work must be developed in order to raise the level of political consciousness of the people in the Liberated Areas and, above all, of the masses of the workers, peasants and soldiers, and in order to train large numbers of cadres. In carrying forward this work, those engaged in it should adopt forms and select contents suited to the existing rural conditions and to the needs and wishes of the people in the countryside.

In all our work in the Liberated Areas, manpower and material resources must be used most sparingly, and in every field long-term plans must be made, and misuse and waste must be avoided. This is needed both for defeating the Japanese aggressors and for building up the new China.

In all our work in the Liberated Areas, we must take great care to help the local people administer local affairs and to cultivate many local cadres from among the best local people. It will be impossible to accomplish the great task of the democratic revolution in the rural areas unless comrades who come from other places identify themselves with the local people and help the local cadres whole-heartedly, painstakingly and in ways that fit the actual conditions, and unless they cherish them like their own brothers and sisters.

When a unit of the Eighth Route Army, the New Fourth Army or any other armed force of the people arrives at a place, it should immediately help the local people to organize forces led by the local cadres, including not only militia and self-defence corps but also local troops and regional forces. This will make possible the eventual creation of regular forces and regular army formations led by local people. This is an extremely important task. Unless it is accomplished, we can neither build stable anti-Japanese base areas nor expand the people's army.

Of course the local people for their part should warmly welcome and help the revolutionary workers and people's forces coming from other areas.

Everybody should be alerted on the question of dealing with covert wreckers. For it is easy to spot and handle overt enemies and wreckers of the national cause, but not those who work under cover. Therefore we should take up this matter in all seriousness and at the same time be very careful in dealing with such people.

All religions are permitted in China's Liberated Areas, in accordance with the principle of freedom of religious belief. All believers in Protestantism, Catholicism, Islamism, Buddhism and other faiths enjoy the protection of the people's government so long as they are abiding by its laws. Everyone is free to believe or not to believe; neither compulsion nor discrimination is permitted.

Our congress should propose to the people of the Liberated Areas that a people's conference of the Chinese Liberated Areas[14] be held in Yenan as soon as possible to discuss the questions of co-ordinating the activities of the various Liberated Areas, strengthening their work in the War of Resistance, helping the people's anti-Japanese democratic movement in the Kuomintang areas, helping the underground armed forces of the people in the occupied areas, and promoting national unity and the formation of a coalition government. Now that China's Liberated Areas have become the centre of gravity in the nation-wide people's struggle to resist Japan and save the country, the broad masses throughout the country pin their hopes on us and it is our duty not to disappoint them. Such a conference would give great impetus to the Chinese people's cause of national liberation.

V. LET THE WHOLE PARTY UNITE AND FIGHT TO ACCOMPLISH ITS TASKS!

Comrades! Now that we understand our tasks and the policies for accomplishing them, what should be our attitude in carrying out these policies and performing these tasks?

The present international and domestic situation opens up bright prospects and provides unprecedentedly favourable conditions for us and the Chinese people as a whole; this is evident and beyond doubt. But at the same time there are still serious difficulties. Anyone who sees only the bright side but not the difficulties cannot fight effectively for the accomplishment of the Party's tasks.

Together with the Chinese people, our Party has built up immense strength for the Chinese nation in the twenty-four years of the Party's history, including the eight years of the War of Resistance Against Japan; the success of our work is obvious and beyond doubt. But at the same time there are still defects in our work. Anyone who sees only the successful side but not the defects likewise cannot fight effectively for the accomplishment of the Party's tasks.

In the twenty-four years since its birth in 1921, the Communist Party of China has gone through three great struggles — the Northern Expedition, the Agrarian Revolutionary War and the War of Resistance Against Japan which is still going on. From its very beginning our Party has based itself on the theory of Marxism-Leninism, for Marxism-Leninism is the crystallization of the most correct and most revolutionary scientific thought of the world proletariat. When the universal truth of Marxism-Leninism began to be integrated with the concrete practice of the Chinese revolution, the Chinese revolution took on an entirely new complexion and the entire historical stage of New Democracy emerged. Armed with Marxist-Leninist theory, the Communist Party of China has brought a new style of work to the Chinese people, a style of work which essentially entails integrating theory with practice, forging close links with the masses and practising self-criticism.

The universal truth of Marxism-Leninism, which reflects the practice of proletarian struggle throughout the world, becomes an invincible weapon for the Chinese people when it is integrated with the concrete practice of the revolutionary struggle of the Chinese proletariat and people. This the Communist Party of China has achieved. Our Party has grown and advanced through staunch struggle against every manifestation of dogmatism and empiricism, which runs counter to this principle. Dogmatism is divorced from concrete practice, while empiricism mistakes fragmentary experience for universal truth; both kinds of opportunist thinking run counter to Marxism. In the course of its twenty-four years of struggle our Party has successfully fought such wrong thinking and it is still doing so, thus greatly consolidating itself ideologically. Our Party now has 1,210,000 members. The overwhelming majority have joined during the War of Resistance, and there are various impurities in their ideology. The same is true of some of the members who joined the Party before the war. The work of rectification in the last few years has been most successful and has gone a long way towards removing these impurities. This work should be continued and ideological education within the Party should be developed still more extensively in the spirit of "learning from past mistakes to avoid future ones" and "curing the sickness to save the patient". We must enable the Party's leading cadres at all levels to understand that close integration of theory and practice is a hallmark distinguishing our Party from all other political parties. Therefore ideological education is the key link to be grasped in uniting the whole Party for great political struggles. Unless this is done, the Party cannot accomplish any of its political tasks.

Another hallmark distinguishing our Party from all other political parties is that we have very close ties with the broadest masses of the people. Our point of departure is to serve the people whole-heartedly and never for a moment divorce ourselves from the masses, to proceed in all cases from the interests of the people and not from the interests of individuals or groups, and to understand the identity of our responsibility to the people and our responsibility to the leading organs of the Party. Communists must be ready at all times to stand up for the truth, because truth is in the interests of the people; Communists must be ready at all times to correct their mistakes, because mistakes are against the interests of the people. Twenty-four years of experience tell us that the right task, policy and style of work invariably conform with the demands of the masses at a given time and place and invariably strengthen our ties with the masses, and the wrong task, policy and style of work invariably disagree with the demands of the masses at a given time and place and invariably alienate us from the masses. The reason why such evils as dogmatism, empiricism, commandism, tailism, sectarianism, bureaucracy and an arrogant attitude in work are definitely harmful and intolerable, and why anyone suffering from these maladies must overcome them, is that they alienate us from the masses. Our congress should call upon the whole Party to be vigilant and to see that no comrade at any post is divorced from the masses. It should teach every comrade to love the people and listen attentively to the voice of the masses; to identify himself with the masses wherever he goes and, instead of standing above them, to immerse himself among them; and, according to their present level, to awaken them or raise their political consciousness and help them gradually to organize themselves voluntarily and to set going all essential struggles permitted by the internal and external circumstances of the given time and place. Commandism is wrong in any type of work, because in overstepping the level of political consciousness of the masses and violating the principle of voluntary mass action it reflects the disease of impetuosity. Our comrades must not assume that everything they themselves understand is understood by the masses. Whether the masses understand it and are ready to take action can be discovered only by going into their midst and making investigations. If we do so, we can avoid commandism. Tailism in any type of work is also wrong, because in falling below the level of political consciousness of the masses and violating the principle of leading the masses forward it reflects the disease of dilatoriness. Our comrades must not assume that the masses have no understanding of what they themselves do not yet understand. It often happens that the masses outstrip us and are eager to advance a step when our comrades are still tailing behind certain backward elements, for instead of acting as leaders of the masses such comrades reflect the views of these backward elements and, moreover, mistake them for those of the broad masses. In a word, every comrade must be brought to understand that the supreme test of the words and deeds of a Communist is whether they conform with the highest interests and enjoy the support of the overwhelming majority of the people. Every comrade must be helped to understand that as long as we rely on the people, believe firmly in the inexhaustible creative power of the masses and hence trust and identify ourselves with them, no enemy can crush us while we can crush every enemy and overcome every difficulty.

Conscientious practice of self-criticism is still another hallmark distinguishing our Party from all other political parties. As we say, dust will accumulate if a room is not cleaned regularly, our faces will get dirty if they are not washed regularly. Our comrades' minds and our Party's work may also collect dust, and also need sweeping and washing. The proverb "Running water is never stale and a door-hinge is never worm-eaten" means that constant motion prevents the inroads of germs and other organisms. To check up regularly on our work and in the process develop a democratic style of work, to fear neither criticism nor self-criticism, and to apply such good popular Chinese maxims as "Say all you know and say it without reserve", "Blame not the speaker but be warned by his words" and "Correct mistakes if you have committed them and guard against them if you have not" —

this is the only effective way to prevent all kinds of political dust and germs from contaminating the minds of our comrades and the body of our Party. The reason for the great effectiveness of the rectification movement, the purpose of which was "to learn from past mistakes to avoid future ones and to cure the sickness to save the patient", was that the criticism and self-criticism we carried out were honest and conscientious, and not perfunctory and distorted. As we Chinese Communists, who base all our actions on the highest interests of the broadest masses of the Chinese people and who are fully convinced of the justice of our cause, never balk at any personal sacrifice and are ready at all times to give our lives for the cause, can we be reluctant to discard any idea, viewpoint, opinion or method which is not suited to the needs of the people? Can we be willing to allow political dust and germs to dirty our clean faces or eat into our healthy organism? Countless revolutionary martyrs have laid down their lives in the interests of the people, and our hearts are filled with pain as we the living think of them — can there be any personal interest, then, that we would not sacrifice or any error that we would not discard?

Comrades! When this congress is over, we shall go to the front and, guided by its resolutions, fight to bring about the final defeat of the Japanese aggressors and to build a new China. To achieve this aim, we shall unite with all the people of our country. Let me repeat: We shall unite with any class, any party, any group or individual if they are for the defeat of the Japanese aggressors and the building of a new China. To achieve this aim, we shall solidly unite all the forces of our Party on democratic centralist principles of organization and discipline. We shall unite with any comrade if he abides by the Party's Programme, Constitution and decisions. In the period of the Northern Expedition our Party had a membership of less than 60,000, most of whom were later dispersed by the enemy; in the period of the Agrarian Revolutionary War we had a membership of less than 300,000, most of whom were likewise dispersed by the enemy. Now we have more than 1,200,000 members; this time we must in no circumstances allow ourselves to be dispersed by the enemy. If we can profit from the experience of these three periods, if we are modest and guard against conceit and are able to strengthen unity among all comrades inside the Party and with all the people outside the Party, we can rest assured that, far from being dispersed by the enemy, we shall destroy the Japanese aggressors and their servile running dogs resolutely, thoroughly, wholly and completely, and thereafter build a new-democratic China.

The experience of the three periods of the revolution, and especially that of the War of Resistance Against Japan, has convinced us and the whole Chinese people that without the efforts of the Chinese Communist Party, without the Chinese Communists as the mainstay of the Chinese people, China can never achieve independence or liberation, or industrialization and the modernization of her agriculture.

Comrades! I firmly believe that with the Communist Party of China armed with the experience of the three revolutions, we can accomplish our great political task.

Thousands upon thousands of martyrs have heroically laid down their lives for the people; let us hold their banner high and march ahead along the path crimson with their blood!

A new-democratic China will soon be born. Let us hail that great day!

NOTES

[1] The Chinese National Liberation Vanguard Corps, or to give its shorter name the National Vanguard Corps, was a revolutionary youth organization formed under the leadership of the Chinese Communist Party in September 1936 by the progressive youth who participated in the December 9th Movement of 1935. After the outbreak of the War of Resistance, many of its members saw action and took part in building base areas behind the enemy lines. The organizations of the National Vanguard Corps in the Kuomintang areas were forcibly dissolved by the Chiang Kai-shek government in 1938; those in the Liberated Areas were later merged into the Association of Youth for National Salvation, an organization of even broader scope.

[2] On July 7, 1937, the Japanese invading forces attacked the Chinese garrison at Lukouchiao, some ten kilometres southwest of Peking. Under the influence of the ardent and nation-wide anti-Japanese movement the Chinese troops put up resistance. This incident marked the beginning of the Chinese people's heroic War of Resistance Against Japan which lasted for eight years.

[3] For a fuller account of the three anti-Communist onslaughts, see "A Comment on the Sessions of the Kuomintang Central Executive Committee and of the People's Political Council", pp. 137-51 of this volume.

[4] These operations to force China's north-south trunk railways open for through traffic constituted the offensive launched in May 1944 by the Japanese army to seize the Canton-Hankow Railway along its entire length and thus secure an uninterrupted land link between northern and southern China.

[5] Scobie was the commander of the British imperialist forces of aggression in Greece. In October 1944, when the German invaders were retreating in defeat on the European continent, Scobie's troops entered the country, bringing with them the reactionary Greek government that had been in exile in London. Scobie directed and assisted this government in attacking the Greek People's Liberation Army, which

had waged a long and heroic struggle against the German invaders, and in massacring Greek patriots, and so plunged Greece into a blood bath.

⁶ *Pao chia* was the administrative system by which the Kuomintang reactionary clique enforced its fascist rule at the primary level. On August 1, 1932, Chiang Kai-shek promulgated his "Regulations for the Organization of *Pao* and *Chia* and for a Population Census in the Counties", covering the provinces of Honan, Hupeh and Anhwei. The "Regulations" provided that "the *pao* and *chia* are to be organized on the basis of households; there is to be a head of each household, of each *chia*, which is made up of ten households, and of each *pao*, which is made up of ten *chia*". Neighbours were required to watch each other's activities and report them to the authorities, and all were punishable when one was found guilty; counter-revolutionary measures for exacting compulsory labour were also laid down. On November 7, 1934, the Kuomintang government officially announced that this system of fascist rule was to be established in all the provinces and municipalities under its rule.

⁷ The Cairo conference, held by China, the United States and Britain in November 1943, issued the Cairo Declaration which clearly stipulated that Taiwan and certain other territories were to be returned to China. In June 1950 the U.S. government sent a fleet to control Taiwan in open repudiation of this agreement, in the attempt to deprive China of her sovereignty over it.

⁸ Yuan Shih-kai was the head of the Northern warlords in the last years of the Ching Dynasty. After the Ching Dynasty was overthrown by the Revolution of 1911, he usurped the presidency of the Republic and organized the first government of the Northern warlords, which represented the big landlord and big comprador classes. He did this by relying on counter-revolutionary armed force and on the support of the imperialists and by taking advantage of the conciliationist character of the bourgeoisie, which was then leading the revolution. In 1915 he wanted to make himself emperor and, to gain the support of the Japanese imperialists, accepted the Twenty-one Demands with which Japan aimed at obtaining exclusive control of all China. In December of the same year an uprising against his assumption of the throne took place in Yunnan Province and promptly won nation-wide response and support. Yuan Shih-kai died in Peking in June 1916.

⁹ Omei is a famous mountain in the southwestern part of Szechuan Province. Here it symbolizes the mountainous areas of Szechuan, the last refuge of the Chiang Kai-shek ruling clique in the War of Resistance Against Japan.

¹⁰ From Dr. Sun Yat-sen's "Statement on My Departure for the North", dated November 10, 1924.

¹¹ For many decades, beginning with the end of the 18th century, Britain exported an increasing quantity of opium to China. This traffic not only subjected the Chinese people to drugging but also plundered China of her silver. It aroused fierce opposition in China. In 1840, under the pretext of safeguarding its trade with China, Britain launched armed aggression against her. The Chinese troops led by Lin Tse-hsu put up resistance, and the people in Canton spontaneously organized the "Quell-the-British Corps", which dealt serious blows to the British forces of aggression. In 1842, however, the corrupt Ching regime signed the Treaty of Nanking with Britain. This treaty provided for the payment of indemnities and the cession of Hongkong to Britain, and stipulated that Shanghai, Foochow, Amoy, Ningpo and Canton were to be opened to British trade and that tariff rates for British goods imported into China were to be jointly fixed by China and Britain.

¹² The Atlantic Charter was issued jointly by the United States and Britain at the conclusion of their Atlantic conference in August 1941. The Moscow con-

ference was held in October 1943 by the foreign ministers of the Soviet Union, the United States and Britain. The Teheran conference of the Soviet Union, the United States and Britain was held in the capital of Iran from November to December 1943. The Crimea conference of the Soviet Union, the United States and Britain took place in February 1945 at Yalta. At all these international conferences the signatories recorded their resolve to defeat fascist Germany and Japan through common endeavour and, after the war, to prevent the revival of the forces of aggression and the remnants of fascism, maintain world peace and help the peoples of all countries to realize their aspirations for independence and democracy. But immediately after the war the U.S. and British governments violated all these international agreements.

[13] As the representative of China's Liberated Areas Comrade Tung Pi-wu attended the United Nations Conference on International Organization which was held at San Francisco from April to June 1945, with the participation of representatives from fifty countries. The proposals for the Organization of the United Nations were drafted at Dumbarton Oaks, U.S.A., where the representatives of the Soviet Union, the United States, Britain and China met from August to October 1944 in accordance with the decisions of the Moscow and Teheran conferences.

[14] With Japan's surrender the situation changed and the people's conference of the Chinese Liberated Areas was not convened, although a Preparatory Committee for this conference was formed in Yenan after the Seventh National Congress of the Chinese Communist Party and held an inaugural meeting which was attended by representatives from all the Liberated Areas.

THE FOOLISH OLD MAN
WHO REMOVED THE MOUNTAINS

June 11, 1945

We have had a very successful congress. We have done three things. First, we have decided on the line of our Party, which is boldly to mobilize the masses and expand the people's forces so that, under the leadership of our Party, they will defeat the Japanese aggressors, liberate the whole people and build a new-democratic China. Second, we have adopted the new Party Constitution. Third, we have elected the leading body of the Party — the Central Committee. Henceforth our task is to lead the whole membership in carrying out the Party line. Ours has been a congress of victory, a congress of unity. The delegates have made excellent comments on the three reports.[1] Many comrades have undertaken self-criticism; with unity as the objective unity has been achieved through self-criticism. This congress is a model of unity, of self-criticism and of inner-Party democracy.

When the congress closes, many comrades will be leaving for their posts and the various war fronts. Comrades, wherever you go, you should propagate the line of the congress and, through the members of the Party, explain it to the broad masses.

Our aim in propagating the line of the congress is to build up the confidence of the whole Party and the entire people in the certain triumph of the revolution. We must first raise the political consciousness of the vanguard so that, resolute and unafraid of sacrifice, they will surmount every difficulty to win victory. But this is not enough; we must also arouse the political consciousness of the entire people so that they may willingly and gladly fight together with us for victory. We should fire the whole people with the conviction that China belongs

---

This was Comrade Mao Tse-tung's concluding speech at the Seventh National Congress of the Communist Party of China.

not to the reactionaries but to the Chinese people. There is an ancient Chinese fable called "The Foolish Old Man Who Removed the Mountains". It tells of an old man who lived in northern China long, long ago and was known as the Foolish Old Man of North Mountain. His house faced south and beyond his doorway stood the two great peaks, Taihang and Wangwu, obstructing the way. He called his sons, and hoe in hand they began to dig up these mountains with great determination. Another greybeard, known as the Wise Old Man, saw them and said derisively, "How silly of you to do this! It is quite impossible for you few to dig up these two huge mountains." The Foolish Old Man replied, "When I die, my sons will carry on; when they die, there will be my grandsons, and then their sons and grandsons, and so on to infinity. High as they are, the mountains cannot grow any higher and with every bit we dig, they will be that much lower. Why can't we clear them away?" Having refuted the Wise Old Man's wrong view, he went on digging every day, unshaken in his conviction. God was moved by this, and he sent down two angels, who carried the mountains away on their backs. Today, two big mountains lie like a dead weight on the Chinese people. One is imperialism, the other is feudalism. The Chinese Communist Party has long made up its mind to dig them up. We must persevere and work unceasingly, and we, too, will touch God's heart. Our God is none other than the masses of the Chinese people. If they stand up and dig together with us, why can't these two mountains be cleared away?

Yesterday, in a talk with two Americans who were leaving for the United States, I said that the U.S. government was trying to undermine us and this would not be permitted. We oppose the U.S. government's policy of supporting Chiang Kai-shek against the Communists. But we must draw a distinction, firstly, between the people of the United States and their government and, secondly, within the U.S. government between the policy-makers and their subordinates. I said to these two Americans, "Tell the policy-makers in your government that we forbid you Americans to enter the Liberated Areas because your policy is to support Chiang Kai-shek against the Communists, and we have to be on our guard. You can come to the Liberated Areas if your purpose is to fight Japan, but there must first be an agreement. We will not permit you to nose around everywhere. Since Patrick J. Hurley[2] has publicly declared against co-operation with the Chinese Communist Party, why do you still want to come and prowl around in our Liberated Areas?"

The U.S. government's policy of supporting Chiang Kai-shek against the Communists shows the brazenness of the U.S. reactionaries. But all the scheming of the reactionaries, whether Chinese or foreign, to prevent the Chinese people from achieving victory is doomed to failure. The democratic forces are the main current in the world today, while reaction is only a counter-current. The reactionary counter-current is trying to swamp the main current of national independence and people's democracy, but it can never become the main current. Today, there are still three major contradictions in the old world, as Stalin pointed out long ago: first, the contradiction between the proletariat and the bourgeoisie in the imperialist countries; second, the contradiction between the various imperialist powers; and third, the contradiction between the colonial and semi-colonial countries and the imperialist metropolitan countries.[3] Not only do these three contradictions continue to exist but they are becoming more acute and widespread. Because of their existence and growth, the time will come when the reactionary anti-Soviet, anti-Communist and anti-democratic counter-current still in existence today will be swept away.

At this moment two congresses are being held in China, the Sixth National Congress of the Kuomintang and the Seventh National Congress of the Communist Party. They have completely different aims: the aim of one is to liquidate the Communist Party and all the other democratic forces in China and thus to plunge China into darkness; the aim of the other is to overthrow Japanese imperialism and its lackeys, the Chinese feudal forces, and build a new-democratic China and thus to lead China to light. These two lines are in conflict with each other. We firmly believe that, led by the Chinese Communist Party and guided by the line of its Seventh Congress, the Chinese people will achieve complete victory, while the Kuomintang's counter-revolutionary line will inevitably fail.

NOTES

[1] The three reports at the Seventh National Congress of the Communist Party of China were Comrade Mao Tse-tung's political report, Comrade Chu Teh's military report and Comrade Liu Shao-chi's report on the revision of the Party Constitution.

[2] Patrick J. Hurley, a reactionary Republican Party politician, was appointed U.S. ambassador to China towards the end of 1944. In November 1945 he was forced to resign because his support for Chiang Kai-shek's anti-Communist policy roused

the firm opposition of the Chinese people. Hurley's open declaration against co-operation with the Chinese Communist Party was made on April 2, 1945 at a U.S. State Department press conference in Washington. For details, see "The Hurley-Chiang Duet Is a Flop", pp. 281-84 of this volume.

³ See J. V. Stalin, "The Foundations of Leninism", *Works*, Eng. ed., FLPH, Moscow, 1953, Vol. VI, pp. 74-82.

ON PRODUCTION BY THE ARMY
FOR ITS OWN SUPPORT
AND ON THE IMPORTANCE OF
THE GREAT MOVEMENTS FOR RECTIFICATION
AND FOR PRODUCTION

April 27, 1945

In the existing circumstances in which our army is facing extreme material difficulties and is engaged in dispersed operations, it is absolutely inadmissible for the leading bodies to assume full responsibility for provisioning the army, for to do so would both hamper the initiative of the large numbers of officers and men at the lower levels and fail to satisfy their needs. We should say, "Comrades, let us all go into action and overcome our difficulties!" If only the leadership at the higher levels sets the tasks well and gives the lower levels a free hand to overcome difficulties by their own efforts, the problem will be solved and, indeed, solved in a more satisfactory way. But if, instead, the higher levels always shoulder loads heavier than they can really carry, dare not give the lower levels a free hand and do not arouse enthusiasm for self-reliance among the broad masses, then in spite of all the efforts of the higher levels the result will be that both the higher and the lower levels will find themselves in a predicament, and the problem will never be solved in the existing circumstances. The experience of the last few years has amply borne this out. The principle of "unified leadership and decentralized management" has proved to be the correct one for organizing all economic activities in our Liberated Areas in the present circumstances.

The armed forces of the Liberated Areas already total more than 900,000 men. To defeat the Japanese aggressors, we must increase

---

This was an editorial written by Comrade Mao Tse-tung for the *Liberation Daily*, Yenan.

them to several times this number. But we have so far received no outside aid. Even if we get it in the future, we shall still have to provide our own means of livelihood; on that score there must be no illusions whatsoever. In the near future we shall have to take the necessary number of military formations from the areas where they are now engaged in dispersed operations, and concentrate them for attack on particular enemy objectives. Such big formations for concentrated action will be unable to engage in production to support themselves, and, what is more, will need large supplies from the rear; only the local troops and regional formations remaining behind (and they will still be considerable) will be able both to fight and to engage in production as before. Such being the case, is there any doubt that, as long as fighting and training are not impeded, all troops without exception should use the present opportunity to learn how to be partially self-supporting through production?

In our circumstances, production by the army for its own support, though backward or retrogressive in form, is progressive in substance and of great historic significance. Formally speaking, we are violating the principle of division of labour. However, in our circumstances — the poverty and disunity of the country (resulting from the crimes of the chief ruling clique of the Kuomintang), and the protracted and dispersed people's guerrilla war — what we are doing is progressive. Look how pale and emaciated the Kuomintang soldiers are, and how robust and strong our soldiers of the Liberated Areas are! Look what difficulties we ourselves had before we started production for self-support, and how much better off we have been since! Let us ask two army units here, say two companies, to choose between the two methods, *i.e.*, between the higher levels supplying them with all their means of livelihood and the higher levels supplying little or nothing but letting them produce for themselves all that they need, or the greater part, or half, or even less than half of what they need. Which method will yield better results? Which will they prefer? After a year's serious experiment in production for self-support, they will surely answer that the second method yields better results and be willing to adopt it, and they will surely answer that the first method yields poorer results and be unwilling to adopt it. The reason is that the second method can improve the living conditions of everyone in the army, whereas the first method can never satisfy their needs in the present difficult material circumstances, however hard the higher levels may try. Because we have adopted what seems to be a "backward" and "retrogressive" method, our troops are able to overcome shortages in the means of livelihood and improve their living conditions, so that every soldier is robust and strong; as a result, we are able to ease the tax burden on the people who are also in difficulties, thus winning their support, and we are able to keep up the protracted war and expand our armed forces, thus extending the Liberated Areas, reducing the enemy-occupied areas and attaining our objective of final victory over the aggressor and the liberation of the whole of China. Is this not of great historic significance?

Production by the army for its own support has not only improved the army's living conditions and lightened the burden on the people, thereby making it possible further to expand the army. In addition, it has had many immediate effects. They are as follows:

(1) Improved relations between officers and men. Officers and men work together in production and become like brothers.

(2) Better attitude to labour. What we now have is neither the old mercenary system nor universal military service, but a third system, the system of mobilizing volunteers. It is better than the mercenary system since it does not produce so many loafers, but it is not so good as universal military service. Nevertheless, our present conditions only allow us to adopt the system of mobilizing volunteers, and not that of universal military service. The mobilized soldiers have to lead an army life for a long time, which may impair their attitude to labour and so turn some of them into loafers or taint them with certain bad habits characteristic of the warlord armies. But since the army began to produce for its own support, the attitude to labour has improved and loafer ways have been overcome.

(3) Strengthened discipline. Far from weakening discipline in battle and in army life, labour discipline in production actually strengthens it.

(4) Improved relations between the army and the people. Once an armed force begins to "keep house" for itself, encroachments upon the property of the people seldom or never occur. As the army and the people exchange labour and help each other in production, the friendship between them is strengthened.

(5) Less grumbling in the army about the government and improved relations between the two.

(6) An impetus to the great production campaign of the people. Once the army engages in production, the need for government

and other organizations to do likewise becomes more obvious, and they do so more energetically; also, the need for a universal campaign of the whole people to increase production naturally becomes more obvious, and this too is carried on more energetically.

The widespread movements for rectification and for production which began in 1942 and 1943 respectively have played and are still playing a decisive role, the one in our ideological and the other in our material life. Unless we grasp these two links at the right time, we shall be unable to grasp the whole chain of the revolution, and our struggle will not advance.

As we know, of the members who joined the Party before 1937, only a few tens of thousands are left, and most of our present membership of 1,200,000 come from the peasantry and other sections of the petty bourgeoisie. The revolutionary fervour of these comrades is admirable and they wish to have Marxist training, but they have brought with them into the Party ideas which are out of keeping or not altogether in keeping with Marxism. The same is true of some people who joined the Party before 1937. It constitutes an extremely serious contradiction, an enormous difficulty. In these circumstances, could we have advanced smoothly if we had not started a widespread movement of Marxist education, that is, the rectification movement? Obviously not. But as we have solved or are in the process of solving this contradiction among large numbers of cadres — the contradiction, within the Party, between the proletarian ideology and non-proletarian ideologies (including those of the petty bourgeoisie, the bourgeoisie and even of the landlord class, but mainly of the petty bourgeoisie), *i.e.*, the contradiction between the Marxist ideology and non-Marxist ideologies — our Party can go forward with great, firm strides in unprecedented (though not complete) ideological, political and organizational unity. From now on our Party can and should grow even larger and, guided by the principles of Marxist ideology, we shall be able to steer its further development still more effectively.

The other link is the movement for production. The War of Resistance has been going on for eight years. When it began we had food and clothing. But things got steadily worse until we were in great difficulty, running short of grain, short of cooking oil and salt, short of bedding and clothing, short of funds. This great difficulty, this great contradiction, came in the wake of the big Japanese offensives and the Kuomintang government's three large-scale attacks on the people (the "anti-Communist onslaughts") in 1940-43. Could our anti-Japanese struggle have progressed if we had not overcome this difficulty, solved this contradiction, grasped this link? Obviously not. But we have learned and are still learning to develop production, and so we are again full of vigour and vitality. Fearing no enemy, we shall prevail over them all in a few years.

Thus there can be no doubt of the historic importance of the two great movements for rectification and production.

Let us go forward and spread these two great movements everywhere as a foundation for the fulfilment of other tasks in our struggle. If we can do so, the complete liberation of the Chinese people will be assured.

Now is the season for spring ploughing, and it is hoped that the leading comrades, all the working personnel and the masses of the people in every Liberated Area will grasp the link of production in good time and strive for even greater achievements than those of last year. Greater efforts must be made this year, particularly in areas which have not yet learned to develop production.

THE HURLEY-CHIANG DUET IS A FLOP

July 10, 1945

Convened to camouflage Chiang Kai-shek's dictatorial regime, the Fourth People's Political Council opened in Chungking on July 7. It was the smallest opening session on record. Not only was nobody present from the Chinese Communist Party, but many members of the Council from other groups were absent too. Out of a total membership of 290, only 180 turned up. Chiang Kai-shek held forth at this opening session as follows:

> The government is not going to submit any specific proposal on questions relating to the convocation of the National Assembly, and you gentlemen can therefore discuss these matters fully. The government is ready to listen to your opinions on these questions in all honesty and sincerity.

This will probably be the end of the whole business about convoking the National Assembly on November 12 this year. The imperialist Patrick J. Hurley has had something to do with this business. At first he strongly encouraged Chiang Kai-shek to make such a move, and it was this that put some stiffening into Chiang Kai-shek's New Year's Day speech,[1] and a great deal more into his March 1 speech[2] in which he announced his determination to "hand state power back to the people" on November 12. In his speech of March 1 he flatly rejected the Chinese Communist Party's proposal, which voiced the general will of the Chinese people, that a conference of all parties be convened and a coalition government established. He gleefully played up the idea of forming a so-called Committee of Three, including an American, to "reorganize" the armed forces of the Chinese Communist Party. He had the audacity to say that the Chinese Communist Party must hand over its troops before he would bestow "legal status" upon it.

Comrade Mao Tse-tung wrote this comment for the Hsinhua News Agency.

In all this, the backing of His Worship Patrick J. Hurley was decisive. In a statement in Washington on April 2, Hurley did his best to boost Chiang Kai-shek's "National Assembly" and other such nasty schemes in addition to denying the role of the Chinese Communist Party, vilifying its activities, declaring against co-operation with it and uttering other such imperialist platitudes. Thus the duet between Hurley in the United States and Chiang Kai-shek in China reached its most raucous pitch, with the sacrifice of the Chinese people as the common objective. Since then the show seems to have flagged. Countless voices have been raised in protest everywhere, among both Chinese and foreigners, both inside and outside the Kuomintang, among people with party affiliations and without. The sole reason is that for all its high-sounding language, the Hurley-Chiang racket is designed to sacrifice the interests of the Chinese people, further wreck their unity, and as it were, lay a mine to set off large-scale civil war in China, thereby damaging the common interests of the people of the United States and other allied countries during the anti-fascist war and the prospects of peaceful coexistence afterwards. At the moment Hurley seems to be lying low, busying himself with no one knows what, with the result that Chiang Kai-shek has to talk twaddle before the People's Political Council. Previously, on March 1, Chiang Kai-shek said:

> The conditions in our country differ from those in other countries: prior to the convocation of the National Assembly, we have no responsible organization which is representative of the people and through which the government can consult the people for their opinions.

If that is so, why does our Generalissimo now go to the People's Political Council to "listen" to "opinions"? According to him, there is no "responsible organization" in the whole of China through which one "can consult the people for their opinions"; it follows that the People's Political Council as an "organization" exists merely to eat, and his "listening" to it has no legal basis. Be that as it may, if the People's Political Council says even a single word against the convocation of the bogus "National" Assembly, it will have done a good deed and merited divine grace, though by so doing it would have violated the Imperial Edict of March 1 and committed *lèse-majesté*. Of course, it is still premature to make any comment on the People's Political Council, as we have to wait a few days to see what it will produce for the Generalissimo to "listen" to. One thing, however, is certain: ever since the Chinese people began raising their voices in protest against this National Assembly, even the enthusiasts for "constitutional monarchy" have been worried about our "monarch", cautioning him not to stick his neck into a noose by convening a "Parliament of Pigs"[3] and warning him of the fate of Yuan Shih-kai. Who knows but that our "monarch" may stay his hand in consequence? But it is absolutely certain that he and his retinue will not allow the people to gain a particle of power, if that would cost them a single hair. The immediate proof is that His Majesty has described the people's justified criticism as "unbridled attacks". He said:

> . . . under war conditions a general election is obviously out of the question in the Japanese-occupied areas. Consequently two years ago the Plenary Session of the Central Executive Committee of the Kuomintang resolved to convoke the National Assembly and institute constitutional government within a year after the conclusion of the war. However, in certain quarters unbridled attacks were made at that time.

And the grounds for these attacks were that this date might be too late. His Majesty thereupon proposed that "the National Assembly be convoked as soon as the war situation is stabilized, in view of the possibility that the final conclusion of the war may be delayed and that order may not be quickly restored everywhere even after the end of the war". Much to his surprise, these people again made "unbridled attacks". This has put His Majesty in a terrible fix. But the Chinese people must teach Chiang Kai-shek and his group a lesson and tell them: Whatever you say or do, no tricks in violation of the people's wishes will be tolerated. What the Chinese people demand is immediate democratic reforms, such as the release of political prisoners, the abolition of the secret service, and the granting of freedoms to the people and of legal status to the political parties. You are doing none of these things and instead are simply juggling with the pseudo-problem of the date of the "National Assembly"; this will not deceive even a three-year-old. Without a minimum of genuine democratic reforms, all your assemblies, large or small, will be thrown into the cesspit. Call this an "unbridled attack" if you like, but every deception of this kind must be exploded resolutely, thoroughly, wholly and completely, with not a trace allowed to remain. The reason is simply that it is a swindle. Whether or not there is a national assembly is one thing and whether or not there is a minimum of democratic reforms is quite another. The former can be dispensed with for the time being, but the latter must be introduced immediately. Since Chiang Kai-shek and his group are willing to "hand state power back to the people sooner", why are they unwilling to carry out a minimum of democratic reforms "sooner"? Gentlemen of the Kuomintang! When you come to these concluding lines, you will have to admit that the Chinese Communists are not in any sense making an "unbridled attack" on you, but are asking you one simple question. May we not even ask a question? Can you brush it aside? The question you must answer is: How is it that you are willing to "hand state power back to the people" but not willing to institute democratic reforms?

NOTES

[1] The radio speech made by Chiang Kai-shek on January 1, 1945 did not even mention the ignominious defeats of the Kuomintang troops at the hands of the Japanese aggressors in the previous year, but maligned the people and opposed the proposal for abolishing the Kuomintang's one-party dictatorship and for setting up a coalition government and a joint supreme command, a proposal supported by all the people and all the anti-Japanese parties in the country. He insisted on continuing the Kuomintang's one-party dictatorship and as a shield against the people's criticism he talked about convening a Kuomintang-controlled "National Assembly" which had been spurned by the whole nation.

[2] On March 1, 1945 Chiang Kai-shek made a speech in Chungking at the Association for the Establishment of Constitutional Government. Besides reiterating the reactionary views of his New Year's Day speech, Chiang proposed the formation of a Committee of Three, including a U.S. representative, to "reorganize" the Eighth Route Army and the New Fourth Army, which amounted to an open invitation to the U.S. imperialists to intervene in China's domestic affairs.

[3] In 1923, the Northern warlord Tsao Kun had himself elected "President of the Republic of China" by giving members of parliament a bribe of 5,000 silver dollars each. He became notorious as the president elected through bribery, and the bribed members came to be called "members of the Parliament of Pigs". Comrade Mao Tse-tung's analogy here likens the Kuomintang's bogus "National Assembly" to the "Parliament of Pigs".

ON THE DANGER OF THE HURLEY POLICY

July 12, 1945

It has become increasingly obvious that the policy of the United States towards China as represented by its ambassador Patrick J. Hurley is creating a civil war crisis in China. Sticking to its reactionary policies, the Kuomintang government has lived on civil war ever since it was set up eighteen years ago; only at the time of the Sian Incident in 1936 and of the Japanese invasion south of the Great Wall in 1937 was it forced to abandon its nation-wide civil war for a time. Since 1939, however, civil war on a local scale has again been waged without interruption. "Fight the Communists first" is the mobilization slogan used by the Kuomintang government among its own people, while it relegates resistance to Japan to a secondary place. At present all its military dispositions are focused not on resisting the Japanese aggressors but on "recovering lost territory" from China's Liberated Areas and on wiping out the Chinese Communist Party. This situation must be taken into serious account in our struggle both for victory in the War of Resistance and for peaceful construction after the war. The late President Roosevelt did take it into account and consequently, in the interests of the United States, refrained from adopting a policy of helping the Kuomintang to undertake armed attacks on the Chinese Communist Party. When Hurley visited Yenan as Roosevelt's personal representative in November 1944, he expressed agreement with the Chinese Communist Party's plan for the abolition of the Kuomintang one-party dictatorship and the establishment of a democratic coalition government. But later he changed his tune and went back on what he had said in Yenan. This change was crudely revealed in his statement in Washington on April 2. In the interim, according to the selfsame Hurley, the Kuomintang government represented by Chiang Kai-shek seems to have turned into the Beauty

---

This comment was written for the Hsinhua News Agency.

and the Chinese Communist Party into the Beast, and he flatly declared that the United States would co-operate with Chiang Kai-shek only and not with the Chinese Communist Party. This, of course, is not just Hurley's personal view but that of a whole group of people in the U.S. government. It is a wrong and dangerous view. At this juncture Roosevelt died, and Hurley returned to the U.S. embassy in Chungking in high spirits. The danger of the China policy of the United States as represented by Hurley is that it is encouraging the Kuomintang government to be still more reactionary and aggravating the civil war crisis. If the Hurley policy continues, the U.S. government will fall irretrievably into the deep stinking cesspool of Chinese reaction; it will put itself in the position of antagonizing the hundreds of millions of awakened and awakening Chinese people and will become a hindrance to the War of Resistance in the present and to world peace in the future. Isn't it clear that this would be the inevitable result? A section of U.S. public opinion is worried about the China policy of the Hurley type with its dangers and wants it changed, because as far as China's future is concerned, it sees clearly that the forces of the Chinese people which demand independence, freedom and unity are irresistible and are bound to burst forth and supplant foreign and feudal oppression. We cannot yet say whether or when the U.S. policy will be changed. But one thing is certain. If the Hurley policy of aiding and abetting the reactionary forces in China and antagonizing the Chinese people with their immense numbers continues unchanged, it will place a crushing burden on the government and people of the United States and plunge them into endless trouble. This point must be brought home to the people of the United States.

TELEGRAM TO COMRADE WILLIAM Z. FOSTER

July 29, 1945

Comrade William Z. Foster and the National Committee of the Communist Party of the United States of America:

We are glad to learn that the special convention of the Communist Political Association of the United States has resolved to repudiate Browder's revisionist, that is, capitulationist line,[1] has re-established Marxist leadership and revived the Communist Party of the United States. We hereby extend to you our warm congratulations on this great victory of the working class and the Marxist movement in the United States. Browder's whole revisionist-capitulationist line (which is fully expressed in his book *Teheran*) in essence reflects the influence of reactionary U.S. capitalist groups on the U.S. workers' movement. These groups are now doing their utmost to extend their influence in China too; they are supporting the erroneous policy of the reactionary clique inside the Kuomintang, a policy which is against the interests of the nation and the people, and are thereby confronting the Chinese people with the grave danger of civil war and jeopardizing the interests of the peoples of our two great countries, China and the United States. Beyond all doubt the victory of the U.S. working class and its vanguard, the Communist Party of the United States, over Browder's revisionist-capitulationist line will contribute signally to the great cause in which the Chinese and American peoples are engaged, the cause of carrying on the war against Japan and of building a peaceful and democratic world after the war.

NOTES

[1] Earl Browder was the General Secretary of the Communist Party of the United States of America from 1930 to 1944. During World War II, the Rightist ideas in the Communist Party of the U.S.A., of which Browder was the chief exponent, developed

into an anti-Marxist revisionist-capitulationist line. From December 1943 onward, Browder advocated this line in a number of speeches and articles and in April 1944 he published *Teheran* as his Right opportunist programme. Revising the basic Leninist thesis that imperialism is monopolistic, decadent and moribund capitalism, and denying the imperialist nature of U.S. capitalism, he declared that U.S. capitalism "retains some of the characteristics of a *young* capitalism" (Browder's italics) and that there is a "common interest" between the proletariat and the big bourgeoisie in the U.S.A. Thus he pleaded for the safeguarding of the system of monopolist trusts and dreamed about saving U.S. capitalism from inevitable crises by means of class conciliation. Basing himself on this absurd appraisal of U.S. capitalism and following a capitulationist line of class collaboration with monopoly capital, Browder in May 1944 presided over the dissolution of the Communist Party of the U.S.A., the party of the U.S. proletariat, and formed a non-Party organization, the Communist Political Association of the U.S.A. From the very beginning, Browder's wrong line met with opposition from many members of the Communist Party of the U.S.A. with Comrade William Z. Foster at their head. Under the leadership of Comrade Foster, the Communist Political Association in June 1945 passed a resolution denouncing Browder's line. In July the association held a special national convention and decided on the thorough liquidation of this line and the re-establishment of the Communist Party of the U.S.A. Browder was expelled from the Party in February 1946 because he persisted in his stand, which was a betrayal of the proletariat, and because he openly supported the imperialist policy of the Truman Administration and engaged in factional activities against the Party.

THE LAST ROUND
WITH THE JAPANESE INVADERS

August 9, 1945

The Chinese people heartily welcome the Soviet government's declaration of war on Japan on August 8. The Soviet Union's action will very much shorten the war against Japan. The war is already in its last stage and the time has come to inflict final defeat on the Japanese aggressors and all their running dogs. In these circumstances, all the anti-Japanese forces of the Chinese people should launch a nation-wide counter-offensive in close and effective co-ordination with the operations of the Soviet Union and the other allied countries. The Eighth Route Army, the New Fourth Army and the other armed forces of the people should seize every opportunity to launch extensive attacks on all the invaders and their running dogs who refuse to surrender, annihilate their forces, capture their arms and *matériel*, vigorously expand the Liberated Areas and reduce the areas under enemy occupation. We must boldly form armed working teams which, by hundreds and by thousands, should penetrate deep into the rear of the enemy-occupied areas, organize the people to wreck the enemy's communication lines and fight in co-ordination with the regular armies. We must boldly arouse the people in the occupied areas in their tens of millions and immediately organize underground forces to prepare armed uprisings and to annihilate the enemy in co-ordination with the troops attacking from without. Meanwhile, the consolidation of the Liberated Areas must not be neglected. Among the 100 million people there, and among the people in all other areas as they are liberated, we should universally carry out the reduction of rent and interest this winter and next spring, increase production, build up the people's political power and armed forces, intensify militia work, strengthen army discipline, persistently develop the united front of all sections of the people and guard against waste of manpower and material resources. All this is designed to put more punch into our army's offensive against the enemy. The people of the whole country must be on their guard to avert the danger of civil war and make efforts to bring about the formation of a democratic coalition government. A new stage in China's war of national liberation has arrived, and the people of the whole country must strengthen their unity and struggle for final victory.

毛 泽 东 选 集

第 三 卷

*

外文出版社出版（北京）

一九六五年第一版

一九六七年第二次印刷

编号：（英）1050—321

49796